EDMONTON

Portrait of a City

Dennis Person and Carin Routledge

©1981 Dennis Person & Carin Routledge

Canadian Cataloguing in Publication Data

Person, Dennis
Edmonton, Portrait of a City
Includes index.
ISBN 0-919091-05-9

Edmonton (Alta.) – Description. – Views. 2. Edmonton (Alta.) –
History. – Pictorial works. I. Routledge, Carin. II. Title.
FC 3696.37.P47   971.23'3   C81-091298-8
F1079.5.E3P47

A REIDMORE BOOK

Distributed in Canada by McClelland & Stewart Limited

Editorial	Marianne Morse
Design	Randy Morse, Marianne Morse, Sheila Scott, Charles Day
Preparation	Great Scott Designs
Production	Randy Morse
Typesetting	The Copyfitters

Printed and bound in Western Canada

Photo Credits

Legend: T-top, C-center, B-bottom,
L-left, R-right

City of Edmonton Archives: 15B, 16T,
16c, 19T, 22, 25B, 28T, 29B, 30C, 30B,
31T, 33, 35, 37B, 38T, 42B, 43B, 46B,
67B, 80B, 83B, 93, 95B, 98T, 104T,
104B, 108B, 110T, 127T, 140, 142T,
143B, 144T, 147, 148C, 149, 152B, 155B,
156B, 158B, 159, 160T, 160B, 161, 163T,
166B, 170L, 170C, 174, 186T, 200C,
202B, 213T, 228T

Provincial Archives of Alberta: 9, 11B, 13,
14, 15T, 16B, 17B, 18, 19B, 20, 21, 23,
24, 27, 28B, 30T, 31B, 32, 34, 36, 37T,
38B, 41B, 43T, 45, 47, 48, 49, 50, 51,
52, 53, 54, 55, 56, 57, 58, 59, 61, 62,
63, 64, 65T, 66, 67A, 68, 69, 71, 72,
73, 74, 75T, 76, 77T, 78, 80T, 80C, 81,
82, 83T, 85, 86, 87B, 88TL, 88B, 89T,
90T, 90B, 91T, 91B, 92, 94, 95T, 96B,
97T, 99T, 100B, 101, 104C, 106B, 108T,
109, 110B, 111, 115T, 116B, 117C, 117B,
122T, 123T, 124T, 125, 126T, 133, 134,
136, 137, 141B, 145C, 145B, 151T, 153,
155T, 157, 160C, 162, 165, 166T, 167,
168, 169T, 170B, 171, 173, 175C, 175B,
176, 177, 178, 179, 180, 181TR, 182,
183T, 184, 185, 186C, 186B, 187, 189,

190, 191, 192, 193, 194, 195, 196, 197,
198TL, 198TR, 199, 200T, 200B, 201,
202T, 203, 204, 205, 207, 208, 209,
210BL, 210BR, 211, 212, 213B, 214, 215,
216, 217, 218, 219, 220, 221, 223, 224,
225, 226, 227, 230C, 230R, 231, 232,
233, 234, 235T, 236, 237T, back
dust jacket

Glenbow-Alberta Institute: 3, 10B, 11T,
17T, 25T, 29T, 39T, 40, 41T, 42T,
46T, 60, 65B, 75B, 77, 78B, 84, 87T,
88TR, 89B, 90C, 91C, 96T, 97B, 98B,
99B, 100T, 103, 105, 106T, 107, 112,
113, 114, 115C, 115B, 116T, 116C, 117T,
118, 119, 120, 121, 123B, 124B, 126B,
127B, 128, 129, 130, 131, 132, 135, 139,
141T, 142B, 143T, 144B, 145T, 146,
148T, 148B, 150, 154, 156T, 158T,
163B, 169B, 198B, front dust jacket,
endpapers

Government of Alberta: 229, 230L,
236L, 237B

University of Alberta Archives: 39B,
122B, 181TL, 181B, 210T

Sunwapta Broadcasting Limited:
151B, 152T

Citadel Theatre: 235B

Jason Woodhead: 228B

Dennis Person: 172, 173T, 183B,
back dust jacket

Provincial Archives of British
Columbia: 142C

Public Archives of Canada: 7, 8, 10T

Uncaptioned Photos

Endpapers: [c 1914] Boarding the tour bus
on 102 Street north of Jasper Avenue.

Page 3: [c 1930] Jasper Avenue east of
101 Street.

Back dust jacket bottom: [April 27, 1981]
Downtown at dusk.

Table of Contents

1. Fort Edmonton (1795-1870)   page 6
2. Beyond the Fort (1871-1891)   page 12
3. Birth of Strathcona (1875-1911)   page 26
4. Edmonton, the Town (1892-1903)   page 44
5. City and Capital (1904-1911)   page 70
6. Amalgamation and Boom (1912-1914)   page 102
7. War, Women and Wings (1915-1929)   page 138
8. Depression and War Again (1930-1946)   page 164
9. Oil Capital (1947-1957)   page 188
10. Growing Up (1958-1970)   page 206
11. Metropolis (1971-1981)   page 222
12. Index   pages 238-40

Preface

With Edmonton's older buildings disappearing a block at a time from the downtown area, even long-time residents find it difficult to maintain a sense of historical heritage. But even as the last physical vestiges of the past are removed, a vivid record of the city and its people survives in photographs. Edmonton is luckier than most cities in having its past so well photographed, almost from its beginnings. These priceless pictures taken over the last hundred years document Edmonton's metamorphosis from a rough-hewn fur trading post to a hub of modern industrial and cultural vitality.

This work is not intended to be a comprehensive analytical history of the city. Instead, it is a pictorial history with enough text to explain each photo as it illustrates some aspect of Edmonton's history.

History does not proceed as tidy chapters with events arranged neatly according to subject matter. In real life, many unrelated things happen simultaneously, and some trends continue into subsequent eras while others disappear. The photographs included here with their related captions, give a basic cross-section of Edmonton's history, and the sometimes disjointed nature of the story actually reflects the way life really is. To ease the burden for the reader, related photos and stories are grouped together as much as possible. The index will be of assistance in piecing together several aspects of a particular story, and the introduction to each chapter should help put each period into perspective.

Of course, not every story could be included in one volume. Many firms, personalities, events, sports, buildings and scenes had to be omitted in order to bring this volume down to a practical size. Similarly, thousands of excellent photos housed in archives had to be set aside. However, the over 400 photographs included in this book give a good cross-section of the Edmonton experience during the last century.

To ensure accuracy, original sources such as newspapers, directories and research reports were consulted as much as possible. Since even these sources can occasionally contain errors and omissions, some mistakes may have slipped through, although a diligent attempt was made to verify all the facts and dates mentioned.

All measurements are in imperial rather than metric units, since these were the norm for most of the years covered by this book. Similarly, Fahrenheit temperatures are used. To assist the reader in locating early sites, street references are given in modern terms rather than the pre-1914 system of names.

The date on which each photograph was taken is given in brackets at the beginning of each caption.

Acknowledgements

This book was prepared with the assistance of over fifty people and several organizations whom the authors wish to acknowledge and sincerely thank. Special thanks must be given to photographers Mathers, Byron and May, Brown, McDermid, Blyth and others who recorded Edmonton's history on film, and to the City of Edmonton Archives, Provincial Archives of Alberta, and the Glenbow-Alberta Institute in Calgary for preserving the photos and making them so readily available. Organizations which kindly and ably gave their assistance include the Provincial Archives of Alberta, City of Edmonton Archives, University of Alberta Archives, Provincial Archives of British Columbia, Historic Sites Services, Edmonton Public Library, The Edmonton *Journal*, Sunwapta Broadcasting Ltd., The Citadel Theatre, Canadian Broadcasting Corporation, and the Glenbow-Alberta Institute. Of the many people who provided valuable assistance, special thanks must be given to Randy Morse for the advice, encouragement and good direction he gave at various stages of this work. Sincere thanks and appreciation must also be given Tony Cashman, John Gilpin, Eric Holmgren, Helen LaRose, Alex Mair and Alan Tovey for taking the time to read preliminary drafts and make many valuable comments and suggestions that helped shape this work into a better form. Special thanks to Sheila Scott and Charles Day for their long hours spent in preparing this book. A special word of thanks to Trudy Cowan and the Alberta Historical Resources Foundation. Special thanks are also given Alan Ridge for his interest and valuable consideration that are so very much appreciated. Lastly, very special thanks must be given Helen LaRose and the staff at the City Archives who not only were most helpful in providing information, but also did much to make research and study so much more enjoyable.

Special acknowledgement must be given to the work of several contemporary Edmonton historians. The many informative and interesting books written by James Macgregor and Tony Cashman, and the excellent papers prepared by John Gilpin and John Day were valuable references that provided both general background information and specific factual data so necessary for this book.

The authors also wish to express their sincere appreciation to the following persons for their assistance and information: Sheila Abercrombie, Ted Ackerman, John Bachinski, Rino Basso, Chris Beckwith, Jim Blower, Kay Brown, Romeo Buchard, Walter Cavalieri, Doris Chapman, Annette Crawley, Pat Garneau, J. Grimble, Judy Harder, June Honey, Philip Johnson, Karl Kaesekamp, Sylvia Kiyansuu, Georgeen Klassen, Dave Lennard, Al Litke, Loyd Loveseth, Mrs. J.C. McGregor, John McIsaac, Alex McNeill, Wendy Medland, Bryan Melnyk, Vern Modine, Quincy Moffat, Les Morgan, Marianne Morse, Adeline Northely, Les Page, Lucy Person, Ivar Person, Pat Peterson, Gertrude Pomahac, Art Potter, John Primrose, Alexander Rattray, Pat Reid, Carolyn Routledge, David Routledge, Richard Secord, Len Semrau, Mike Shandro, Don Smith, Lana Yakimishyn; those who wish to remain anonymous; and those whose names may have slipped our memories at this time.

1 Fort Edmonton (1795-1870)

In 1795, competition for furs between the British Hudson's Bay Company and the Montreal-based North West Company was intense. As the Fort George area (now eastern Alberta) was becoming depleted of furs, the Nor'Westers secretly built a new post further west at the junction of the North Saskatchewan and Sturgeon rivers, near modern Fort Saskatchewan. The new post was named Fort Augustus and Angus Shaw was put in charge. When the Hudson's Bay Co. learned of this, they immediately set to work close by erecting their new fort, which they called Edmonton House after London's north suburb, home of the Company's deputy governor, Sir James Winter Lake. In the spring of 1796, William Tomison took charge of the new post and began trading with the Woods Indians to the north and their traditional enemies, the Plains Indians to the south.

The shortage of firewood in 1802 in the vicinity of the forts became so acute that both companies decided to build new posts 20 miles upstream at the site now occupied by Edmonton's power plant near the 105 Street bridge. These new forts retained the old names and were built side by side on the north bank of the river as protection against the more war-like Plains Indians. These Plains Indians traded not only furs, but buffalo meat and pemmican, which had become the staple diet of the voyageurs. It saved them hunting for food during the five-month journey each summer to take the furs to Hudson's Bay or Montreal and return with trade goods.

In 1810, the forts moved again, 65 miles down-river to the mouth of White Earth Creek near modern Smoky Lake. Three years later they were rebuilt back at the power house site.

The bitter rivalry between the two companies brought the North West Co. near bankruptcy, forcing amalgamation with the Hudson's Bay Co. in 1821. George Simpson became governor of the H.B.C. and quickly took advantage of its new monopoly to make the fur trade profitable once more. In 1823, he put ex-Nor'Wester John Rowand in charge of the whole Saskatchewan District, making Fort Edmonton (which now included Fort Augustus) the administrative centre for all the western prairies.

Rowand demonstrated to Governor Simpson that the North Saskatchewan River, with an 80-mile portage to the Athabasca River, was the fastest route across the prairies for brigades headed either to the Pacific or to the fur-rich North. Edmonton, situated at the end of practical navigation on the North Saskatchewan, became a key fort on the major trans-Canada route and a supply base for brigades heading east, west and north.

Floods in 1825 and 1829 forced the final move of Fort Edmonton to higher ground just below the present Legislative Building. Here Rowand built an imposing new fort to impress upon the Indians the power of the Company and its chief officer. Under Rowand, Fort Edmonton reached the height of its importance. It was the seat of government of the district, the main trading post for seven Indian tribes, the major supply centre on the North Saskatchewan, the principal provider of York boats for the annual trip to the Bay, and the largest population centre in the district with about 130 inhabitants.

In the late 1850s, however, the fashion in Europe changed from felted fur to silk hats, leaving the fur trade with much reduced markets. Also, American settlers were pushing westward into the Oregon Territory. American annexationists were using the cry of *Manifest Destiny* to demand the ousting of the British from North America. This threat was eased for a time by the Treaty of Oregon in 1846 which extended the boundary along the 49th Parallel, west of the Rockies, depriving H.B.C. of the Pacific Northwest south of the border, but leaving it all of present Canada west of Ontario and part of northern Quebec. Meanwhile, American traders in Montana were making generous use of liquor to lure the Blackfoot away from the H.B.C. This forced the Company to continue its use of liquor, contributing further to violence and degradation among the Indians. By 1869, American whisky traders had begun to establish posts in southern Alberta. As H.B.C. power eroded, law and order disappeared. Worse, the 1869-70 smallpox plague killed almost half the Indian population, and depletion of the buffalo herds left those who survived to face starvation.

With American settlers pouring westward and pressing against the 49th Parallel, the need was becoming urgent for Canada to claim and populate the prairies. In 1869, the weakened H.B.C. agreed to sell its rights to Rupert's Land to the new Dominion of Canada.

[December, 1871] **One of the earliest photographs of Fort Edmonton** shows the fifth Fort Edmonton built by the Hudson's Bay Company. Two earlier forts had been built further downstream and two more had been built near the foreground of this picture, where the Rossdale power plant stands now. Flooding in 1825 and 1829 forced a move to higher ground and gave Chief Factor John Rowand the opportunity to plan a better and more impressive fort, which he wished to name "Fort Sanspareil" (Fort Without Equal). Some frowned upon that name and countered by nicknaming his Big House "Rowand's Folly". The Cree Indians called the fort "Amisk Wutchee Waskahegan", meaning Beaver Hills House.

[December, 1871] **John Rowand's Big House** was the largest and most expensive building west of Hudson's Bay. Its windows contained the first glass panes to be used in the West and amazed the Indians. In addition to being the home of the chief factor and his family, some employees and visitors, it served as an office, warehouse, reception hall and seat of government for the Hudson's Bay Company's Saskatchewan District. The smaller building served as living quarters for other employees at the fort.

[1879] **This panorama shows all of Edmonton** in 1879. Rowand's Big House is gone, replaced by Chief Factor Richard Hardisty's new Big House, built outside the palisade of the fort higher up the hill to the left. On the horizon above the Big House is the fledgling settlement of Edmonton near Rev. George McDougall's Methodist church. On the south side of the river, across from the steamboat *Lily* moored on the bank, is John Walter's house.

Rev. William Newton of the Anglican Church in Edmonton described the settlement in 1879: "We have nothing like a town. As we said, there is the fort, then if you had a telescope and could look around the corner into a valley you would see a hotel. Then if there was no fog you could see the Methodist chapel and parsonage and scattered houses on that side; and on the other, All Saints English Church, a few Indian tents and again a few settlers' houses up the river. This is Edmonton proper."

[n.d.] **John Rowand** (1789-1854) **was a Nor'Wester** until the amalgamation of the North West and the Hudson's Bay Companies in 1821. From 1823 to 1854, he reigned as head of the Hudson's Bay Company's Saskatchewan District (roughly the present Alberta and Saskatchewan) with his headquarters at Fort Edmonton.

Sir George Simpson, governor of the Hudson's Bay Company, described Rowand as "One of the most pushing bustling Men in the Service whose zeal and ambition in the discharge of his duty is unequalled, rendering him totally regardless of every personal Comfort and indulgence. Warm hearted and Friendly in an extraordinary degree where he takes a liking, but on the contrary his prejudices exceedingly strong. Of a fiery disposition and as bold as a Lion. An excellent Trader who has the peculiar talent of attracting the fiercest Indians to him while he rules them with a Rod of Iron and so daring that he beards their Chiefs in the open camp while surrounded by their Warriors: has likewise a Wonderful influence over his people. Has by his superior management realized more money for the concern than any three of his Colleagues since the Coalition; and altho' his Education has been defective is a very clear headed clever fellow. Will not tell a lie (which is very uncommon in this Country) but has sufficient address to evade the truth when it suits his purpose: full of drollery and humour and generally liked and respected by Indians, Servants and his own equals."

[1884] **This is a later view** inside the palisade of Fort Edmonton. The large building on the left is the Far North Building, built when the fort was enlarged in 1861 and used as a warehouse by the Hudson's Bay Company. The small building in the centre was used as the North West Mounted Police Commanding Officer's house. In front with the men are two small brass cannons available for the defence of the fort and used to fire a welcoming salute to Indian bands coming to trade. On the hill outside the stockade is Chief Factor Richard Hardisty's Big House, which he had built around 1874 with the logs from Rowand's earlier Big House.

[1905] **In 1905, the Cree Indians** set up this camp on Ross Flats below the Hardisty Big House. Over a century had passed already since their ancestors began to come to the North West Company's Fort Augustus and the Hudson's Bay Company's Edmonton House to trade. The Cree came from the woods to the north, while the Assiniboine, Blackfoot, Blood, Sarcee, Piegan and Gros Ventre tribes came from the plains to the south to swap their furs, pemmican and buffalo meat for tomahawks, rifles, beads, cooking pots, blankets, tobacco and rum.

[n.d.] **After the merger** of the North West Company with the Hudson's Bay Company in 1821, the voyageurs' swift canoes were replaced by slower but more efficient York boats that could carry more cargo, including bulkier items like stoves, while requiring fewer men. These large, flat-bottomed boats, equipped with oars, sail and rudder, were used on the North Saskatchewan to take the Company's furs to York Factory on Hudson's Bay and to bring back trade goods. When the wind was favourable, large square sails were used.

Most of these boats were built at Fort Edmonton. This was a continuous occupation at the fort, because more boats were needed to carry the furs to Hudson's Bay than ever returned.

[n.d.] **Brigades of ox-drawn Red River carts** were the main form of transportation in the Northwest in the days before the railway. They were used to freight goods along the Carlton Trail between Fort Edmonton and Fort Garry, and along the Calgary and Whoop-Up Trails to Fort Benton in Montana.

The carts were simply a light wooden box set on an axle attached to two tall wheels, with two shafts connecting the box to the ox. They were made entirely of wood and "shaganappi" – strands of fresh, raw buffalo hide. This simple design had definite advantages: It could be easily repaired, even when no trees were available for wood, by using strands of fresh buffalo hide to bind the broken pieces together. It could also be taken apart and the wooden box, with the wheels lashed underneath, be used as a raft to float the goods across a stream too deep to ford. It had one outstanding disadvantage, however: The wheels could not be greased, because of the thick prairie dust, and the result was an ear-piercing screeching that had to be endured for the length of the journey!

2 Beyond the Fort (1871-1891)

The transfer of Rupert's Land and the North-Western Territory from the Hudson's Bay Company to the Dominion of Canada was concluded in May, 1870. From the sale, the H.B.C. received £300,000 plus huge grants of land, including several acres around each of its trading posts. At Edmonton, the boundaries of this H.B.C. Reserve around the old fort were established along roughly the modern 101 Street on the east, 121 Street on the west, the river on the south and 118 Avenue on the north.

With the end of H.B.C. rule, men with an eye to the future looked beyond the fort to the rich land and the possibilities it held for settlement. Malcolm Groat chose the land west of the fort, and since there was no one between him and the Rocky Mountains, he staked a square mile. Rev. George McDougall claimed land on the high bank just east of the reserve for the new Methodist mission he was building. Soon other settlers began to cultivate the virgin soil around Edmonton, but most had other jobs as well, as H.B.C. packers or as guides for the survey crews now working in the West.

Times were changing, though. The Industrial Revolution in Europe and the eastern United States was causing a shift in population from the farm to the city, creating a market for farm produce. The development of Red Fife wheat, which could mature before the early prairie frosts, and the new steel-roller milling process that made premium flour from this hard northern wheat, were making commercial wheat growing possible on the Canadian prairie. Mechanization was making large-scale farming feasible and the promised C.P.R. would provide the necessary transport.

To prepare for the influx of settlers, who would people the prairies for Canada, the Dominion Land Survey was working slowly westward, dividing the vast prairie into quarter sections, so settlers could have legal title to their land. The Dominion Lands Act of 1872 allowed a settler to claim a quarter section (160 acres) for a fee of $10 on condition that he live on it and work it for three years. And the C.P.R. survey under Sandford Fleming was at work planning the route for the trans-Canada railway. In 1875, indications were that the route would pass through Edmonton on its way to the Yellowhead Pass. Prospects looked very bright for Edmonton.

In spite of the worldwide depression at the time, progress was being made in Edmonton. The North West Mounted Police arrived in 1874 to curb the whisky trade and restore law and order. In 1875, steamboats quickened the pace of river transport from Winnipeg to Edmonton. The Dominion telegraph line along the proposed C.P.R. route reached Hay Lakes, 20 miles away, in 1877, and two years later the line was extended to Edmonton's

south bank with Alex Taylor as operator. An official post office was established at the fort in 1878, with Chief Factor Richard Hardisty as postmaster. The Edmonton Agricultural Society held its first exhibition in 1879. The H.B.C. subdivided the southern portion of its reserve in 1880 and built Jasper Avenue across it. Frank Oliver and Alex Taylor launched Alberta's first newspaper, The *Bulletin*, in December, 1880. In 1881, John Walter inaugurated the first cable ferry and Matt McCauley organized the first public school, funded until 1884 by private subscription.

The C.P.R. reached Winnipeg in 1881, where the population mushroomed as settlers began to claim the land. While Edmontonians were rubbing their hands in anticipation of a similar boom, the C.P.R. announced that the route would be changed to traverse the southern prairies toward the Kicking Horse Pass. While Edmonton reeled in shock, the C.P.R. reached the NWMP Fort Calgary in 1883 and a rival town boomed and replaced Edmonton as the heart of the western prairies, while the railway replaced the North Saskatchewan River as the main trans-Canada route. Edmonton was now isolated and in the doldrums. It was still the Gateway to the North, however, and northern freight traffic was increasing. This, and the tenacity of the Edmonton settlers, enabled Edmonton to survive while other settlements along the North Saskatchewan faded.

In the midst of this, Edmonton's No. 1 Liberal Frank Oliver was elected to the North West Territories Council in Regina, where he could hammer John A. Macdonald's Conservative representatives for a better deal for Edmonton and responsible government for the West.

Meanwhile, the Dominion Land Survey finally reached Edmonton in 1882 and enabled the early settlers to claim legal title to their land, putting an end to the problem of claim jumpers. The trail to Athabasca Landing was upgraded with bridges and ferries, and stagecoaches began to travel the trail to Calgary, carrying mail, passengers and goods to the new iron-railed lifeline to the outside world.

Riel's North West Rebellion in 1885 caused panic in Edmonton for a few weeks, when an attack by the local Indians and Métis was feared; in fact, Edmonton was never in danger and life soon returned to normal.

Although Alex Taylor introduced telephones to the community in 1886 and electric lights in 1891, little else was happening in Edmonton during this period before the arrival of the Calgary & Edmonton Railway on the south bank of the river in 1891. With the railway came settlers. Over 300 homestead entries were filed at Edmonton during the summer of 1891. Optimism was returning to the settlement.

[n.d.] **Among the first to settle** beyond the fort were Kenneth McDonald (1828-1906), a saddler and harness-maker for the Hudson's Bay Company, and his brother-in-law, William Rowland, who staked their claims in July, 1870. Kenneth McDonald, on the right, is shown contemplating the construction of a new barn on his homestead, which was east of what became 92 Street and included the land now occupied by Clarke Stadium and the Commonwealth Stadium. One of his houses, similar to that shown in the background, now stands on 1885 Street in Fort Edmonton Park as an example of an early settler's home.

[n.d.] **Malcolm Alexander Groat** (1836-1912) was another employee of the Hudson's Bay Company who became an early settler outside the fort.

He came to Edmonton by Red River cart from Fort Garry in 1861. At Fort Edmonton, he served as second in command to Chief Factor William J. Christie, whose daughter he married in 1870. He was in charge of the Company's farm and pack horses, used for freighting goods along the Athabasca Trail to Fort Assiniboine.

In 1878, he left the Company to farm land he had staked in 1870 just west of the Hudson's Bay Reserve. This land extended from the river to 111 Avenue and from 121 Street to 149 Street. During the land boom, after the turn of the century, he subdivided part of this estate for lots. He also donated land for the first Roman Catholic and Anglican churches built outside the fort. He served on the first school board in 1881 and was a founder of the Northern Alberta Pioneers and Old Timers Association. Groat Estates, Groat Ravine, Groat Road and Groat Bridge are all memorials to this pioneer, who saw Fort Edmonton become a major city.

[1895] **Malcolm Groat, on the left,** soon expanded his farm to include cattle raising at a time when Edmonton's beef and meat-packing industries were still in a primitive state. Beefing about meat prices was probably not so new, though, when this item appeared in the *Bulletin* in 1882: "Fresh beef steak is 20 cents a pound and roast fifteen. Some people are thinking of substituting dollar bills for beef steak, in order to live more cheaply."

14

[n.d.] **Rev. George Millward McDougall** (1821-1876) brought his family to the West in 1863 and established a Methodist mission at Victoria (now Pakan), about eighty miles down-river from Fort Edmonton. There he worked tirelessly among the Indians until recurring outbreaks of smallpox, which claimed the lives of three of his daughters and a daughter-in-law and decimated the native population, made continuing his work at Victoria impossible. In 1871, he moved his family to Fort Edmonton, where the Hudson's Bay Company's quarantine precautions had proven effective against the disease. Here he established a new Methodist mission to carry on his work among the Indians and Métis. Rev. McDougall's parsonage was among the first buildings erected outside the palisades of the fort. In 1875, when the mission was well established, he moved again to join his son, John, at the Morley mission among the Stony Indians on the Bow River. The following January, Rev. George McDougall perished in a blizzard while hunting for buffalo. His wife and daughters were among the first white women to live in this area. Three of his daughters married Hudson's Bay Company officers. Two of these, Richard Hardisty and Harrison Young, later became chief factors at Fort Edmonton.

[c1892] **Rev. McDougall's little Wesleyan church,** built in 1873, was the first Protestant church in Alberta and is the oldest surviving building in Edmonton. It originally stood facing the river near the site of the present McDougall United Church. Built of hand-hewn squared timbers, it was later given a clapboard covering, although the original logs still form the inside walls. This little church formed the nucleus of the emerging settlement of Edmonton and was used by other denominations as well for services and social gatherings.

The building was relocated several times. This photo shows it around 1892, when it was moved across 101 Street to the site later occupied by the Journal Building, in order that a new frame church could replace it on the original site near the College Avenue School shown in the background. In 1893, it was moved again and used by the Salvation Army. In 1904, it was moved behind Alberta College to serve as a boys' dormitory and later a storehouse. In 1946, it was relocated next to McDougall United Church and restored as a memorial to the Rev. George McDougall. Finally, in 1978, it made its last move to Fort Edmonton Park.

[c1883] **This was John A. McDougall's third store** in Edmonton, opened on the northwest corner of Jasper Avenue and 98 Street in the summer of 1883 with the backing of Stewart and Bannerman of Winnipeg. Here Mr. McDougall sold goods of every sort. On the main floor, two counters ran the length of the building with groceries on one side, dry goods on the other and hardware at the rear. Upstairs were the hats, boots, shoes and ready-made clothing. The wide platform out front, on which the men are standing, was one of the first sidewalks in town.

John A. McDougall's store was one of the first to introduce the use of paper bags and wrapping paper to its customers, as former Chief Factor Harrison Young

recalled: "The old style of things was if you bought a pound of tea and some sugar, you tied it up in your handkerchief, if you had one. If not, you bought something to tie it up in. A shirt came in handy for that. With a string tied round the wrist of the shirt you put the sugar in one sleeve and the tea in the other. Another string tied round made all secure. If you were dead broke and could buy no more, it was not considered out of the way to take off the shirt you had on and use it."

In 1885, Mr. McDougall sold out and this store was run by Stewart and Bannerman until it was sold to the Hudson's Bay Company as their first retail store outside the fort.

[n.d.] **John A. McDougall** (1854-1928) first came to the Edmonton area around 1877 as a free trader, bringing supplies west from Winnipeg to the Indian camps, where he would trade his goods for furs. When his supplies ran out, he would return to Winnipeg to trade his furs and re-outfit. In 1879, he decided to settle in Edmonton and open a trading store. From these modest beginnings, in partnership with Richard Secord, he built up an impressive department store, fur trade, real estate business and financial empire. He was also active in community affairs, serving as chairman of the Public School Board in 1893, as alderman in 1894, as president of the Board of Trade in 1895, as mayor in 1897 and again in 1908, as Liberal MLA for Edmonton 1909-1913, and as a member of the first Senate of the University of Alberta.

[c1890] By 1890, the commercial core of the new settlement, composed mainly of two-storey frame buildings, was emerging along Main Street (now Jasper Avenue). East of 99 Street stand, on the north side, Raymer's jewellery store with the clock sign, Patrick Byrnes shoe shop, Ross Brothers' hardware, the Hudson's Bay Company store (formerly McDougall's), the Alberta Hotel with the pitched roof, John Brown's store sitting forward onto the street with Mather's photographic studio barely visible behind it, A. MacDonald's store with the pitched roof and the false-fronted Columbia House hotel. On the south side of the street, across from the Columbia House, is Robertson's Hall and further west are Xavier St. Jean's Hotel du Canada and the Masonic Hall. The little whitewashed log building at the far right is the old Bulletin Building, built for Frank Oliver in 1878 as a general store with his living quarters on the upper floor. It was later used as a print shop for the *Bulletin* until 1894.

[c1890s] **Another of Edmonton's early settlers** was Matthew McCauley (1850-1930), who came to the Edmonton area in 1879 and settled on a farm near Fort Saskatchewan until 1881. He then moved into Edmonton and built a house and barn east of Mc Dougall's Methodist Church where McCauley Plaza now honors his memory. From here, he operated the first livery stable in Edmonton in partnership with Bill Ibbotson. In addition to caring for horses and offering horses for hire, they ran a cartage service, a stagecoach service to St. Albert and handled a mail contract.

It was not surprising that Matt, with eight children already, soon agitated for a school. As chairman of the trustees' committee, he organized Edmonton's first school, which was financed by voluntary donations. He continued as chairman of the school board and as trustee for many years after.

In 1882, when squatters refused to recognize the land claims of Edmonton's first settlers (for want of an official survey of the settlement, they could not hold legal title to their land) Matt McCauley led a group of vigilantes and threw the

squatters' shacks tumbling over a cliff in the defence of justice – if not of the law.

In 1892, when Edmonton was incorporated as a town and Matt was unanimously chosen to be its first mayor, he led his vigilantes again, this time against what was perceived to be Strathcona's attempt to steal the Dominion Land Office from its rightful

place on the north bank. Matt's show of strength and determination convinced the federal government to keep the main Land Office in Edmonton and add a branch office across the river in Strathcona.

Matt served three terms as mayor before being elected to succeed Frank Oliver as Edmonton's delegate to the Northwest Territories Assembly in Regina in 1896. That same year, his first wife died and he later remarried and raised four more children. In 1901, he took up ranching at Beaver Lake and in 1905 returned to Edmonton as Liberal MLA for Vermilion in Alberta's first Legislature. He resigned in 1906 to become warden of the new federal penitentiary in Edmonton. When the Conservatives came to power in Ottawa and dismissed him from that position in 1911, he left for Penticton to grow apples until 1925 when, at age 75, he took up a homestead near Sexsmith and worked it until his death in 1930.

[c1886] **Edmonton's first public school** was built in 1881, when a group of interested citizens led by Matt McCauley donated funds for a building and for the teacher's salary of $500 a year. The Hudson's Bay Company donated four lots on the Hudson's Bay Reserve for the school house, where the McKay Avenue School is now. The 24-foot by 30-foot

building cost $968 and was one of the first frame buildings in the settlement. It was sparsely furnished with a teacher's desk, twelve student desks (each four feet long), a blackboard, a small hand bell, a coal stove, a water pail and a tin cup. A water barrel outside was filled regularly by the water man, as he made his rounds.

When the Northwest Territories set up a public school system, this school became Edmonton Protestant School District No. 7, the first officially established school in Alberta. Later, after the construction of the new brick McKay Avenue School, the old frame schoolhouse was moved to Ross Flats where it was used as a residence at 9647 100 Street until 1980.

This photo shows the teacher, Mr. W.H. Carson, with his class of fifty-two pupils of various ages and grade levels. For coping with this awesome task, he was rewarded with a handsome salary of $75 a month.

[n.d.] **Hon. Frank Oliver** (1853-1933). On December 6, 1880, Frank Oliver and telegraph operator Alex Taylor began publishing the *Bulletin*, the first newspaper in Alberta. In its pages, Frank championed the cause of western rights and responsible government for the prairies and launched his political career, which began in 1883 with his election as Edmonton's representative to the North West Territories Council in Regina. He was defeated in 1885 but re-elected in 1888 and served in Regina until 1896, when he went to Ottawa as the Liberal Member of Parliament for Alberta. In 1904, he was re-elected as MP for Edmonton and in 1905 became Laurier's Minister of the Interior in charge of immigration policy when the influx of settlers to the West was at its height. He was in a position to see to it that Edmonton was chosen as capital of the new province of Alberta. In 1911, Laurier's Liberals were defeated and Frank Oliver remained as a member of the Opposition until his own defeat in 1917.

[n.d.] **Alex Taylor** (1854-1916). When the Dominion telegraph line was extended from Hay Lakes into Edmonton in 1879, Alex Taylor came too as its first operator, with his office in John Walter's old log house across the river from the fort. That winter, he arranged for weekly news bulletins to be wired to him from Winnipeg. He wrote out these bulletins and left them in Frank Oliver's store, where customers could read them. This was Edmonton's first "newspaper". It soon became the *Bulletin*, with Alex supplying the telegraph news to Frank Oliver, who had been a printer and newspaperman in Winnipeg before coming to Edmonton.

The telegraph business also led to the telephone business. In 1884, only eight years after Alexander Graham Bell's historic call from Brantford to Paris, Ontario, Alex Taylor encouraged the Dominion Telegraph Service to build a telephone link between his telegraph office in Edmonton and St. Albert. This, Alberta's first telephone line, began operation in January, 1885. Soon after, Alex had telephone connections from his office to the fort and to various businesses and Edmonton's first telephone system was launched. This was sold to the city in 1904 and became the municipally owned Edmonton Telephones of today.

Alex Taylor also set up Edmonton's first electric light company in 1891, using a coal-burning boiler to make electricity. As well, he was the Dominion weatherman, postmaster, clerk of the court and chairman of the public school board for several years. Even though in later life he lost the use of both arms, he remained active in serving the community and set a fine example of dignity and courage.

[c1890] **Donald Ross** (1840-1915) established his homestead on River Lot 4, on the flats below Rev. McDougall's Methodist mission. It was Saskatchewan River gold that first lured him here, via New York, California, Nevada and Peace River. Arriving in 1872, he panned the sandbars for a time, earning about five dollars a day, before deciding to put down roots and try farming the area now known as Rossdale. As settlers began to trickle into the new settlement, the need for food and accommodation became pressing and soon Donald's log house became Edmonton's first hotel, when he converted the second floor into a dormitory and began serving meals for 50 cents. In 1882, he added the two-and-a-half storey addition seen here in front of the original log building.

[1902] **Donald Ross (on the right)**, son of a Scottish gardener, proudly displays the fruits of his labour. As early as 1874, he was experimenting with growing vegetables on a plot just below his log house. Soon, his was the first garden to produce vegetables for sale and he became a familiar sight on local streets driving a wagon full of produce pulled by a team of snow-white mules. The market garden and greenhouses also supplied fresh vegetables for his hotel kitchen and won him prizes at the annual Exhibition. Gardening also kindled a friendship between Donald and his hotel's most famous guest, the botanist Luther Burbank, who occasionally visited here looking for wild plants to invigorate his cultivated species.

[c1902] **Donald Ross's Edmonton Hotel** was a popular community gathering place during the settlement's early days, and soon Donald had to build this three-storey addition. Public meetings were sometimes held here to discuss such current issues as hiring a school teacher or deciding to incorporate Edmonton as a town. At other times, it was simply a popular spot for an evening's entertainment over a game of pool or billiards. When times were hectic at the hotel, even the billiard tables were used as extra beds. One morning a guest complained at having to pay 50¢ for such a night's accommodation. His host obligingly offered to let him pay the usual billiard table rate instead, 75¢ an hour. Or, if he preferred, he could move on to the next hotel – in Portage la Prairie.

The hotel burned down in 1925 and today a park bench and a concrete replica of the old fireplace, made of river clay and Saskatoon bushes, marks the original site of Edmonton's "pioneer house of entertainment" and serves as a memorial to its convivial landlord.

[1903] **The bar of the Edmonton Hotel** was a favourite gathering place for the hamlet's menfolk. Although the decor was stylish, with an ornate pressed-metal wall serving as backdrop to stuffed birds, deer heads and palms, it was undoubtedly whisky and the landlord's ready wit that were the main attractions. Since the hotel was located at the bottom of the hairpin turn in the road up the steep McDougall Hill, it was a convenient stopping place for teams hauling goods to Edmonton from the railway station in Strathcona. Giving the horses a rest before heading up the hill gave the driver an excuse to rest his foot on the brass rail, his elbow on the oak bar and enjoy a quick one and an exchange of pleasantries with innkeeper Donald Ross (on the far right).

[1890] **Edmonton's second hotel** was Jasper House, shown here as it looked in 1890. It was built on the north side of Jasper Avenue, just east of 97 Street, in 1882 by James Goodridge (1852-1900) to replace his earlier boarding house. The hotel business has flourished there ever since, although the building has undergone extensive alterations, eventually becoming the Hub Hotel.

For many years, Jasper House was Edmonton's first and only brick building. Besides offering accommodation, food and drink, the hotel was used as temporary business quarters for newly arrived entrepreneurs, such as Emanuel Raymer, jeweller, and J.C.F. Bowen, lawyer and later Alberta's Lieutenant-Governor. As well as being the headquarters for the Edmonton-Calgary stagecoach and a

meeting place for many early sports clubs, it was home to the Goodridge family.

The upstairs door with the treacherous landing was used for getting furniture up to the second floor. It was over fourteen years before a balcony was added.

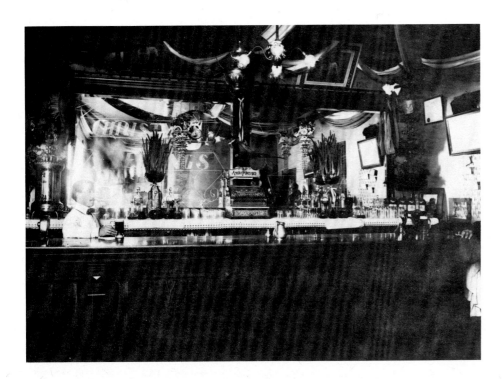

[c1905] **The feature that attracted** the most business at the Jasper House was the bar. Although the North West Territories was supposed to be under strict prohibition until 1892, liquor was seldom hard to find, even if it sometimes had to be disguised as patent medicine. In this photograph, taken after laws were introduced to allow licensed saloons, a few bottles of the real brew are visible. In earlier times, they would have been kept well out of sight – but not out of reach.

[1893-94] **H.A. Finch's Saddle and Harness Shop,** on Jasper Avenue between 99 and 100 Streets, sold harness for horses and oxen, saddles, bits, leather suitcases, axle grease and harness oils, in addition to making and repairing harnesses. Mr. Finch had been manager for Hutchings and Riley, a Calgary harness and saddlery firm, which opened an Edmonton branch in 1891 below Mrs. Kernohan's millinery shop. In 1893, Mr. Finch bought out the business and carried on under his own name.

[1884] **In the days of the horse and buggy,** blacksmith shops were essential. Besides shoeing horses and oxen, Sanderson & Looby's shop also repaired carriages, mending tires, spokes, rims and axles.

George Sanderson (1850-1940) and Edward Looby (1855-1914), standing in their shirtsleeves in the centre foreground, came to Edmonton in 1881 and established their smithy, Edmonton's second, just west of Jasper House on the northwest corner of Jasper Avenue and Namayo Avenue

(now 97 Street). Living in quarters above the shop, they carried on their business in partnership until 1887 when George sold out and set up a shop of his own. Edward carried on at the old shop, expanding the business into harnessmaking as well. George branched out too, handling bicycles for a while before turning to locksmithing. He was also active in local politics, serving as alderman in 1893 and as Edmonton's first fire chief 1892-94. Edward was a sportsman, active in cricket, curling and the rifle club.

[1889] **Edmonton's first cricket team** assembled for this photo at the old downtown sports ground northwest of the present Hudson's Bay store.

With so many of Edmonton's early settlers coming from the British Isles, it is not surprising that cricket got an early start here. The game was played as early as October, 1881, when this ten-year-old hamlet had an adult population of only 263, and became the first sport to be officially organized in the community when the Edmonton Cricket Club was formed in May, 1882, with Dr. Wilson as president. The new club declared itself "the boss of any similar organization within a radius of 500 miles", since it was two years before any mention was made of the sport in Calgary and six years before the Vancouver Cricket Club was formed. In 1884, though, Fort Saskatchewan formed a club, which briefly provided out-of-town competition until the Riel Rebellion of 1885. After five years of inactivity, the Edmonton club reorganized in March, 1889, and annual games were played against Fort Saskatchewan and Clover Bar. The first Edmonton vs. Calgary game, on August 16, 1892, resulted in a 106 - 59 victory for the visiting Calgary eleven.

[n.d.] **Here are the members of Edmonton's** first rugby club. In the back row, captain Campbell Young holds the ball as he stands beside the well dressed referee, Herbert Edmiston.

Although a few enthusiasts played football by moonlight in February, 1882, the first newspaper account of a rugby football game in Edmonton was of one that took place on Christmas Day, 1882, on the Hudson's Bay Reserve. It resulted in a pane of glass being knocked out of Mr. A. Dunlop's window. The following game, played on New Year's Day, "ended without accident". The next mention is of a New Year's game, 1884, played on Main Street.

The first serious challenge game came shortly after the railroad arrived at South Edmonton in 1891. That October, the Edmonton boys challenged Calgary. After losing the first game in Calgary 4 - 1 (two tries and a goal to one try), the heavier Edmonton team won the rematch on the Edmonton Hudson's Bay Reserve race track grounds 5 - 0 (three ties and one goal). The next autumn, Calgary refused to reply to a new challenge.

[1890] **Baseball got started here** in May, 1884, with a club consisting of thirty-six members, including twenty-five players. The first game was played at the race track grounds on May 24, 1884. After a five-year interval, the club was reorganized in March, 1889. On August 11, 1891, the Calgary team came by stagecoach to play the local team and won 28-22. The Edmonton boys got some measure of satisfaction, however, when, in a 100-yard footrace, Torrance of the Calgary baseball team was beaten by the local Indian speedster, Moosewa, and an estimated $1000 changed hands in favor of the local bettors. The return match at Calgary in late October also resulted in a Calgary victory, 26-19. The first Edmonton win against their southern rivals occurred in August, 1892, when a stronger Edmonton team won 20-17. The following October, Calgary won both ball games, but Moosewa again put another $1000 into the pockets of the northern visitors by easily beating Calgary's sprinter in the 100-yard race.

[November 9, 1891] **With moustaches finely groomed** and guns brightly polished, here are the members of the Edmonton rifle team.

Prior to the organization of the Edmonton Rifle Association on July 3, 1886 with forty members, a few informal shooting matches were held by local sharpshooters. On December 17, 1885, the turkey shoot at the Long Lake Hotel provided an eight-inch bull's-eye at the end of a 200-yard range. Out of 164 shots, ten turkeys were won. In September, 1886, the Rifle Association set up shooting ranges varying from 200 to 800 yards on Ross Flats below the old fort. On November 8, 1886, the first annual match was held for both men and women members over distances of 200, 400, 500 and 600 yards, with five shots at each range position. To officially open the affair, Mrs. Richard Hardisty, wife of the fort's chief factor, fired the first shot.

After several matches between the Edmonton club and the North West Mounted Police stationed at Fort Saskatchewan, the North West Rifle League held their first inter-association matches in July, 1889, with the teams from Edmonton, Prince Albert, Battleford, Calgary and Lethbridge each using their home ranges and telegraphing the results to the other towns. In 1891, the Edmonton team took the third place trophy in the North West Rifle League's series of summer matches.

Trapshooting got started when the Edmonton Gun Club was formed in 1889. The targets were tin pigeons and the chief competition came from members of the Fort Saskatchewan Gun Club.

[1885] **Bringing supplies to the growing** settlement of Edmonton became more efficient with the introduction of steam-powered paddlewheelers to the river transportation system. These flat-bottomed riverboats, designed to operate in shallow waters, had long been churning the waters of the Mississippi and the Missouri, but it was not until 1875 that the *Northcote*, pictured here, made the first successful journey on the North Saskatchewan River upstream to Edmonton. Although the Saskatchewan, with its low water level and shifting sandbars, was never an easy river to navigate, the comparative speed of these vessels and the large cargoes of over a hundred tons that they could handle made them much favored over brigades of oxcarts trudging along a thousand miles of prairie trails. For the next fifteen years, the sound of the steam whistle brought townsfolk scurrying to the shore to greet passengers and to witness the unloading of building materials, merchandise, flour and other supplies. In 1891, though, the sound of another steam whistle, that of the railway, announced the doom of the riverboats.

Today the only remains in Edmonton of the steamboat era are two plaques, in the Chateau Lacombe and Macdonald Hotel, made from pieces of Minnesota oak retrieved from the hull of the disintegrating *Northcote*, which tell the story of the historic ship that pioneered steam navigation on the Saskatchewan and served as a make-shift gunboat at the Battle of Batoche in 1885.

[1889] Upon seeing the Calgary-Edmonton stage try to make its way through the mire of the Calgary Trail, it is not surprising that the two-hundred-mile journey took a full five days each way. When Donald McLeod initiated the service in August, 1883, the stage left Jasper House on Monday morning and arrived in Calgary late Friday. The fare of $25 each way included four overnight reprieves at stopping houses along the way and entitled the traveller to a hundred pounds of baggage. Fording rivers, losing the trail in a fog, or setting out from Edmonton with sleigh runners only to find that a chinook had left the trail bare further south were elements that added to the adventure of the journey.

3 Birth of Strathcona (1875-1911)

From the time the C.P.R. reached Calgary in 1883, creating a rival boomtown there, Edmontonians demanded a branch line linking Edmonton to the mainline. This was finally achieved in 1891 with the arrival of the Calgary & Edmonton Railway on the south bank across from Fort Edmonton. Nothing, however, could induce the railway company to go to the expense of building a bridge across the broad, deep river valley to bring the trains into Edmonton proper. Instead, the company was promoting a new townsite on the south side, where they were now the major landowners. Moreover, they expected this new townsite to replace the established settlement on the north bank, which they referred to as "the former Edmonton Settlement".

This state of affairs naturally rankled the old settlers on the north shore who had invested their toil and capital in building a community at what had always been the hub of the district. All these vexations came to a head in June, 1892, when Tom Anderson, the Dominion land and timber agent at Edmonton, attempted to remove the land office to the south side. To Edmontonians, the removal of an established government office to the new townsite was not only a nasty precedent that would hasten the demise of their town, but a breach of promise by the federal government who had given assurances that such a shift would not take place. And since Tom Anderson was also the owner of River Lot 13 on which a large portion of the new townsite was situated, he stood to gain from any appreciation in the value of land there, as did Osler, Hammond & Nanton, townsite agents for the C & E Railway Co. To Edmontonians, therefore, the removal of the land office was not a sincere effort to provide convenience for incoming settlers, but rather another ruse by the C & E to increase profits.

So, when bystanders noticed Mr. Anderson loading record books and furniture from the land office onto a wagon, they quickly sounded the alarm and soon an angry mob surrounded the wagon, unhitched the horses and removed all nuts from the wheels so it could not be moved. Later scathing telegrams were sent to Ottawa demanding the retention of the land office and the removal of Tom Anderson as agent instead. Anderson in turn called out the Mounties who could do little in the face of "five hundred men with blood in both eyes", as Frank Oliver described them. When it was feared that reinforcements from the NWMP post in Fort Saskatchewan might try to assist the move, Edmonton's Mayor McCauley called out the armed home guards, organized by Gen. Strange during the Riel Rebellion, "to keep the peace – that is, the land office". But Supt. Griesbach wisely chose to await word from Ottawa before risking a showdown, and the mob vented its fury by burning the land agent in effigy.

In a couple of days a telegram arrived from Prime Minister Laurier assuring Edmonton that the land office would remain in Edmonton and only a branch would be set up in South Edmonton. The "Land Office Steal" was over and peace – but not love – was restored between the two communities.

The C & E Railway Co. had built the rail line but leased it to the C.P.R. to operate while the C & E shareholders looked to profits from their land holdings along the route. In South Edmonton they put lots up for sale and set about building streets, many named after C.P.R. officials like Sir William Whyte. They also built a railway station and a hotel at the corner of Whyte Avenue and 1st Street SE (103 Street today), thereby establishing the location of the town's commercial centre.

Before long, stores, hotels, a livery stable, blacksmith shop and similar essential services lined Whyte Avenue west of the railway. To serve the area's agricultural community, grain elevators and two large flour mills were built. Livestock were brought here for shipment to market, and meat packing plants were soon established by John Gainer, Gallagher and Hull, Vogel and Calgary's Pat Burns. Jackson Brothers set up a foundry and machine shop and Robert Ochsner began the Strathcona Brewing and Malting Co. Down in Walterdale, John Walter's sawmill, boat-building and lumber business flourished, and the Pollard Brothers' brickyard and several coal mines were also busy. In 1894, the South Edmonton *News* (later the Strathcona *Plaindealer)* began publishing and the Agricultural Society held its first annual fair at the fair grounds near University Avenue and 104 Street.

In June, 1899, the community reluctantly gave in to incorporation as a town and changed its name to Strathcona in an attempt to distinguish it from the north side community that refused to wither away. In March, 1907, with a population of 3,500, Strathcona became a city and set to work building a city hall, a new fire hall, a library, a hospital, parks and boulevards. At this time too, it was selected as the site for the new provincial university and River Lot 5 was purchased for the new campus.

In spite of Strathcona's steady growth and development, Edmonton had grown faster. In 1911, while Strathcona's population was 5,579, Edmonton's was 24,900. In Strathcona's 1910 civic election, amalgamation was a key issue. The pro-amalgamation candidates won heavily and immediately set to work negotiating the union. On September 26, 1911, the Strathcona ratepayers voted 518 to 178 in favour of amalgamation and on February 1, 1912, Strathcona became a part of Greater Edmonton.

[c1904] **John Walter** (1850-1920) was the
first to settle on the south bank of the
river across from Fort Edmonton. There
he applied his able skills as a carpenter
and boatbuilder and became one of
Edmonton's first wealthy businessmen.

He came to Edmonton from the
Orkneys in 1870 as an employee of the
Hudson's Bay Company and worked at
the fort for five years, building York boats
and doing other carpentry jobs. After
leaving the Company and settling on the
south bank, he continued to build York
boats for the H.B.C. under contract at
$220 a boat.

As his boatbuilding business increased
and expanded into other areas, including
the manufacture of buckboards and
sleighs as well as scows for gold dredges,
it led naturally into the lumber business.
Although he had supplied his own lumber
all along from timber stands upstream, in
1893, in partnership with William
Humberstone, he established a sawmill
and lumber business that in time grew to
become the largest in Edmonton. Around
1900, he bought out Humberstone's share
of the business, and in 1907 he added a
second mill across the river on Ross Flats.
These industries brought in vast amounts

of money when the Klondikers were
clamouring for means of transport to the
Yukon goldfields.

John Walter also owned large amounts
of land. In what later became Strathcona,
he owned all of River Lot 9, which
extended from the river to University
Avenue between approximately 107 and
109 Streets, as well as other property in
town and in rural areas. In addition, he
built and operated two ferries and a
sternwheeler, the *City of Edmonton*,
which he used both as a freighter for his
lumber business and as an excursion boat
on holidays. For a time around 1880, he
ran a general store too. Twice he ventured
into coal mining, but without great
success.

The coming of bridges and the railway,
the end of the land and building boom,
and the disastrous flood of 1915 (that
wiped out both his sawmills) contributed
to a sharp decline in his business fortunes,
but he remained much admired and
respected by his contemporaries as a
compassionate and generous employer
and friend.

[1887] **John Walter, shown here in 1887** with his wife Annie on the far left holding their infant son, built this log house, his second one, in 1884 at a cost of $800. It is now preserved along with his other two houses at the John Walter Historic Site on the flats now known as Walterdale.

[n.d.] **In April, 1882,** at a spot near the present 105 Street bridge, not far from the ford that had served as the earliest river crossing to the fort, John Walter launched Edmonton's first cable ferry. In 1884, a little downstream, he added a second one that travelled between Ross Flats and Cloverdale, near where the Low Level bridge now crosses the river. During spring break-up and fall freeze-up, when the ferries could not operate, a basket was attached to the cable to transport the mail and, in emergencies, passengers across the river. The upper ferry, shown here, was taken out of service in 1913 when the High Level and Fifth Street bridges were opened.

On the south bank are Walter and Humberstone's lumber mill and Walter's whitewashed log house. In 1903, the mill employed 100 men and processed 6 million board feet of timber. At its peak in 1912, that output had more than doubled.

[c1906] **James McKernan** (1852-1934) was part of the famous North West Mounted Police trek to Fort Macleod in 1874. When he took his discharge in 1876, he returned to Ontario with stories of the great prospects in the Edmonton area. The following year he and his brother Robert (c1846-1908), returned to maintain the first telegraph line from Battleford to Hay Lakes, near Edmonton. In 1878, Robert brought his family west in a three-month trudge by covered wagon and Red River carts from Winnipeg. They settled on the south side of the river near a little lake that came to be known as McKernan's Lake, where the McKernan subdivision is now. Here they built up a homestead that served as the family home for half a century.

[n.d.] **McKernan's Lake became** one of Edmonton's most popular recreation areas – for picnics in the summer, and for skating and curling in the winter.

[1891] **In 1880, Edmonton was riding high** on the tide of optimism created by the building of the C.P.R. westward toward Edmonton and the Yellowhead Pass. The coming of the railway assured Edmonton of a bright future and rapid growth. But in 1881 the bubble burst, when the C.P.R. route was diverted southward, through Calgary and the Kicking Horse Pass. Edmonton, however, would not give up easily. It continued to demand a rail link from Edmonton to the C.P.R. mainline in Calgary.

In 1891, construction of this crucial link, the Calgary and Edmonton Railway, was nearing completion, but the task was arduous, relying on horse and man power. The grade was built with horse-drawn ploughs and scrapers. Here the rough-hewn ties are being transferred from flat car to wagon to be distributed along the road bed where another crew will lay the ties in place.

[1891] **Since manpower was a chief source** of energy in building the C & E, travelling bunk cars were needed to house the crews as they progressed slowly northward. Here the bunk cars are decorated to celebrate their arrival at the end of the line – the job is completed! The larger one measures 60 feet long, 19-1/2 feet high, and 10 feet wide. The pattern of little windows is fair indication of the amount of space allotted each of the ninety men it could house.

[July 25, 1891] **When this little wood-burning engine** rolled into South Edmonton on July 25, 1891, it marked a joyous beginning for the new railway settlement on the south bank of the North Saskatchewan River. But, for the older settlement on the north bank, it meant dashed hopes and frustrated plans yet again, as it became clear that the railway had no intention of crossing the river. In fact, the owners of the C & E were calling their new southside townsite "Edmonton" in the belief that this new site, in which they were the major landowners, would replace the settlement on the north bank.

[November, 1891] **Here is the embryonic town** of South Edmonton, showing the Hotel Edmonton and the C & E Railway station around which the future town grew. This station served the C & E, which was operated by the C.P.R., until 1908 when it was moved and converted into a residence. (It is now being restored to its original form by the Old Strathcona Foundation.) Hotel Edmonton, later called the Strathcona Hotel, was built by the C & E Railway Co. in 1891 on the northwest corner of Whyte Avenue and 103 Street, thereby fixing this location for the development of the commercial district of the new town. The hotel was leased to W.J. Sharples, a Liverpudlian, who entertained his guests in the bar with piano and song in the liveliest pub tradition.

[July 1, 1895] **This view of Whyte Avenue** on Dominion Day, 1895, shows the commercial hub of South Edmonton developing westward from the railway station, on the left, and the Hotel Edmonton, on the right. The Parrish Block was built for Sam Parrish, a Calgary businessman, who was quick to invest in South Edmonton real estate when the lots were first offered for sale by the railway and to open a South Edmonton branch of his general store business. Next to the Parrish Block is MacLaren's general store, William Ross's hardware store, LaRose's livery stable, a blacksmith shop and the Commercial Hotel. The large building toward the end of the street is the Raymond Hotel.

[c1906] **The stately Raymond Hotel,** later called the Royal Hotel, was located on the south side of Whyte Avenue at 105 Street. It was built in 1893 by a wealthy Englishman, Erskine N. Raymond, who spared no expense in furnishing it luxuriously as one of the most elegant hotels in the Territories.

The interior was finished in fir and cedar, and stained glass was used in the windows. In addition to 22 bedrooms, the hotel featured a billiard room with full-sized English billiard table, an oak bar complete with brass rail, a large dining room, a drawing room with a piano and French doors opening onto the gallery surrounding the second floor. Since it was one of the tallest buildings in town at the time, its third-floor balcony offered an impressive view of the surrounding countryside and the river valley. In 1894, it was taken over by William H. Sheppard who later bought the Strathcona Hotel and served as mayor of the town in 1906.

[c1903] **The dining room** of the Raymond Hotel could comfortably accommodate 100 guests and was the first dining salon in northern Alberta to be well suited for dances and concerts. The floors throughout the hotel were of double thickness, faced with British Columbia fir. Lace curtains over the windows softened the visual effect.

[1893] **In 1892, the trustees** of the new South Edmonton School District No. 216 of the North West Territories borrowed $800 to buy a site and erect this one-room frame school, South Edmonton's first, on the northwest corner of Whyte Avenue and 105 Street. While awaiting construction of the new school, classes were held temporarily in the Ontario House hotel and later in a log building owned by Vic Anderson. In January, 1893, the new school was ready, with Miss M.C. Clark as teacher. The enrolment grew rapidly. By 1894, this building was already over-crowded and work began on the new brick Niblock Street School. Later this frame school was used as a Baptist church.

[c1897] **In 1894, it cost $4,000** to build the four-room Niblock Street School, one of the first brick buildings in South Edmonton, at 84 Avenue and 105 Street where Old Scona stands now. In 1895, there were only two teachers here, Miss M.C. Clark and Miss A.H. Short, who taught all the elementary grades. In 1896, Duncan S. MacKenzie joined them as principal and high school teacher at a salary of $660 for the year. The enrolment continued to grow rapidly, and although more teachers joined the staff, the building was again too small by 1899 and classes had to expand into temporary quarters once more until completion of the Grandin Street School (old King Edward School) in 1901. In 1906, the Niblock Street School was demolished to make way for the new high school, Strathcona Collegiate Institute.

First Mayor and Council of Strathcona.
1899.

[1899] **In 1899, the C.P.R. town** of South Edmonton was incorporated and its name changed to honour Donald Smith, Lord Strathcona, a prosperous and influential director of the C.P.R. and of the Hudson's Bay Company.

The first mayor of the new town was Thomas Bennett, who had been mayor of Bury, Quebec, before coming to South Edmonton in 1895 to serve as immigration agent. He also served as chairman of the School Board for many years.

John Joseph Duggan (1867-1952) established his lumber business in South Edmonton in 1891 and later expanded into the McCormick farm implement dealership. In addition, he owned much of the land of the present Duggan subdivision. Besides serving on the first Town Council in 1899, he also served as mayor in 1902 and 1908-10.

John James McKenzie (c1863-1952) worked as a ferry hand for John Walter until the fall of 1891 when he opened his own blacksmith business in South Edmonton. Later, he too expanded into the farm implement business, representing Massey Harris. He was elected to South Edmonton's first School Board in 1892 and served for many years as school trustee, both for Strathcona and for Edmonton after the two cities amalgamated. In

addition, he served on Strathcona's Town Council for several years and as its mayor in 1904. After amalgamation, he was an Edmonton alderman from 1919-21.

Malcolm McIntyre managed a general store for Sam Parrish for a few years until he was able to buy the business and operate it under his own name. By 1899, he too had a Massey-Harris dealership. He was a Town Councillor in 1899 and 1902.

William Henry Sheppard (1862-1944) bought the Raymond Hotel in 1894 and the Strathcona Hotel in 1904. He was a director of Edmonton Brewing and Malting Co. and later vice-president of Associated Breweries of Canada. He served on the Town Council for several years and was mayor in 1906.

Russell A. Hulbert (1861-1934) who ran a general store and a real estate business, served on Council in 1899 and again in 1907.

John Walter was one of Strathcona's first citizens, having established his boatmaking business here in 1875. He led the campaign to establish a public school in South Edmonton and was chairman of its first School Board in 1892. Later he served on this first Town Council in 1899.

Alexander Cameron Rutherford (1857-1941) was one of Strathcona's most prominent citizens. He brought his family to the young settlement in 1895 and set up a law practice. He quickly became active in community and business affairs and served as secretary-treasurer on the first Town Council.

[1900] **A.C. Rutherford progressed** to the Legislative Assembly of the North West Territories in 1902 and served as Deputy Speaker until 1905, when he became the first Premier of the new province of Alberta, as well as its Minister of Education and its Provincial Treasurer. In 1906, he urged the establishment of the University of Alberta and staunchly supported it against all criticism. In 1910, in the face of allegations of profiteering by his cabinet, he resigned as Premier, although the allegations were later disproved. He continued in the Legislature as a private member until 1913 and remained active in community affairs, serving on the university senate, and later as its chancellor from 1927 until his death in 1941.

During his most active years in Alberta politics, 1895-1911, Hon. A.C. Rutherford and his family lived in this house at 104 Street and Saskatchewan Drive. Mr. Rutherford and his son, Cecil, are standing out front, while his daughter, Hazel, and his wife, Mattie, are on the verandah. This house was moved to Fort Edmonton Park for preservation in 1967.

[1913] **The artwork and books** in Mr. Rutherford's study reflect the learned character of the man who did much to improve the education of many other Albertans.

[1913] **The sculpture, vases,** paintings and piano that are prominent in the Rutherford living room and dining room reveal the love for fine living that was manifested by the Rutherford family.

[1901] **In 1901, when Strathcona's** population was 1,550, most buildings along Whyte Avenue were still wooden one- or two-storey structures, as shown in this view of the south side of the avenue between 103 and 104 Streets. W.E. Ross's hardware store, whose twin arches can be seen near the extreme left, was one of the few exceptions, being of brick.

[September 4, 1912] **The people of Strathcona** seem only mildly interested in the royal visitors as H.R.H. the Duke of Connaught, Governor-General of Canada, and his daughter, Princess Patricia, pass by in the leading car. The Governor-General was in town to open the new Legislative Building across the river.

Since fire regulations prohibiting the use of wood as a major building material in the business core were long in effect by 1912, brick buildings were beginning to dominate the scene along Whyte Avenue. One notable example was the recently opened post office, whose clock tower dominated the street. On the other side of the street, the white wooden building on the northwest corner of 104 Street was Douglas Brothers department store.

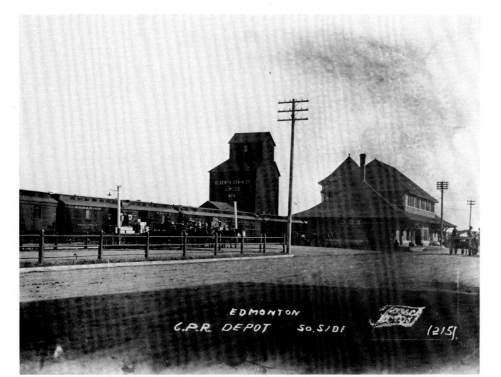

[1910] **In 1907, the C.P.R.** upgraded its facilities in Strathcona to serve as its chief divisional point in northern Alberta and the old wooden railway station was replaced by this stylish red brick structure. Thousands of immigrants passed through its doors on their way to free land and new lives in northern Alberta.

The grain elevator was built in 1898 by the Winnipeg-based Dominion Milling Co. and was later taken over by the Alberta Grain Co.

[1906] **With the arrival of each train,** the railway station became a hive of activity. Each hotel sent a horse-drawn bus or carriage to the station with a driver eager to help alighting passengers into his particular conveyance for the trip across town or across the river to his hotel. Competition was keen in 1908, with eight hotels in Strathcona and twenty more in Edmonton competing for the business. The shortest ride was to the Windsor Hotel just across the street, on the corner of Whyte Avenue and 102 Street. To the right of the Windsor is the farm machinery business owned by J.J. Duggan, four times mayor of Strathcona.

[c1908] **Another hotel was Robert McKernan's** ornate Dominion Hotel, built in 1903 on the north side of Whyte Avenue, between 103 and 104 Streets, where it still stands today. It had 33 bedrooms, a barroom at the front on the left with its own separate entrance, and a dining room at the rear, boasting a private staircase for the ladies who could come down to dinner without having to pass through the more public areas of the hotel. As a precaution against disorder, no drinks or cigars were served in the dining room.

[c1908] **By 1908, the horse and wagon** had to contend with streetcars on Whyte Avenue. On October 31, 1908, Streetcar No. 1, the first streetcar to run in the prairie provinces, crossed the Low Level Bridge and entered Strathcona on its trial run. On November 9, the two-tone brown cars of the Edmonton Radial Railway began regular service in Edmonton and Strathcona. For a 5¢ fare one could ride the full length of track along Whyte Avenue from 110 Street to 99 Street and along 99 Street and Scona Road to the bridge. To carry on to Edmonton, though, an additional 5¢ had to be deposited. When the two cities amalgamated in 1912, the double fare was dropped.

The Hotel Edmonton became the Strathcona Hotel when the town was incorporated as Strathcona in 1899. The square tower of the Dominion Hotel adds a flamboyant variation to the streetscape of awninged storefronts.

[n.d.] **In 1907 the Alberta Government** at the instigation of Premier Rutherford, bought the Isaac Simpson farm, River Lot 5, as the site for the new university. This secluded farmland offered a wonderful view of the river valley and the growing capital city across the river. The Premier was unable to resist buying the adjoining 1.3 acres for himself. Here he would be able to watch the capital and his favourite achievement, the university, grow up around him.

[1909] **In keeping with the farm setting** chosen for the university, the turning of the sod was done with a team of horses and plough, and not with a mere shovel. Naturally, it was Premier Rutherford who ploughed the first furrow on September 29, 1909, to mark the beginning of construction of the Arts Building. Assisting him by holding the reins are John A. McDougall and Dr. W.D. Ferris, members of the university senate. Dr. Henry Marshall Tory, first president of the university, ploughed the second furrow.

As events turned out, several years passed before the Arts Building was actually built. In the meantime, Athabasca Hall became the first University building to be completed.

[1913] **On Dominion Day, 1913,** this drinking fountain at the end of the central boulevard on 104 Street and 83 Avenue was unveiled as a memorial to Dr. Wilbert McIntyre, Liberal Member of Parliament for Strathcona from 1906 until his death in 1909. Dr. McIntyre opened his medical practice in Strathcona in 1902 and, between sessions at Ottawa, continued the practice from his office in the back of Duncan's drugstore.

The 15-foot high fountain of bronze and cast iron contained three ornamental electric lamps, four drinking fountains, and two basins at the bottom for dogs. After this fountain was smashed by a car in 1952, it was replaced by a new granite fountain in Queen Elizabeth Park, which bears the brass plaque from the original fountain.

The white frame building to the right is the Orange Hall, built in 1903 by the members of the Strathcona Orange Lodge, a religious fraternal organization, to house their meetings. This building remains on its original site in essentially its original condition; even the original plumbing still exists.

[c1913] **Strathcona's civic core** was compactly situated along 83 Avenue between 103 and 104 Streets. The City Hall, in the foreground, was built in 1909 to house the municipal offices and the jail. Looming above it is the town's water tower, a free-standing structure behind the City Hall.

The next building, with the square bell tower, is the old fire hall, built in 1901. The upper storey contained sleeping quarters for the fire chief, who was the department's only full-time member. The rest were volunteers who, in 1902, received 50¢ per practice and 50¢ per fire.

Further east is Fire Hall No. 6 with three double doors. It was built in 1909-10 for $15,000 and is the oldest remaining firehall in Edmonton, although it is now used as a theatre for the Walterdale Playhouse. In its heyday, it housed the very latest horse-drawn fire-fighting equipment and had stables at the rear for nine horses. The octagonal bell tower in its northeast corner was used to dry the hoses. The upper floor contained bedrooms, the chief's office, a band room and the general hall, with two sliding poles.

[c1913] **Knox Presbyterian Church,** on 104 Street at 84 Avenue, was built in 1907 to replace an earlier frame church on the same site. It is now the oldest Presbyterian church in Edmonton.

The Strathcona Public Library was built with the aid of a $15,000 grant from Andrew Carnegie and was opened in March, 1913, by ex-mayor Duggan.

The building in the background, between the church and the library, is the Connaught Armoury, home of the 19th Alberta Dragoons and the Department of National Defence until 1965. It has now been restored by the Old Strathcona Foundation as the Armoury Restaurant.

[c1906] **Built at a cost of $27,000**, the new six-room Duggan Street School opened in February, 1906, on 78 Avenue between 106 and 107 Streets. It was here, on the top floor, that the fledgling University of Alberta – comprised of the president, Dr. Henry Marshall Tory, four professors, and 45 students – held its first classes in September, 1908. In 1912 the building was twinned. The enlarged structure with two towers is still ringing with the sounds of young school children today, although it now goes by the name of Queen Alexandra School.

[c1913] **Strathcona Collegiate Institute** replaced the old Niblock Street School in 1908 at a cost of $100,000. It provided eight classrooms, a science laboratory, a library and, on the top floor, an assembly hall. Initially, only the main floor was used as a high school. The second floor was used for two years to house the University of Alberta while the first campus buildings were being built. Here, in the fall of 1909, the University conferred an honorary Doctor of Laws degree on Lord Strathcona. This school is now the Old Scona Academic High School.

[1903] **Instructor Mr. Wild prepares** an experiment in the science room of the Strathcona Collegiate Institute. The wrought iron and wooden forms (desks) were typical in all schools until after the Second World War.

[1898] **Due to the popularity of tennis** at private lawn parties, permanent courts were built to accommodate the clubs, which were organized on each side of the river. In South Edmonton, one tennis court was located across the lane from Holy Trinity Church at 83 Avenue and 101 Street and another was built behind the Baptist Church at 84 Avenue and 104 Street.

The first lawn tennis club in Edmonton was organized in May, 1891. In the following year, a court was built east of McDougall's Methodist Church for the use of club members.

[1901] **Here, in their smart new uniforms,** are members of the Strathcona ladies' hockey team that was formed in 1901. This is actually the second team; the first ladies' team, composed entirely of married women, played only a short time. This second squad really came to play, and succeeded in taking their Edmonton rivals in a game that was long remembered as one of the roughest to be seen in decades. The north-side ladies had previously held the upper hand for some time, so the Strathcona side, like wolves dressed in sheep's clothing, put up a determined battle and won a hard-fought game.

[1907] **Shortly before midnight** on Saturday, June 8, 1907, fire broke out at the mouth of Walter's coal mine on the river bank below 108 Street, where five men were working the night shift. The foreman, George Lamb, sounded the alarm and descended the shaft to warn the men below, but before they could escape, the fire engulfed all three openings. Lamb emerged in flames and collapsed outside the burning engine house. He died in hospital the next day. The five miners died at the foot of the shaft.

Local businesses remained closed on the morning of the funeral. The service for the five Englishmen was conducted by Rev. W.R. George on an improvised platform in front of Wainwright's undertaking parlors on the corner of Whyte Avenue and 104 Street. The funeral of the sixth victim, a Catholic, was held in St. Anthony's Church. The two processions united to form a mile-long cortege that made its way to the cemeteries amid the slow tolling of churchbells.

[1912] **On September 26, 1911**, by a vote of 518 in favour versus 178 against, the citizens of Strathcona decided to cast their lot with Edmonton and amalgamate with their former rival. The final meeting of the City of Strathcona Council was held in City Hall on 104 Street on January 31, 1912, the evening before amalgamation. When the council adjourned for the last time, after the obituary speeches, all joined hands and sang Auld Lang Syne and For He's a Jolly Good Fellow, followed by rousing cheers for the old administration. Mayor Arthur Davies then invited the aldermen, officials and reporters to continue their wake at a dinner in the Strathcona Hotel.

4 Edmonton, the Town (1892-1903)

When the railway arrived at the south bank and a rival settlement emerged with notions of becoming the "new Edmonton", northern businessmen felt a need to consolidate forces to resist this new threat and to firmly establish the north-side community as Edmonton proper. Action was quickly taken to incorporate Edmonton as a town in February, 1892, with Matt McCauley elected mayor by acclamation.

Progress was slow in the early 1890s, since the country was still in the grip of the great worldwide depression that began in 1873. In eastern Canada, hot, dry summers ruined crops; factories and stores closed and there were more Canadians emigrating to the United States in search of jobs than there were immigrants coming in.

This trend quickly reversed when word reached the outside world that in the summer of 1896 George Carmack had struck gold in abundance in a tributary of the Yukon's Klondike River. The stampede to the goldfields was on.

As Gateway to the North, Edmonton was accustomed to traders, trappers and miners trekking to and from the North and quickly began to promote its location at the continent's northernmost railway terminus as the "back door" entrance to the Klondike. Several routes were possible from Edmonton, but by any route it was a dangerous journey of some 1,500 miles. For the inexperienced it usually led to misery – not wealth. However, these back door routes seemed to have some advantages. Since they followed the river valleys, they eliminated the necessity of packing hundreds of pounds of gear over treacherous mountain passes. And they were the only all-Canadian routes to the goldfields, which were in Canadian territory. To ensure that goldseekers entering the Yukon had a reasonable chance of survival, the Mounties checked each prospector's outfit at the Alaska-Yukon border and unless it contained a year's supply of food, he would be turned back. In addition, if the goods were purchased in the United States, 10% customs duty would have to be paid. On the other hand, goods bought in Canada faced duty charges when they passed through Alaska. Outfitting at Edmonton and taking a back-door route to the Klondike was the only way to get around this dilemma.

As a result, in the summer of 1897, Edmonton began to swarm with would-be sourdoughs and business boomed for local outfitters. But the stampede ended as quickly as it had begun. A year later the rush was over. Its effects on Edmonton, though, were longer lasting. Merchants prospered and new business and

investment were attracted to the town. The population more than doubled, from 1,165 in 1885 to 2,626 in 1901. Edmonton received enormous publicity, not only from its own promotion of the all-Canadian route, but from the eye-witness accounts of the hundreds who passed through and saw the vast regions of unclaimed, fertile soil and the opportunities they offered. Some Klondikers returned to take up homesteads themselves. The influx of gold and the new flow of money through merchants' tills put fresh capital into circulation and helped to revive the lagging economy. Furthermore, a new railway was conceived: The Edmonton, Yukon and Pacific.

Mackenzie and Mann (who had been shareholders in the C & E Railway Co. and were now building a rival railway, the Canadian Northern, along roughly the route first considered by the C.P.R. toward the Yellowhead Pass) acquired the charter for the E. Y. & P. in 1898. By that time, the town of Edmonton had finally coerced the federal government into building a bridge at Edmonton and in April, 1900, the Low Level Bridge, Edmonton's first, was opened. It was not until 1902 that tracks were laid on it, and the E. Y. & P. made its momentous first crossing. With the gold rush over, the grand plan to continue the line to the Yukon and Pacific ended too. The railway began at a junction with the C.P.R. just south of Strathcona, wound along Mill Creek, crossed the Low Level and halted abruptly at a little frame station at the foot of McDougall Hill – a grand four miles in all. At long last, however, a railway had reached Edmonton and the inconvenience of freighting goods by wagon down the slithery south bank to the ferry was no longer necessary. Since the new station was built on the flats instead of the high bank, however, the labourious trip up the steep McDougall Hill was still a constant nuisance, much to Edmontonian's chagrin.

In 1896, after the death of Sir John A. Macdonald and a succession of four different prime ministers who completed his term of office, Wilfrid Laurier and his Liberals were elected and stability returned to the federal government. For his minister of the interior, Laurier appointed Clifford Sifton of Manitoba, who at age 35 became the first westerner to receive a cabinet post. Sifton immediately launched a vigorous campaign to recruit settlers to fill the western plains. Throughout the farm belts of Europe, the U.S.A. and eastern Canada, posters, pamphlets and newspaper ads extolled the "Last Best West", 160 acres of free land for the taking. Soon trainloads of immigrants were spilling over the West and the massive land boom was on.

[November 25, 1894] **Along Jasper Avenue,** east of 99 Street, respectful townsfolk huddled on the snow-covered sidewalks to view the funeral cortege of one of the town's well known old-timers, Donald McLeod. The two-storey building at the rear of the procession is the Columbia House hotel, once owned by him, formerly called the Mammoth Hotel, where several early concerts and theatrical performances were held.

Donald McLeod first came to Fort Edmonton in the service of the Hudson's Bay Company around 1865. He left the Company in 1869 to become a free trader and settled on River Lot 14 in 1872. Three years later, he took up freighting and established the largest freighting outfit along the Carlton Trail between Winnipeg and Edmonton. When the railway reached Calgary in 1883, the freighting business declined and McLeod launched the Calgary-Edmonton stagecoach. Later he turned his enterprising attention to railway contracting, ranching, saw and grist mills and real estate.

In the left foreground, next to the druggist's, is Lauder's new bakery and fruit store, run by Tommy Lauder who later became the Fire Chief at the first fire hall, whose towers can be seen behind the bakery.

[c1917] **Fire Hall No. 1**, built in 1893, also served as the first town hall and police station. By 1904, the 50-foot by 50-foot building could no longer accommodate the full civic government and an annex (shown on the right) was built to serve as town hall, police station and court house, leaving only the fire department in the old building.

Fire Hall No. 1, on Fraser Avenue (98 Street) across from the Alberta Hotel, was built by contractor Kenny McLeod who later built the McLeod Building and also served as chief of the Volunteer Fire Brigade from 1894 to 1897. The domed tower on the roof held the bell that sounded the alarm to summon the Volunteer Fire Brigade until it was replaced by the concrete tower behind it, which also served as a hosedrying tower.

When the Volunteer Fire Brigade was organized in 1892, the volunteers were paid 30¢ per hour of fire-fighting and the first citizen to supply a team of horses to pull the fire engine received $5 for his trouble. After 1903, the town kept its own team at the ready. In 1906, a professional fire chief was hired and the Volunteer Brigade disbanded. Around 1917, motorized equipment began to replace horse-drawn machinery.

[June 29, 1894] **Edmonton's pioneer photographer** C.W. Mathers got the town's Fire Brigade Band to pose for his camera before they set out to take part in Dominion Day celebrations in Fort Saskatchewan in 1894. By this time, membership in the band was no longer restricted to volunteer firefighters, so presumably someone was left behind to man the firewagons!

The Fire Brigade Band was organized in 1892 as a way to keep the men occupied while remaining on hand at the Fire Hall. In September their instruments arrived and by November they were giving public performances at community functions. In 1893, their efforts were rewarded with smart new uniforms and a band stand on the corner of Jasper Avenue and 97 Street, near the Jasper House hotel. Here they serenaded the townsfolk with open-air concerts. Although this band had competition from the Edmonton Brass Band, it survived many vicissitudes and continued for several years.

[c1899] **Tommy Lauder became a partner** in his father's bakery business and, by 1891, expanded the business to include confectionery, fruit, vegetables and tobacco. He opened a new store on Jasper Avenue east of 99 Street, as shown in a previous photo. By 1896, the upper floor of the new store was enlarged and became the Lauder family residence. The wagon, proudly proclaiming "Lauder Scotch Baker", was used to deliver bread at ten loaves for a dollar to homes in all parts of town. In 1897, Jim Lauder suffered a disabling stroke. The family struggled to continue the business a few years longer, but in 1900 it was sold.

[n.d.] **James Lauder** (1843-1924) and his family emigrated from Scotland in 1874 settling first in Winnipeg and then in Edmonton in 1881. Jim first tried his hand at the hotel business and at homesteading in the area now called Lauderdale before he decided to return to the trade he had practised in Scotland by opening a new bake shop on 98 Street, behind the Alberta Hotel. Bread from his small brick oven first went on sale in November, 1885. In addition, he supplied loaves to the St. Albert Mission, the Hudson's Bay Company and the North West Mounted Police at Fort Saskatchewan.

[c1900] **Gilbert Berg was another baker** who expanded into the grocery, fruit and confectionery business in his store on the south side of Jasper Avenue at 98 Street. He also sold soft drinks in assorted flavours: orange cider, apple cider, lime juice, champagne cider, and raspberry vinegar!

Many items illustrated here were common in stores at the turn of the century. These included the cast-iron, wood-and-coal-burning stove, the broad scoop scale (to the right of the stove), the platform scale (on the counter), the roll of heavy brown wrapping paper (behind the platform scale), the ball of string hung from the ceiling, the cookie bins, the large glass storage jars, the wooden barrel full of cider and the many open boxes of fruit and vegetables.

[1896] **Edmonton's first drugstore** was built in 1882 for Dr. Herbert C. Wilson, a pharmacist and medical doctor, who operated the drugstore in conjunction with his medical practice. He had his medical office at the rear of the drugstore and his residence above it. In 1886, when he was becoming increasingly busy as Edmonton's representative to the North West Territories Council, he sold the drugstore business to Philip Daly, while retaining his medical office and residence as before.

The drug business changed hands several times, with George Graydon taking it over in 1894. In 1888, the building was moved from its original site at 106 Street and 98 Avenue to a more central location on the south side of Jasper Avenue near 99 Street. Here it continued for many years, serving as home to a succession of Edmonton businesses.

[1903] **In 1896, when D.W. Macdonald** moved from his earlier store into this new, fully modern drugstore at 9974 Jasper Avenue, it was described as "one of the smartest looking" and "perhaps the most tastefully fixed store in town." Particularly impressive were the pressed metal ceiling and cove and the attractive wooden cabinets. Here he intended to maintain his reputation "as a dealer in HIGH CLASS DRUGS AND CHEMICALS." Patent medicines and wonder cures were prominently and prolifically advertised in the newspapers at the turn of the century.

[1903] **Luxury items also found a market** in early Edmonton and Emanuel Raymer's jewellery store thrived in the young town. He established his business in 1886, admonishing the townspeople to "Bring your tired watches and lame clocks to E. Raymer."

Mr. Raymer moved his business into this building on the northeast corner of Jasper Avenue and 99 Street, across from the Bulletin office, in 1888 when he required more space for his expanded line of merchandise, which now included books, magazines, comic papers, stationery and toys as well as eyeglasses, clocks, watches, jewellery, silverware and other luxury goods. In addition to selling imported merchandise, he made jewellery, notably rings, from gold and crystal quartz "diamonds" panned from the North Saskatchewan River. In 1892, he sold out his stock of books and stationery and built an addition to his store, which he remodelled again in 1899. In 1906, he sold the business to Jackson Brothers, who continued his tradition of fine jewellery and watch-repair in Edmonton.

Mr. Raymer was also active in community affairs, being a charter member of the Board of Trade, the Edmonton Club, and the Curling Club, and a tenor in the Methodist church choir and the Edmonton Glee Club.

[1903] **In addition to a dazzling array** of silverware, jewellery, clocks and keys, Raymer's store also featured a pleasing pressed-metal ceiling and cove, and handsome wood and glass cabinets. By contrast, the bare lightbulbs seem starkly incongruous.

[n.d.] **As Edmonton's population increased,** so did its demand for coal. Many small mining companies tunnelled into the river bank at the outcrops of the coal seams. In 1888, about six mines were operating in Edmonton and Strathcona, but by 1907 the number had grown to over twenty in Edmonton, Strathcona, Clover Bar and Namao.

Edmonton's first coal miner seems to have been Donald Ross, who first burrowed into the south bank of the river and later into the north bank near his hotel below McDougall Hill. Other early coal miners were William Humberstone, John Walter, F.H. Sache, Frank Hall, C. Sanderson and E. Caverhill. The earliest issues of the *Bulletin,* in 1880, announced that the Hudson's Bay Co. was having coal dug from the south bank and that the coal and lumber industries were keeping the local men employed. By 1910, most of the river flat area east of 101 Street to Clover Bar was mined. In later years, some of these mine shafts caused problems with cave-ins along the river bank.

Edmonton's most unusual mine was the one under the federal penitentiary, operated by the inmates. Since the prison was situated on a coal seam, it was logical that it should supply its own coal to fire its power house boilers.

[n.d.] **Some mines found it more practical** to sink a shaft from above, rather than tunnelling in from the river bank. The Edmonton Coal Co. mine, shown here, used gravity to help load the coal into sleighs waiting on the frozen river. After the Grand Trunk Pacific Railway was built through Clover Bar in 1909, some mines had spur lines put in or relocated their pit heads where a rail line could be built to give them ready access to the ever-increasing export market. Alberta, meanwhile, was acknowledged as having at least half of Canada's known coal deposits.

[n.d.] **This Edmonton Coal Co. team** is travelling along the frozen river as it sets out to deliver its load to Edmonton homes. In 1892, Donald Ross was offering coal for sale from his mine under McDougall Hill at $3.00 a ton delivered or $2.50 a ton at the pit. Twelve years later, S.H. Smith & Co. were charging $3.50 a ton.

[n.d.] **W. Johnstone Walker** came to Edmonton in 1885 shortly after the North-West Rebellion. With the help of his friend John A. McDougall, Mr. Walker opened a general store on 98 Street in 1886, offering a wide range of quality goods, many imported from Manchester, the centre of Britain's textile industry. His stock, transported to Edmonton by a train of oxcarts, included clothing, woollens, fabrics, laces, ribbons, books, stationery, toys, carpets, bedding and chinaware – "terms strictly cash". In 1891, he moved the business into his new store, called Manchester House, on Jasper Avenue, where it thrived and expanded under the management of Cecil Sutherland, who joined the firm in 1896 at the age of seventeen. Two years later, he became manager for Mr. Walker, whose deteriorating health forced his retirement in 1902. Mr. Sutherland continued to run the business for well over half a century.

[February, 1898] **This Klondike party**, led by Hastings and Crozier, set out with sleighs too, but instead of oxen they selected horses and mules to pull their winter variation of a covered wagon.

The frame building behind them had been Johnstone Walker's first store and residence on Fraser Avenue (now 98 Street) and was later used as a primary school.

[May 29, 1899] **Many of the Klondikers** pouring through northern Alberta were less than civil toward the Indians and Métis of the area, aggravating the unrest already engendered by the intrusion of white trappers. This hastened Ottawa's effort to negotiate a treaty with the northern tribes, as had already been done with the tribes of southern Alberta. On May 29, 1899, the treaty commissioners seen here, accompanied by Father Lacombe, set out along Fraser Avenue (98 Street) to meet the Indian tribes of the north for the signing of Treaty No. 8, by which the Indians were given reserves and treaty money in return for their land. Another commission, under Major James Walker of Calgary, went along to issue scrip to the Métis, entitling them to land for homesteading. Much of this scrip, however, was subsequently sold to speculators and profited the Métis little.

The Alberta Hotel shown here began life in 1883 as Luke Kelly's saloon and billiard hall, which has now been reconstructed at Fort Edmonton Park. In 1885, a restaurant was added and in 1887 a two-storey addition was built, while the upper floor meeting hall was converted into hotel rooms and the whole renamed the Alberta Hotel. It stood on the northeast corner of Jasper and 98 Street, where the brick Alberta Hotel later replaced it.

[August 18, 1899] **In August, 1899,** the North Saskatchewan River rose in one of its record floods, the worst one the inhabitants of the young town had yet witnessed. Mr. Durdle, the ferryman, hauled his household effects out through the roof of his house on Ross Flats and tethered the building to nearby trees before it was completely submerged by the deluge.

The river had been high all summer, but after heavy rains it rose, at a rate of six inches an hour, by another 35 feet, reaching a total depth of 41 feet. Ross's, Walter's and Gallagher's flats were submerged. Although Donald Ross's residence and hotel and John Walter's house were spared, Walter and Humberstone's saw mill was inundated, as were Gallagher's pork packing plant, Omand's and Cairn's breweries, Dowling's mill, and the electric light powerhouse, leaving the townspeople without power for three weeks. The ferries were also out of operation, leaving people stranded on each side of the river. Another casualty was the old Hudson's Bay Company steamer *Northwest,* which slipped its moorings on Ross Flats, and floated off down-river after first colliding with the newly built piers of the Low Level Bridge. The piers withstood the buffeting of the *Northwest* and of loose logs and driftwood, but found themselves deluged 6-1/2 feet below water level! This experience encouraged the engineers to increase the height of the piers before adding the bridge's superstructure.

[1902] **Before the advent** of water and sewer mains, Edmontonians were dependent for their water on "the water man", his wagon, and his faithful mules. One particularly famous long-eared worker was eulogized in the *Bulletin,* December 8, 1883: "It is with the most profound regret that we are obliged to chronicle the collapse of one section of Edmonton's very complete system of waterworks. Donald McLeod's historic mule, which for the past year has been actively engaged in forwarding the cold water movement in town, departed this life on Saturday last. Words are inadequate to express the loss thus sustained by our rising and hopeful burgh. Suffice it to say that in the not distant future, when Edmonton has distanced the petty rivalries of Winnipeg, Montreal or Chicago, and stands forth the champion city of the North American continent, when the history of its early days is written on scrolls of silk in letters of gold, the place of honor will be accorded to an engraving of this lamented mule painfully dragging his cart load of water up the hill in the early dawn, wherewith to slake the raging thirst of the hardy pioneers who have put in the previous night on permit whiskey. But alas how the great world rolls on without regard to the living or the dead. Pig Kenny now drives an ox in the water cart and Donald McLeod has bought another mule. Even the greatest and best are soon replaced and as soon forgotten."

[1903] **Before the introduction** of modern refrigeration techniques, ice boxes were the order of the day and the source of ice was the frozen North Saskatchewan River. Here J.W. Huff's ice gang harvests the river's crop and loads the blocks onto horse-drawn sleighs for delivery to homes or for storage in sawdust-insulated ice houses. In 1883, a two-foot-square block of ice sold for ten cents, cut and delivered.

[c1895] **Edmonton's first regular hospital** was the General, built in 1895 at 100 Avenue and 111 Street for the Grey Nuns, the Sisters of Charity of Ville-Marie.

Before 1895, Edmonton doctors had to send their patients to the small hospital operated by the Grey Nuns at the St. Albert Mission, and the doctors had to traverse the rough nine-mile trail there and back each time they visited their patients. Around 1893, six Edmonton doctors urged the Mission authorities to build a new hospital closer to the centre of population emerging in Edmonton. The Grey Nuns soon purchased a whole block from the Hudson's Bay Company for $2,300 and began plans for their $30,000, 36-bed General Hospital which, when it opened, was one of the largest and most expensive buildings in town, offering a splendid view from its attic balconies.

A stable was built at the back of the hospital to accommodate the horses of the staff and visitors.

[c1904] **Edmonton's second hospital**, the Public Hospital on Boyle Street, located at 103A Avenue and 96 Street, opened in December, 1900.

The hospital had three private rooms, one public ward and a dispensary on the ground floor. The operating room was on the second floor, along with five private rooms, one public ward and a bath.

The first superintendant, Miss Jessie Turnbull, received $35 a month as salary. Patients were charged $1 a day or $6 a week for a bed in a public ward, and $2 a day or $12 a week for a private room. Many patients could not afford to pay and the hospital had difficulty collecting the fees, so it began to demand a deposit before a patient would be admitted. Medicare was still far in the future!

In 1901, the verandah was added, plus an annex to provide a new kitchen and an isolation ward for infectious diseases.

The Public Hospital was in operation until 1912, when it was replaced by the new Royal Alexandra Hospital, now known as the Glenrose.

[1902] **The operating room** of the General Hospital boasted the most up-to-date equipment and was a source of pride to its founders, if not to the patients.

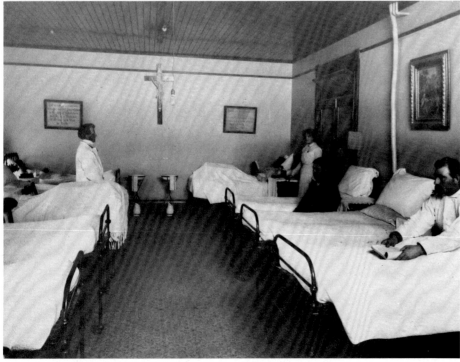

[1902] **This is one of the larger** public wards in the General in 1902, the men's ward. There were two smaller public wards for women, plus several private rooms. The attic storey contained three general wards for infectious diseases, one for men, one for women and one for children.

[c1902] **Looking northwest across** the river in 1902, a new brick skyline is seen emerging on the Hudson's Bay Reserve above the remnants of the old fort. The spire of St. Joachim's Church identifies 110 Street and 99 Avenue. Just west of St. Joachim's is the convent of the Rev. Sisters of the Faithful Companions of Jesus and the belfry-topped General Hospital. In the centre front, commanding an excellent view of the river valley, is the Hardisty Big House, recently used as an isolation hospital during the smallpox epidemic. At the right, all roads lead to the ferry landing near 105 Street.

[1902] **Along 110 Street** north of 99 Avenue in 1902 stand the buildings of the Roman Catholic Mission, the heart of the early French community in Edmonton, along what was then effectively the western edge of the town. St. Joachim's Church was built in 1899 to replace the earlier frame church of 1882 whose steeple and chimney can be seen in the background. On the far left is the convent, built in 1896, of the Sisters of the Faithful Companions of Jesus, a teaching order.

The Sisters came to Edmonton in 1888 and built a small two-storey frame school on this property. On November 2, 1882, they started classes in Edmonton's first tax-supported separate school, St. Joachim's Catholic Separate School District No. 7. Previously, Brother Scollen had taught school inside the fort to children of Hudson's Bay Company employees from 1862 to 1868, and in 1882 he began teaching commercial classes in mathematics, bookkeeping and business

practice, in the old St. Joachim's church. Meanwhile, from 1881 to 1888, Catholic children attended Edmonton's public school. In 1900, a second separate school, for boys only, opened on 103 Street, south of Jasper Avenue, with its first teacher being William McNamara, who in 1914 served as mayor of Edmonton.

[1902] **East of 101 Street** along College Avenue (now called Macdonald Drive) was the Methodist Mission property. In 1892-93, this frame church and the brick parsonage next to it replaced the original church and mission house erected by Rev. George McDougall. The four-room College Avenue School, at the right, was

Edmonton's first brick school, completed in 1895. All three buildings were designed by William Edmiston, the town's first architect and its mayor in 1898-99. The College Avenue School later became the town's first high school, when the larger Queen's Avenue School opened and took over the lower grades. In the background between the parsonage and the school can be seen the Grandview Hotel, the first licensed hotel in town, on the site of the present Macdonald Hotel.

[*October 22, 1902*] **October 29, 1902,** was a momentous day for Edmonton, for at 3:45 that afternoon the very first train chugged across the Low Level Bridge and wheezed to a stop on Edmonton's side of the river. To celebrate this long-awaited and vigorously sought achievement, October 22 was declared a civic holiday and for a 25¢ fare, engine No. 26 of the Edmonton, Yukon & Pacific Railway shuttled the jubilant townsfolk back and forth along its four miles of track aboard two flat cars fitted with seats, a box car (whose roof offered a more exciting vantage point) and a coach. Since not everyone managed a turn that Wednesday, the excursions were scheduled again on Saturday.

Edmonton's rail link with the outside world was finally a reality! This was definitely something to cheer about, because it marked the victorious conclusion to a long and hard-fought battle. One of the last skirmishes occurred on another Wednesday, October 8, 1902, when only the switch connecting the Edmonton, Yukon & Pacific to the Calgary & Edmonton rail line south of

Strathcona remained to be installed. Since the railway committee of the Privy Council had approved the connection, it was simply a matter of putting in the switch and the crew of the E.Y. & P., owned by Mackenzie and Mann of the Canadian Northern Railway, set out to do just that. The C.P.R., who operated the C. & E., had other ideas, however, and sent a switch engine, manned with as many C.P.R. employees as could be mustered, to busy itself making up a train on exactly the section of track where the switch was to be installed. When word of this reached Edmonton, tempers soared, and in the afternoon Edmonton's vigilantes rallied once more and poured across the bridge in a counter demonstration of muscle to match Strathcona's. But all day the train served guard duty and would not budge – until it had to make way for the regular train arriving from Calgary. E.Y. & P. manager, W.J. Pace, quickly took advantage of the break in the enemy ranks, and as soon as the regular train passed by, his crew yanked out the track and connected the contentious switch! Edmontonians had

clamoured for years for a bridge and a railway, and when at long last the Low Level was ready and waiting, they were not to be easily put off.

After all, the financing of the Low Level Bridge had in itself been a coup for Edmonton. After years of prodding by the Town Council and the Board of Trade to build a bridge at Edmonton, in 1897 the federal government finally made an offer, which mayor John A. McDougall took to be a bluff: If Edmonton would put up $25,000 (a huge sum in those days) towards the cost, the federal government would build the bridge. McDougall quickly called a meeting of Edmonton's richest and most influential citizens and they decided to call Ottawa's bluff by raising the money. With the help of bank manager Kirkpatrick, they wired the money to Ottawa immediately. The local ratepayers took over this debt in due course, but in the meantime the federal government was bound to keep its end of the bargain and build the Low Level Bridge.

The bridge opened on April 4, 1900, after Donald Ross installed the ceremonial final rivet.

[1903] **In this 1903 view** looking east from 101 Street, two-storey frame buildings still dominate Jasper Avenue. The notable exception is McDougall and Secord's store on the northwest corner, built in 1897 alongside one of John A. McDougall's earlier frame stores. McDougall had bought these lots on the corner of 101 Street and Jasper in the Hudson's Bay land sale of 1881, paying $50 for the corner lot and $25 each for the two adjacent ones!

The firm of McDougall & Secord Ltd. began in 1897, when John A. McDougall, the enterprising merchant and realtor, went into partnership with his one-time employee and long-time business associate, Richard Secord, whose highly successful fur-trade business was eating into Hudson's Bay Company profits. The new partnership carried on these enterprises, with Secord travelling the north country buying furs and outfitting trappers and miners as well as helping McDougall with the wholesale and retail general store business at home.

Real estate played an increasingly important part in the company's affairs. Vast amounts of Edmonton property, including the Norwood subdivision, passed through their hands. In addition, they acquired thousands of acres of land in the Northwest by buying scrip from the Métis and selling the land to new settlers. As a result, in 1909 they sold the merchandising and fur businesses and carried on in real estate and private banking. The financial firm of McDougall & Secord Ltd. is still in business in Edmonton today, in the hands of descendants of the two pioneers.

[1903] **In the grocery department** of McDougall and Secord's general store, canned goods lined the walls right up to the wooden ceilings. Many items were not pre-packaged, though, so stools instead of shopping carts were provided for the convenience of the customers, who had to wait for bulk goods to be weighed and wrapped. At the turn of the century sugar cost 6¢ a pound, tea 50¢/lb., coffee 40¢/lb., rice 25¢/4 lb., raisins and dates 10¢/lb., bread 5¢ a loaf, eggs 30¢/doz., milk 12 qts. for a dollar, clams and oysters 25¢ per one-pound tin, steak 15¢/lb., pork chops 10¢/lb., chickens 33¢ each and Christmas turkeys around $2.50 each.

[1902] **Sunlight and shadows cast** interesting patterns on Jasper Avenue in 1902, as photographer Mathers focussed his camera looking westward from 99 Street. Hitching posts and power poles lined the broad wooden sidewalks and an abundance of tastefully simple signs, without benefit of neon, announced the businessmen's readiness to serve the needs of long-skirted or black-suited customers. But only a year later, John I. Mills erected the town's first electric sign which, located at the bend in the street, was legible the length of Jasper. At the end of the street is the brick steeple of First Presbyterian Church on the southwest corner of Jasper Avenue and 103 Street.

[May 25, 1903] **Edmonton's population was nearing** 8,000 in 1903, but Main Street (east Jasper Ave.) was still a muddy road pock-marked by horses' hooves, accentuated here by a heavy mid-May snowfall a few days earlier. By then, though, broad wooden sidewalks ran the full length of the street and occasionally even spanned the street itself for the convenience of the ladies whose hemlines always covered the ankles.

The pipes lying along the side of the street are ready for installation as part of the town's new waterworks system. On the extreme right is the new balcony of James Goodridge's Jasper House hotel. Across the street, above The People's Mint, is Robertson Hall. Built for Sheriff Scott Robertson in 1892, it served as a ballroom, concert hall, opera house, theatre, public meeting hall and court room until it burned to the ground in 1906. It was also used as a town hall by the newly incorporated town in 1893, while the fire hall was under construction.

[February 19, 1897] **For the second annual** Old Timers' Ball on February 19, 1897, the stage of Robertson Hall became Leeson's Halfway House in remembrance of the old stage line linking Edmonton to the C.P.R. at Calgary before the railway reached Strathcona. A bark canoe was suspended above the log shanty and fur pelts, traps, miners' tools, snowshoes, lanterns, a toboggan and a stuffed lynx helped to conjure up memories of bygone days. Inside the shanty, some of the older pioneers passed the evening the way they used to, playing cards, while the more energetic ones danced the reels, cotillions and other old-fashioned dances played by the three-piece "band" consisting of violin, piano and whistle. Supper was served at the Jasper House across the street. About two hundred old-timers and tenderfeet attended the celebration, including Kenneth McDonald, John Norris, John A. McDougall, Donald Ross, Malcolm Groat and several scarlet-coated Mounties from Fort Saskatchewan.

[1897] **The cast of the play** *Our Regiment* strike up a scene for one of the earliest photos of live theatre in Edmonton.

In the early days, dramatic entertainment depended upon the talents and imagination of the various townsfolk. In November, 1886, an amateur dramatic club was organized and performed occasionally for fun or charity. The following spring, Simcoe Lee provided the first professional entertainment in the form of literary and musical selections, assisted by the local amateurs.

After the arrival of the railway in 1891, touring professional companies began to include Edmonton on their circuit. In May, 1892, the first professional theatre troupe to arrive, the Caroline Gage Company of Players, came with ten people and sixteen sets of scenery for a four-day stand. In July, 1899, the touring Lyceum Company performed *Othello*, the first full-length Shakespearean play presented in Edmonton.

The first Edmonton-based professional theatre company, called La Cigale, was formed in 1896 and disbanded the following summer after a tour of western Canada.

[n.d.] **With the arrival** of the young Vernon Barford (1876-1963) early in 1900, the cultural life of Edmonton found the able leadership it needed. A dapper Englishman trained in the choir of Worcester Cathedral and at Oxford University, he brought skill and high standards to his new role as organist and choir master of All Saints' Anglican Cathedral, a position he honoured for the next fifty-six years.

He soon took the lead in the town's secular musical endeavors as well. In 1903, he organized the Edmonton Amateur Operatic Society and a year later produced, in Robertson Hall, the first opera seen in Edmonton, *The Chimes of Normandie*. On the eve of Alberta's inauguration as a province, he conducted the chorus and orchestra in a gala concert at the Thistle Rink, and fifty years later he conducted again for the province's Golden Jubilee celebrations. In May, 1908, he was a founder of the Alberta Music Festival, the first regional music festival in North America. He conducted the University Glee Club, the Edmonton Male Chorus and, in the 1920s, the Edmonton Symphony Orchestra. He was also active as a composer of over fifty original works, including songs, piano pieces and an operetta.

He was granted an honorary degree by the University of Alberta, made an honorary fellow of St. John's College, Winnipeg, and had the unusual distinction of being the only male member of the Women's Musical Club.

[1902] **Vernon Barford gave lessons** in piano and organ. His studio in the Macdonald Block on 102 Street and Jasper was typically Victorian with its dark colours and clutter. The Victorian fascination with photography, a comparatively new invention at the time, is amply in evidence here, and the Union Jack cushion reflects the pride of Empire still strongly felt in the colonies.

[1903] **In 1903, the old wood-frame** Alberta Hotel was moved from the corner onto the back of the lot, facing 98 Street, replaced by this posh new brick hotel on the corner.

The new Alberta Hotel, made of local pressed brick and Calgary sandstone at a cost of $55,000, was sumptuously furnished as Edmonton's most prestigious hotel, having the first call-bell system linking the rooms with the main desk, the first shower bath and the first passenger elevator. Its 75-foot-high turret also afforded the finest view in town. In 1905, Prime Minister Sir Wilfrid Laurier stayed here when in town for Alberta's inauguration ceremony. Single rooms rented for $2 a night, or $2.50 with bath, and a suite of rooms with bath could be had for $4.

The large striped barber pole on the street drew attention to the fully modern barber shop in the basement of the hotel. The three-storey brick building behind the barber pole was an 1897 addition to the earlier frame hotel. The old frame building burned down in 1930.

[n.d.] **The barroom of the Alberta Hotel** was also lavishly decorated at a cost of $2,500. Adjoining it was a billiard room and a card room.

[c1904] **These were among the first** horseless carriages to puff along Edmonton streets and everyone was eager for a ride. In the leading car, department store owner Joe Morris is driving his red two-cylinder Ford with the steering wheel on its right and the engine under the seat. This was the first motor car to make an appearance in Edmonton when Joe brought it back with him from Winnipeg aboard the C.P.R. and then, on May 25, 1904, chugged across the Low Level into Edmonton, startling horses and attracting quite a crowd as he went. The Edmonton *Journal* described this new-fangled contraption as being "of the noiseless type with gasoline motive power" and predicted that "this vehicle of pleasurable outings or rich man's toy will become common in the town."

In the second car, with the steering wheel on its left, Malcolm Groat is giving this new sport of automobiling a try on his estate near 124 Street on this sunny summer afternoon.

Windshields and license plates were still things of the future. When the registering and licensing of motor vehicles came into effect in 1906, license No. 1 went, appropriately, to Joe Morris. At that time, motorists sent in the three-dollar fee and were allocated a license number, but received no plates. They were responsible for displaying the number prominently on their vehicle, however, and a great variety of styles of number tags resulted. One of the most popular employed brass thumb tacks arranged on a piece of leather.

[1903] **At the turn of the century,** a Galician hay market operated south of Jasper Avenue near where the Macdonald Hotel is now. The Galicians and Bukovinians were Ukrainian-speaking immigrants from the Austrian provinces of Galicia and Bukovina who first migrated to this area between 1895 and 1902 and settled on the fertile farmland of central Alberta. Since Edmonton was the largest settlement in the district, it was here that they came to buy supplies, to sell their produce, including hay and to take temporary jobs for extra cash during the difficult early years. Their fur hats and colourful costumes made them highly visible in the predominantly Anglo-Saxon Edmonton of 1903.

[May 24, 1895] **Spectators and participants** are ready for another May 24 sports day at the fair grounds at 103 Street north of 102 Avenue.

A few horse and foot races were traditionally held at the fort on New Year's Day to provide recreation and amusement for the holiday. This tradition was continued in the 1880s and was supplemented by challenges and match races, both on foot and on horse, that were usually held on Main Street. The major sports day each year was July 1, Dominion Day. In 1884 as many as 300 people, equivalent to the town's entire population, assembled for the Dominion Day races, which included as the principal event a tug-of-war match with twelve men per side. Betting was indulged in cautiously, with one person losing as much as two dollars on the day.

By 1892, the May 24 and July 1 sports days included horse races, foot races, lacrosse, baseball and trapshooting on these sports grounds on the Hudson's Bay Reserve. That year the riders and drivers in the horse races had to wear colors for the first time. The next year, musical concerts by the 20-piece Fire Brigade Band and smaller Edmonton Brass Band added to the sports day festivities.

[July 1, 1904] **In June, 1899,** the town moved the old grandstand from north of the Hudson's Bay store down to this site north of the river's edge between 101 Street and 104 Street and graded a new half-mile race track on the river flats just northeast of the municipal power plant. A baseball diamond was also finished nearby in time for the 1899 Dominion Day crowd of over 3,000 persons.

In addition to games and races on sports days, the track also was the location of the annual fair or Exhibition until the permanent grounds were opened north of Borden Park in 1909.

[October 12, 1892] **Track star D. Moosewa,** poses for the camera while his friend looks on.

Challenges of swiftness afoot were common even before the town began and continued long after. The first organized track and field meet was held on July 1, 1885, with several running, jumping, vaulting and throwing events. In the early 1890s, the consistent winner, year after year, of all races from 100 yards to one mile, was an Indian runner from Lac Ste. Anne called Moosewa *(The Moose)*. Since no one else was fast enough to win the prize money, in 1895 it was decided to bar Moosewa from the regular May 24 and July 1 races. The betting was high, though, on all the match races staged over the next few years between Moosewa and John Allen, a Toronto professional who moved to Calgary. Both athletes won their share of races, with Moosewa usually winning the 220-yard and mile events and Allen the 100 and 440-yard sprints. Their winning times for these races were not far from the world records for these distances and the difference between winning and losing was never more than a very few feet in any race.

[August 19, 1898] **The Edmonton Golf and Country Club,** founded in April, 1896, used as its first clubhouse the old Hardisty Big House. Shown here viewing their first five-hole course are some club members, including Mr. and Mrs. Alex Taylor and Mrs. G.R.F. Kirkpatrick on the balcony (fifth, sixth and seventh from the left) and banker G.R.F. Kirkpatrick standing on the verandah below (extreme left).

On the afternoons of club tournaments, the ladies, active competitive golfers themselves, served lunch at this historic, if not up-to-date, clubhouse. By 1907, Edmonton golfers were represented in the first Alberta championship. That same year, the city started the first municipal golf course in Canada on the north river flats west of the High Level Bridge. The golfers welcomed this new seven-hole course and the new clubhouse on its eastern end, because the dilapidated Big House burned down in 1906 and construction of the Legislative Building disrupted the original course.

Edmonton's second golf facility did not appear until the Mayfair Golf and Country Club opened its first nine holes in 1921.

[1899] **The Edmonton girls' hockey team** suit up in their red toques and dark skirts for their game at the old outdoor Thistle Rink at 97 Street just north of Jasper Avenue. Their chief rivals were the aggressive Strathcona ladies. Because of the outdoor rinks, the uniforms were designed for warmth, and because tubular skates were not in use anywhere until 1900, these ladies are fastening on the old flat blades. Standing ready at the right, behind her sister Clara, is Edmonton's first telephone operator, Jennie Lauder. At the far left is captain Annie Robertson, who later married Dr. J.D. Harrison. Standing behind the eager team is Mrs. Joe H. Morris, wife of the department store owner, who brought the first car to Edmonton in 1904.

[c1903] **A men's hockey team,** attired in tight-fitting breeches, takes to the ice for a practice at the Thistle Rink.

Although ice skating on the river took place as early as New Year's Day, 1883, hockey did not get started in Edmonton until teams were organized on both sides of the river in November, 1894. Within a week, goalkeeper J.R. Boyle had to miss a few days work as a teller in the Imperial Bank because of an injury to his eye.

In the early years of hockey, each team played seven players on the ice and the game consisted of two 30-minute periods. In the first game ever played in this city, on Christmas Day, 1894, on a 150-by-75 foot rink erected on the river ice, the Fort Saskatchewan policemen defeated the Edmonton seven by a score of 3-2.

Very soon a hotly contested rivalry developed between Edmonton's first official team, the Thistles, and their South Edmonton rivals, the Shamrocks. The Edmonton Thistle club opened its covered rink on 102 Street north of Jasper Avenue in December, 1902; the cross-river rivals erected their South Side Covered Rink beside the C.P.R. tracks north of Whyte Avenue in 1904. Richard Secord not only put up the money for the Thistle Rink, but he also supported the team and contributed the trophy, the Secord Shield, for the hockey championship of the North West Territories. The twin-city rivalry was so intense that Secord erected a sturdy wire screen all around his rink so that the irate, even vicious, fans could not endanger the lives of his players with their canes and parasols.

The hockey season opened on Christmas Day within the relatively safe confines of the Thistle Rink. But the return match on New Year's Day in Strathcona was quite another matter, for there was no such protection above the boards of the southern rink. Secord's boys had to skate with their heads up, and preferably in the center of the rink. In those days before the slapshot, the goal tenders wore only slim cricket pads. The fans were much more dangerous than shifty centres, rovers and wingers!

5 City and Capital (1904-1911)

A new period began for Edmonton in 1904. The community of 8,350 persons became a city, ambitious and determined to move ahead and capitalize on its assets. The worldwide depression had ended in 1896 and by 1904 Europe was prospering and in need of bread. The Canadian northwest, the last undeveloped wheatland in the world, was now rapidly being developed by immigrants. At the turn of the century, when Prime Minister Laurier appointed Clifford Sifton as the minister of the interior, the world knew little of Canada. That soon changed as Sifton carried out the most successful immigration campaign in Canadian history. Throughout northern Europe and the United States, Sifton offered potential immigrants the lure of free land on the Canadian prairies. In a decade, the population of the area tripled. The new immigrants quintupled wheat production, making Canada the leading exporter of wheat in the world. Wheat made this country rich and stimulated the last great railway era that saw the Grand Trunk Pacific and Canadian Northern Railways reach across the northern prairies to rival the world's biggest railway, to the south, the C.P.R.

When Sifton resigned in 1905, his successor was Frank Oliver of Edmonton. Oliver saw to it that when Alberta was proclaimed a province in 1905, Edmonton became the temporary capital. The following year, it was made the permanent capital. With the arrival in 1905 of the northern railroads and thousands of new wheat farmers, Edmonton was well on its way to catch up with its chief rival, Calgary.

Immigration was the most impressive achievement of the decade, during a period generally characterized by growth and change. This city of small buildings, wooden sidewalks, dirt streets, picket fences, outhouses and backyard gardens saw its first automobile in 1904. Along with the arrival of Buicks and Fords in 1906 came speed limits and license plates. By 1907, the city had 29 autos, one more than Calgary. During 1907 and 1908, Edmonton's population increased about 30 percent each year. Living accommodation was in great demand; thousands had to live in tents. In 1907, Strathcona became a city and the university was established there. The next year, streetcars were added to city traffic, automatic telephones were installed, and the population of Edmonton and Strathcona grew to 18,500 and 4,500 respectively. In 1909, when construction began on the Royal George Hotel, the C.P.R. Building, the High Level Bridge and the Macdonald Hotel, the Legislative Building was already well on its way to produce a distinctive skyline for the city.

This was a period when a proud, aggressive man could manage the company he owned and become a magnate. Government regulations were simple, unions were weak or non-existent and the poor had little help from the law. Men made up 90 percent of the labour force. Although wages were low – $3 for an eight-hour day for carpenters, 25¢ per hour for labourers – a man could provide for his family and still have something left over for a few luxuries. Theatres and sports and the Edmonton Exhibition expanded with the wealth and population of the city. By the end of this period, Edmonton with its various ethnic groups was a multilingual, cosmopolitan city. Building contractors and real estate agents were plentiful. Prosperity and opportunity seemed endless.

[November 7, 1904] **Edmonton became a city** on November 7, 1904, by ordinance of the North West Territories Legislature, and at the Thistle Rink everything was ready for the civic banquet. The roof and upper walls were elaborately decorated with flags, deer and buffalo heads, and bunting hanging in great streamers, while the lower walls and galleries were decked with $10,000 worth of furs and musk-ox robes. At the north end was an imitation old-timer's log cabin with a teepee on one side and a late model car on the other, symbolizing the growth of Edmonton from an Indian camping ground and trading post to the full estate of a progressive city.

After over one hundred men had finished dinner, the ladies arrived to hear the evening speeches. Their seats in the galleries were made comfortable and luxurious by the abundance of musk-ox robes. William Short and Matt McCauley then presided over the various toasts, speech-making and singing to the accompaniment of Walter Clarke's orchestra. Mayor Short remarked that "The citizens of Edmonton have faith in their city and are aiding the making of what will inevitably become one of the most important business centers of Canada...Broad and deep foundations for a great city are being laid..." Frank Oliver added that "Edmonton old-timers are intensely proud of their city... Edmonton is destined to be one of the greatest cities of our great Dominion."

[1910] **The Thistle Rink**, on the east side of 102 Street just north of the Jasper Avenue business establishments, was in its time the largest closed building on the prairies west of Winnipeg. Built by Richard Secord in 1902, the 204-foot-long building was spanned by nine 83 1/2-foot-diameter wooden Howe trusses. Inside, four rows of seats flanked each side of the hockey rink. Attached on the east side was a three-sheet covered curling rink.

In addition to providing a covered area for hockey and curling, the Thistle Rink, with a capacity of 1500 persons, was the community meeting place for exhibitions, concerts, carnivals, parties, receptions and political rallies. Prime Ministers Borden and Laurier, as well as Governor-General Earl Grey, spoke from its platform. The first great actress to visit the city, Minnie Maddern Fiske, presented her theatrical production there to a late summer night crowd.

Fire destroyed the building on October 30, 1913, thereby handing its mantel over to the newly completed Exhibition Stock Pavilion (later called the Edmonton Gardens).

[September 1, 1905] **On a gaily
decorated platform** at the old Exhibition
Grounds in Rossdale, Prime Minister and
Lady Laurier, Governor-General Earl
Grey, Lord Strathcona, Mayor K. W.
Mackenzie and other distinguished visitors
watched Hon. G.H.V. Bulyea as he signed
the register of the crown to officially
become the Lieutenant-Governor of the
Province of Alberta. This was immediately followed by the reading of the King's
proclamation which inaugurated Alberta
as a province at noon on September 1,
1905.

The following day's newspaper
described the occasion: "With glorious
Alberta sunshine, amid the cheers of
thousands of the strong-armed, loyal and
true-hearted citizens of the new province,
before a sea of expectant faces of the fair
daughters of a fair land, Alberta was
proclaimed a province yesterday, a new
state in the confederacy of the Dominion,
a bright jewel in the constellation of the
Empire. With imposing ceremony amid
military pomp and brilliancy and the no
less significant and interesting marks of
national advancement and prosperity, the
Lieutenant-Governor of the new province,
Hon. G.H.V. Bulyea, was clothed with his
authority as the representative of His
Majesty, King Edward VII".

[September 1, 1905] **At 100 Street and Jasper Avenue,** crowds of happy sight-seers, dressed in their Friday finest, crowded to catch a sight of the inaugural parade.

The mid-morning procession paraded from Immigration Hall down Jasper Avenue past the Edmonton Club to 102 Street, then circled back on Jasper Avenue to promenade down the Ross Grade in time for the noon-time inaugural ceremonies at the fair grounds. Following the flag bearers and the Calgary Military band, the parade was headed by a rattling old Red River cart bearing two distinguished old-timers, Kenneth McDonald, the first to homestead in the Edmonton settlement, and Murdoch McLeod, who was taken prisoner by Riel in the rebellion. Next came other old-timers of Edmonton, led by James Macdonald. After this fitting tribute to the pioneers, whose vision, determination and hard work made the occasion possible, came several other bands and floats and the 50-member fire brigade with their new uniforms and brightly burnished brass machinery. Earl Grey and Sir Wilfrid Laurier with Lady Laurier watched the great procession in comfort from the Edmonton Club balcony.

ERNEST BROWN
Photo No. 130.

EMMIGRATION OFFICE SHOW SEPT. 1ST/05
EDMONTON.

[September 1, 1905] **Fruits of the harvest** decorated the old Immigration Office at Jasper Avenue and 96 Street in celebration of the provincial inauguration. The wealth of the new province had obviously turned from furs to farming, even though Edmonton still handled the greatest traffic in raw furs on the continent. As late as 1910, it was estimated that over two million dollars worth of ermine, black and silver fox, mink and other pelts passed through Edmonton each year to eastern markets. To celebrate the beginning of a new future, the fruits of the field gave portents of richer times ahead, as many more immigrants would arrive to develop the vast agricultural potential of central and northern Alberta.

[September 1, 1905] **Polished carriages wait** outside, as Lieutenant-Governor Bulyea makes a visit to Alberta College on 101 Street south of Jasper Avenue.

This insitution was formed in May, 1903, by Rev. T.C. Buchanan to fulfill the will of pioneer Rev. George McDougall, who stated that part of his land was to be devoted to education. This original building opened in November, 1904, and the adjoining 50-room addition (on the left) was erected the following summer in time for Bulyea's inauguration day visit. This first building, along with others built on the site in 1926, 1950, 1951 and 1959, served growing numbers of students, who took courses in academic, commercial and musical disciplines, until it was finally demolished in 1961 to make way for the new administration building which opened in 1964.

[September 1, 1905] **While over a thousand guests** danced until 2 a.m. to the music of Clarke's orchestra at the inaugural ball held at the elaborately decorated Thistle Rink, Edmonton's downtown buildings enlivened the night scene with a lavish display of electric lights. Here, advertising both itself and the provincial inauguration, is the third W. Johnstone Walker store at 9930 Jasper Avenue. This building replaced Manchester House and was used by the firm from 1902 to 1915, before moving to their new location at the southeast corner of 102 Street and Jasper Avenue. On that inauguration night, many buildings of the new city put on their first electric light display.

[March 15, 1906] **Four days after the last** hockey game of the season, the Thistle Rink was decked with flags and bunting to host the momentous first session of the Legislative Assembly of Alberta. More than 4,000 people jammed the rink to hear Lieutenant-Governor George Bulyea read Alberta's first Speech from the Throne. Immediately following this speech, photographer C.M. Tait turned on his powerful electric arc light, with large reflector, and asked all to straighten their collars, smile and sit motionless while he took this historic time exposure photograph. That evening, Mayor May, Lieutenant-Governor Bulyea and Premier Rutherford headed the list of 500 people who attended the "conversazione" held in the rink and danced until midnight to Clarke's ten-piece orchestra.

[May, 1906] **After the initial sessions** of the Legislature held in the Thistle Rink, subsequent sessions were housed in the more comfortable assembly room on the top floor of the McKay Avenue School. One of the early topics for discussion was the selection of an official capital city for the new province. After much heated debate, Edmonton was finally chosen over Calgary, Red Deer, Banff and other communities.

While the design and construction of the permanent Legislative Building progressed, the Legislature met in this schoolroom from April, 1906 until November, 1907, when the sessions were held in the newly completed Terrace Building just east of the old fort. The first session held in the Legislative Building took place on November 30, 1911, almost a year before the building was completed for the official opening.

[September, 1907] **As the new city** was getting used to the title of Capital of Alberta, attention shifted to the construction of the new Legislative Building. In August, 1907, steam shovel and horse power began excavation work just west of where Hardisty's Big House stood on the hill north of the old fort.

The following spring, the contractor encountered quicksand. Engineer Chalmers wrestled with the problem of how to firmly place the province's largest and heaviest structure on less-than-firm ground, and finally chose to place the footings on concrete pilings reinforcd with steel channel beams. The delay consumed much of the 1908 building season, and structural steel fabrication and foundation work occupied most of the 1909 season. The base of the building, the first storey and the steps were constructed of Vancouver Island granite.

[October 1, 1909] **The whole city buzzed** with excitement on the occasion of the cornerstone laying. With impressive pomp and ceremony, the four-by-five-foot cornerstone was laid at the northeast corner of the building with a brass plaque bearing the inscription: "This cornerstone was laid by His Excellency the Right Honorable Albert Henry George, Earl Grey, G.C.B., G.C.M.G., G.C.V.O., Governor-General of Canada, October 1, 1909". Under the stone were laid the Holy Bible, copies of each of the three Edmonton newspapers, plans of the building, coins and currency, a copy of the pay sheet and a list of officials who had supervised the construction work.

Here we see parked beside the huge entrance arch, bearing the motto "We Reap, We Sow", the teams of the Hardisty Cartage Co. which brought 1,600 children to witness the event. The impressive mile-long street procession from east Jasper Avenue to the building site featured 2,500 children from the city's four large public schools and one separate school.

[August 9, 1910] **In the sweltering heat** of the August sun, thousands of Edmontonians crowded the streets around the Yale Hotel to get a glimpse of Sir Wilfrid Laurier as he visited the city for yet another time. The citizens were dressed in their very finest, and had made the streets resplendent with bunting, evergreens and ripening grain, even outdoing the displays mounted on the occasion of the provincial inauguration five years before, when Laurier made his previous visit. In his kind and sympathetic speech, the Prime Minister predicted that Edmonton would not only be a worthy capital of Alberta, but would be one of the greatest cities on the continent.

ell's Photo

Driving the last Spike on C.N.R. at Edmonton

[November 24, 1905] **Thousands of Edmontonians** sought every possible vantage point from which to see the driving of the last spike on November 24, 1905 to commemorate the completion of the Canadian Northern Railway from Winnipeg to Edmonton. Somewhere in the center of this mass of cheering citizens, who also enjoyed a declared half-day holiday to mark the occasion, Lieutenant-Governor Bulyea drives the ceremonial silver spike at 2:15 in the afternoon.

This was a long-awaited and highly significant event in the history of the city, for it was now linked directly with the commercial east, and it was now a city on a transcontinental railway. In his speech, after the cheering and engine whistling ceased, Bulyea recalled the vast difference between the three months it took the Red River carts to squeak across the prairie from Winnipeg and the twenty-eight hours it took the first C.N.R. special train to arrive for this historic occasion. Commenting on the effect the railway would have on the city, he added, "I believe in the next ten years that we will see far more development than in the past twenty."

[c.1911] **After the reception** and tea party held in the unfinished station following the driving of the silver spike, the construction of Edmonton's first C.N.R. station was hastened to completion by the year's end on the site where only ten years previously Indians had pitched their teepees and tethered their ponies. On November 30, 1905, the six-mile rail connection was made between the station and the Edmonton, Yukon and Pacific Railway which in turn crossed the Low Level Bridge to connect with the C.P.R. at Strathcona.

Although the city was now connected to both the east and west coasts of Canada, the first regular passenger train did not arrive in Edmonton until December 16, 1905. The next day, 145 passengers boarded the train for Winnipeg

and other eastern points and remarked about the coaches being splendidly appointed with acetylene gas lamps, upholstered seats, and comfortable sleepers, while the dining car provided a superb cuisine.

In July, 1909, the rival Grand Trunk Pacific Railway arrived and connected with the C.N.R. line in North Edmonton. While both companies shared this station, the G.T.P. company laid out its railyards, roundhouse and shops in Calder. The first G.T.P. train left Union Station for Wainwright on November 23, 1909, just three weeks after the company announced it had purchased a large block of land just east of the 101 Street station. The G.T.P. plans for their own station on this eastern site never materialized, so Union Station was kept busy servicing passengers and freight until a new C.N.R. station was opened on the original G.T.P. site in 1928. The first C.N.R. station was finally demolished in 1952, almost a half-century after the first train entered the city called "The Gateway to the North".

[May 1, 1908] **Immigration Hall, on the west side** of 101 Street just north of the C.N.R. tracks, was the first home in Edmonton for thousands of immigrants. This building replaced the former small shelter on Jasper Avenue and 96 Street in 1907. After temporary quarters here, the next homes for many newcomers were small frame shacks – or even tents. Men without families to house often stayed in the hotels, rooming houses and the cheaper, bedbug-infested flophouses. Many others of course stayed here only long enough to move onto their rural homesteads where hard work and long-term rewards awaited them.

As a result of extensive immigration from the British Isles, United States, Scandinavia, Germany, Holland and the Ukraine, Alberta's population expanded between 1906 and 1914 from 185,000 to 470,000, of which 62 percent were farmers. During this same period, immigration increased Edmonton's population from 14,000 to over 72,000. During 1912 alone, over 20,000 people poured into the newly amalgamated twin cities of Edmonton and Strathcona. That summer, the city used the Granite Curling Club and several school buildings as temporary sleeping quarters for newcomers, while 2,671 people were camped in tents on the river flats or on vacant lots around the fringes of the city.

[c1912] **A new Alberta family** quietly awaits dinner inside the Immigration Hall. For some families, running cold water, electric lights and the large wood-burning cookstove (with upper warming oven and far end hot water reservoir) were modern conveniences much better than what they had left behind in their homeland. For others, such meagre accommodation was the introduction to a life far different from the well-established, cultured civilizations of their European ancestry. For most, the journey to Edmonton had been a long and tiring one. Now there was no turning back, only the determination to make a new start in a new land and work toward potential wealth and happiness.

[April 10, 1909] **Homesteaders queue** at the Dominion Land Registry Office at 10522 100 Avenue. Some waited all night for an early opportunity to register land at the Saddle Lake Reserve.

This building, constructed in 1893, served for fifteen years as the crown land, timber and registry office. From these offices, Georges Roy registered lands for the new immigrants. With their claims in their hands and high hopes in their hearts, these hardy homesteaders set off for the bushy regions around Camrose, Lloydminster, Vegreville, Smoky Lake, Westlock, Entwistle, Calmar and later further north into the Grande Prairie and Peace River country.

By the fall of 1909, this building had become far too small and the land offices were moved to the new Jasper Block on the corner of 105 Street and Jasper Avenue. For three decades from the time of the First World War, this sturdy brick building was occupied by the 19th Alberta Dragoons, the Edmonton Fusiliers, and the 19th Armoured Car Regiment of the Canadian Army, and was called then the Victoria Armories, named after the avenue on which it fronted. After the Second World War, the provincial government used the premises for offices and health department laboratories.

[n.d.] **Many homesteaders and immigrants** to the Edmonton area started from such meagre beginnings as this. With the large influx of settlers, the demand for housing was so great that in the summer of 1907, 3,294 people, a fifth of the city's growing population, were living in 1,098 tents. Some had been badly misinformed by locquatious real estate sharks, who advertised in eastern Canadian and European newspapers. Others came to join relatives here. Most came because the new land and the new start gave them an opportunity that was not available in their homeland. Perseverance, patience and perspiration finally paid off for most, who progressed from tents and tar-paper shacks to more prosperous-looking houses and business establishments.

[n.d.] **The John A. McDougall residence,** built in 1900 at 9936 103 Street, was one of the first of Edmonton's large, elegant mansions. Surrounded by lawns, formal gardens, a tennis court and stables, the imposing home reflected the prosperity of one of Edmonton's successful early entrepreneurs.

Inside, the oak panelled hall with its superb wooden staircase led to a luxurious white and gold drawing room which featured an elaborate chandelier that hung from the gilded ceiling. Across the hall was the library with cedar bookcases and splendid cedar ceiling. In addition to a large billiard room on the third floor, the house boasted a central vacuum cleaning system, surely one of Edmonton's first.

[n.d.] **Although he was never mayor,** Richard Secord (1860-1935) must be included as one of the founding fathers of the City of Edmonton. This great-grand-nephew of Laura Secord came to Edmonton in 1881, at the age of 21, taking three months to walk with a team of Red River carts from Winnipeg. That fall, he helped survey and stake out the townsite and build the first school. Later he taught there at a salary of $800 per year. He married school teacher Anna Ada York, then worked as a free trader at Athabasca Landing for a few years. In 1897, the partnership of McDougall and Secord Ltd. was established. From 1902 to 1904, Mr. Secord was a member of the North West Territories Assembly in Regina. While serving on this assembly, he introduced the bill which resulted in Edmonton becoming a city in 1904. He and his partner, John A. McDougall, also played a major part in arranging the financing for the Low Level Bridge. In addition, Mr. Secord financially supported the covered Thistle Rink, the Misericordia Hospital, the incline railway at the foot of 101 Street and many other worthy projects in the rapidly developing city. He died in January, 1935, at the age of 74, after serving Edmonton generously for over half a century.

Everywhere, the house reflected the personality of its owner, a largely self-educated man who read and travelled widely and pursued his keen interest in the fine arts by bringing back from his European travels the many fine paintings and *objets d'art* that adorned his palatial dwelling. While the McDougall family lived in the house, and particularly before Government House was erected in 1913, the spacious mansion served as one of the leading centres of formal entertainment among the city's active social circle.

In 1946, the house was donated to the provincial government as a home for ex-servicemen's children. The building was demolished in 1974, but a few of its orange-red bricks still can be seen on the new Y.W.C.A. building which now occupies the site.

[c1908] **In 1907 McDougall's business partner,** Richard Secord, had the same architect, Henry D. Johnson, design this beautiful home at 9842 105 Street. The Secord family moved into their brick and sandstone home in 1908; it remained the family residence until the death of Mrs. Secord in 1950. From 1951 until its demolition in 1968, the spacious house accommodated the Edmonton Art Gallery.

[1906] **In 1905, prominent old-timer,** newspaperman and politician Frank Oliver, built this compact brick house just across the street from McDougall's monumental mansion. Before the house was completed, Mr. Oliver, Alberta's first member of Parliament, was appointed Minister of the Interior in the cabinet of Sir Wilfrid Laurier, making him also the first federal cabinet minister from the province. The Oliver family moved to Ottawa, where they resided until 1916; this new house at 9937 103 Street served as the first Government House. As the official residence of Alberta's first lieutenant-governor, G.H.V. Bulyea, the building witnessed many famous government social functions. From 1916 until the death of Mrs. Oliver in January, 1943, the house was the private residence of the Oliver family. It was then taken over by the federal government for use as the headquarters for the Canadian army's defense office for the North West. This Edmonton landmark was demolished in July, 1957, and replaced by a two-storey federal government office building, fittingly named the Oliver Building.

[c1911] **At the edge of the river valley** at 11523 100 Avenue, the proprietor of a small Jasper Avenue store and former valet to a nobleman in France, René LeMarchand, was able to raise enough French capital to erect one of the largest and most modern luxury apartment buildings in western Canada. When completed in the summer of 1910, the $200,000 apartment house was the first in the city to have an elevator and the only one in which the kitchen ranges were supplied with gas produced in a special plant located behind the building. (This innovation came thirteen years before natural gas was first supplied to the city on November 9, 1923.) Every suite had a fireplace, custom storm windows and dumbwaiter service from the delivery area. The 43-suite apartment block was for a long time *the* elite multiple residence in the city. Some of Edmonton's exclusive tenants paid from forty to one hundred dollars a month to enjoy its convenience, its prestige and its fine valley view.

After many renovations since the 1940s, when most suites on the lower floors were converted to professional offices, the building was completely refurbished in 1980 at a cost of approximately two million dollars, to convert the entire building to commercial and professional offices.

[1906] **This was downtown Edmonton** as viewed northeast from the roof of McKay Avenue School at 104 Street (left) and 99 Avenue (right). At the intersection of 104 Street and 100 Avenue (left) is the conical-roofed tower of the Gariepy house, above which is seen the tower and roof of First Presbyterian Church at the corner of Jasper Avenue and 103 Street. To the right of this church is the Hudson's Bay store with its central triangular pediment. To its right, behind the tower of All Saints Anglican church, is the round-roofed Thistle Rink. Emerging above the Revillon warehouse is the Empire Block at 101 Street and Jasper Avenue. At the right, in the flats below McDougall Hill, is Donald Ross's original log hotel with the two large additions seen behind. The building with the four Gothic windows, in the right foreground, is Edmonton's earliest Presbyterian Church, completed in November, 1882. In the centre of the photo, below the Revillon warehouse, is John A. McDougall's large brick mansion. Further to the right is Frank Oliver's three-storey house, above which can be seen the white facade of Alberta College. Nearby is the steeple of McDougall Methodist Church, while further to the right is the College Avenue School.

[1907] **East along Jasper Avenue** past 101 Street, at the left, are the McDougall & Secord store and the Empire Block on opposite sides of 101 Street. The verandah on the right identifies the Windsor Hotel.

By the time Edmonton became a city in 1904, most of the stores and many of the houses and streets in the central area of the city had electric lights. Although the offices of the city-owned electric light and power company were prominently situated near the main intersection of the city, the street lights were few and far between. In 1905, only 53 carbon arc street lamps spotted the night sky. By 1911, these had increased to 209. Good news came in 1906, when power rates were reduced from sixteen to fourteen cents per kilowatt hour on the top end of the billings and from five to four cents at the bottom end of the city's scale of charges.

[1903] **With its taxi team standing ready,** the Windsor Hotel sits alone at the southwest corner of Jasper Avenue and 101 Street. To add to the comfort of guests, whose arrivals were announced daily in the newspapers, a local beer wagon pulls up for another delivery of barrels for the popular barroom inside.

The 40-room hotel was formally opened on February 9, 1903, and with a change in ownership in 1914, it became the Selkirk Hotel. In 1950, additions were made to increase the capacity to 97 rooms. Though modest in size, the hotel was a very popular meeting place, particularly with the sports set, due to its central location, convenience to taxis, comfortable pub and classy basement restaurant known as Johnson's Cafe. The well-worn landmark was severely damaged by fire on December 18, 1962, and was consequently demolished the following September to make way for the Royal Bank of Canada tower.

[1906] **The Windsor Hotel and Empire Block** at 101 Street frame the view along Jasper Avenue toward the tower of First Presbyterian Church, located on the southwest corner of 103 Street and Jasper Avenue. On this cold winter day, few sleighs and cutters use the wide city streets.

In July, 1906, the city commissioners decided to ask city council to amend the building bylaw limiting the height of all buildings to six storeys. Commissioner Candy remarked: "I do not see how such high buildings do any good. It makes a few wealthy people, but it is not to the welfare of the community to make a millionaire out of anyone."

[n.d.] **The spacious Windsor Hotel lobby** was richly decorated with a panelled ceiling, tiled floor, warm wainscotting, heavy chandeliers and polished brass spittoons. Large windows afforded a good view of the action on Jasper Avenue.

[n.d.] Numerous mirrors increased the spaciousness of the narrow 18-foot-wide barroom, while several spittoons and a polished brass foot-rail added to the convenience of the thirsty, tobacco-chewing patrons. Adding to the warmth and luxury of the room was the dark mahogany woodwork, rich in colour and detail. The room was demolished in 1950, when a new owner made extensive renovations to the hotel.

[1909] **The Imperial Bank and the**
Jackson Brothers building loom large on
the left in this view of Jasper Avenue east
of 100 Street. Behind the pole on the right
sidewalk is the glassy Blowey Henry
furniture store, while beside the pole at
the southeast corner of 100 Street and
Jasper Avenue, is the Cristall Palace, the
men's clothing store owned by Abe
Cristall, the city's first Jewish resident.
On the far right side of the photo are
(from the 100 Street corner) the Dominion
Bank Building, P. Burns & Co. meat
market and Edmonton Drug Co. Ltd. with
the large sale sign.

What street traffic lacked in density was
made up by diversity, as horse-drawn
drays, wagons, buggies, surreys and
democrats mingled with a few motor cars
and electrically powered streetcars.

[c1910] **In the rapidly expanding** new
city, the Imperial Bank rises like a temple
of commerce on the northeast corner of
100 Street and Jasper Avenue. This
$90,000 sandstone building, which opened
in September, 1907, replaced the first brick
bank in Edmonton, erected on this site. In
a corner of its impressively marbled
interior, the bank had an alcove reserved
for women customers only. This unique
feature enabled ambitious ladies playing
the real estate game to deposit their gains
without the knowledge of their husbands.
The large rear door on 100 Street
provided access to the second-floor law
offices of Beck, Emery, Newall and Bolton
and third-floor living quarters for
bank clerks.

[c1911] **In this view of Jasper Avenue**
west of 99 Street, the Dominion Bank
Building and First Presbyterian Church are
seen at the left along with the Empire
Block, bearing the Campbell Furniture
Co. advertisement. As the streetcars pass
by the Gariepy Block and the Imperial
Bank, on opposite sides of 100 Street,
workers are busy erecting the Tegler
Building seen past the clock tower of the
Post Office. Behind the Johnstone Walker
flag, construction begins on the McLeod
Building just north of the tiny Canada
Permanent Building on 100 Street. (This
last building, built in 1910 at a cost of
$70,000, was the first entirely reinforced-
concrete structure in the city.) Few traffic
problems exist to prevent pedestrians from
promenading where they wish along
Jasper Avenue.

[1909] **To ease the burden** of horses bringing their heavy loads up the steep north river bank, entrprising local businessmen erected an incline railway at the foot of 101 Street. The two steam-powered cable cars could hold two teams each or twelve tons at a time. As one car went up the 45-degree slope, the other went down the wide tracks. The innovation was designed by Charles Taylor, brother of Alex Taylor of local telegraph fame. At a round-trip fare of five cents for passengers and fifteen cents for teams, the 290-foot railway operated from 1908 until 1913, when the completion of the High Level Bridge eliminated the slow and arduous trips through the broad valley between the twin cities.

[n.d.] **Horses had to work hard** to pull their heavy loads up the Ross Grade. Even teams of huge grey Percherons and golden Clydesdales took twenty minutes to haul their loads of merchandise and building materials up the steep ten-percent incline. At the bottom of the hill were Donald Ross's Edmonton Hotel and Diamond Park baseball field (left).

[1906] **Behind a harvesting binder** at one side of the city market square, an auctioneer attracts a sizeable crowd. Or is it Dr. True selling his bottled cure-all wonder tonic? Behind the implement dealership, the 70-foot-high fire-bell tower obscures the tower of the Alberta Hotel. The large three-storey white building is the 30-room Imperial Hotel, which opened in 1903. At the Dominion Dining Hall, meals can be had for 25 cents, or, if you pay in advance, you can get five meal tickets for a dollar. If the cook's specials particularly appeal to you, you can enjoy the weekly board for $3.50 – paid in advance, of course.

[c. 1912] **In November, 1906,** another first-class hotel opened in Edmonton on the southwest corner of 101 Street and 102 Avenue. Conveniently located just two blocks south of the busy railroad station, the King Edward Hotel did a thriving business under the ownership of Jack Cahoun and R.B. Ferguson, who formerly had a miners' outfitting business on the site. By January, 1910, they had sold the rest of their corrals on this property and had built the south addition, at the left, thereby increasing the size to 110 rooms from the original 50. Named after the reigning monarch of the time, the hotel had a dining room that could accommodate up to 200 people. Until the opening of the Macdonald Hotel in 1915, the King Edward was *the* prestige hotel in the city. It was host to most of the noteworthy banquets, public functions and visiting dignitaries of the time, including Sir Wilfrid Laurier. It was the first hotel in Edmonton to introduce bed-sitting-room furnishings especially designed for hotel use.

[c1914] **Two superfluous pediments** and one awkward column mar the otherwise impressive commercial facades of the new Hudson's Bay Company store at the northeast corner of 103 Street and Jasper Avenue. The original wooden building erected on this corner was moved northward to allow the construction of this $75,000 brick structure, which opened for business in 1905 with a staff of seventeen. In 1911, the round corner column was covered with brick to relate more closely to the corner above, and the pediments were removed to make way for a Mansard-roofed fourth floor. The following year, the original frame building was removed and replaced with a six-storey annex.

[June 24, 1912] **With the temporary platform** in place, the new Court House at the southwest corner of 100 Street and 102 Avenue sits ready for its official opening.

Edmonton's first court hearings were held in the public school house. Later they were moved to Sheriff W. Scott Robertson's Hall, until a permanent room was established in 1901 in the Sandison Block.

On June 24, 1912, this new $250,000 sandstone edifice, set on a foundation of B.C. granite, opened with four court-rooms. These were increased to eight with an addition completed in 1954. The last cases were held here in early June, 1972, prior to demolition of the building in July, 1972, to make way for Edmonton Centre.

On June 26, 1972, the new six-storey, $10 million concrete Law Courts Building at 97 Street and 103 Avenue was formally opened with twenty new courtrooms. In April, 1978, plans were announced for the construction of a $25 million annex to the Law Courts Building that would add another 38 courtrooms when it opened in 1981.

[c1912] **While the external facades** of the Court House were formal and heavy, the internal skylit space over the grand staircase was much more light and delicate in appearance. Off the upper gallery were doors leading to the library and four oak-panelled court rooms.

[1906] **When the Edmonton settlement** was surveyed in 1881 and the streets were all given names, one avenue was named in respectful memory of the Hudson's Bay Company doctor for the Northwest, Dr. William M. MacKay, who practiced in Edmonton from 1898 to 1916. When the first public school was built in 1881, it had the honour of being located on McKay Avenue. (This is the traditional and official spelling, but not the spelling used by the physician.)

In 1904, the first frame school was moved off this site at 10425 99 Avenue (the correct address since the city adopted the present street numbering system in 1914). In its place, this eight-room brick school was built and soon it became associated with other impressive people. The cornerstone was laid by the Governor-General of Canada, Lord Minto, and the first two sessions of the Alberta Legislature (1906 and 1907) were held in the top floor assembly room, with Premier A.C. Rutherford and Lieutenant-Governor George Bulyea presiding over the formalities. In 1912, four more classrooms were added to the west end of the building (right), and the incorrect spelling was placed for posterity over the matching entry. In May, 1976, the historic structure was designated an Alberta historic site.

[1911] **Neatly dressed students congregate** in front of the new Victoria High School which opened on May 9, 1911, at 102 Street and 108 Avenue.

In addition to having twelve regular classrooms, the decorative brick structure of "modern collegiate Renaissance style" had facilities for studying physics, chemistry, domestic science, manual training, music, art, commercial courses, and physical education. A 600-seat auditorium and a finely equipped gymnasium were important assets the school provided for both students and the community. Physical culture was given top consideration by the Board. The course included class tactics, marching, elementary drill, fire drill, stationary apparatus work, track and field athletics, basketball, hockey and other league sports, squad drill, skirmishing, rifle drill and company drill.

[May, 1908] **Not all schools were** prestigious brick buildings. This modest frame school is not the 14 Street School, as photographer Brown indicates, but the Donald Ross School at 101 Street and 97 Avenue. It was typical of many elementary schools in the new city, where children were taught the basic subjects: reading, writing, spelling, calculation, history and geography.

[1906] **Like a dignified Victorian dowager,** the Misericordia Hospital stands impressively in the bush at 98 Avenue and 111 Street. The Roman Catholic Sisters of Misericorde ("compassion"), ministering mainly to unwed mothers, opened a house shelter on this site in 1900. In 1904, a maternity hospital was added. The new 60-bed hospital opened in March, 1906, and after successive additions in 1922, 1939 and 1955, it reached a final capacity of 400 beds. Edmonton's third oldest hospital closed its 63 years of service when the new 550-bed Misericordia Hospital opened on July 18, 1969, at 170 Street and 87 Avenue.

The hospital's nursing school was established with one student in 1907. The school soon changed from obstetrical to general nursing and graduated three nurses in the first class in 1910.

[c1913] **The 122-bed first stage** of the new Royal Alexandra Hospital, which officially opened in April, 1912, likewise stood alone at 10230 111 Avenue. Built at a cost of $225,000, this building replaced the old Public Hospital on Boyle Street (now 103A Avenue). In 1918, a west wing was added to the left to complete the initial expansion plans. The building nearing completion to the right, connected to the hospital by a covered walkway, was the nurses' residence.

The old Public Hospital started Edmonton's first training school for nurses in December, 1905, the same year as the Strathcona Municipal Hospital began its nurses' training program.

[1923] **Several years after** it opened, the 20-bed men's public ward remained austere and inhospitable in spite of the abundance of sunlight which bathed the spacious room.

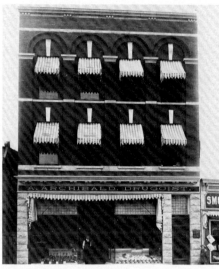

[1910] **When pharmacist Arthur Archibald** opened this neat office block at 9832 Jasper Avenue in March, 1910, he operated the largest and finest pharmacy west of Toronto. He came to Edmonton from Nelson, B.C., in October, 1902, and within eight years was able to erect his own impressive building.

[1910] **The interior of Archibald's Drugstore** was finished in quartered red oak painted in a silver-grey tone to resemble dark marble. Lining the walls were cupboards and cases broken visually by recessed oval plateglass mirrors. Some of the recesses were furnished with cushioned seats covered in claret-coloured leather. Seven plateglass display cases sitting on marble bases housed tempting displays of elaborate toilet articles and other expensive dainties that one would find in only the most up-to-date of posh drugstores. Behind the pillared rear wall of silver-grey oak and huge oval mirror was the dispensing laboratory. The light cream-tinted ceiling contained an improved lighting system consisting of prismatic glass fixtures which shed an even flood of mellow light over the handsomely furnished interior.

[December, 1905] **An abundance of fresh turkeys** and sides of beef hung along with the Christmas decorations in the P. Burns Co. meat market at 10009 Jasper Avenue. The metal tiled ceiling and varnished wooden counter added a touch of sanitation to this spacious butcher shop.

[n.d.] **Wagon chassis and chimney hoods** were just as common as steel anvils and leather aprons in the many blacksmith shops found in the new city. The sweaty, muscular and usually jovial smiths worked hard repairing vehicles and farm machinery and shoeing the hooves of the numerous horses that kept the city moving.

Just as plentiful as the blacksmith shops, and not far from them, were the saddleries, harness shops and livery stables with their lofts filled with hay. Adding to these sights and smells of the horse-drawn city were the veterinarians' offices with their bottles of iodine and creolin.

[n.d.] **On July 19, 1907,** the 200-member Edmonton Club opened this grandiose clubhouse on the brow of the hill at the corner of Macdonald Drive and 100 Street. Built at a cost of $22,000 and furnished for another $8,000, the luxurious accommodation featured on the second floor a large billiard room, card rooms, dining room and a spacious balcony which offered an impressive view of the river valley and the wooded city of Strathcona. In September, 1968, this building was demolished and replaced with a new concrete building which opened in 1969 at approximately the same site. This exclusive business and professional men's club was formed on April 29, 1899, and is the city's oldest private club.

[February 10, 1968] **In the dining room** of the Edmonton Club, little changed from the time of its opening and its closing 61 years later. The warm mahogany panelling and white linen tablecloths greeted many of the city's leading citizens as they gathered for their noon-time luncheons, where they could eat and smoke and discuss the affairs of the day without the presence of ladies or wives. Women were only allowed on designated parts of the premises after 4:30 in the afternoon.

[1908] **The well-dressed staff** paused to stand proudly for this historic photo in front of Edmonton's first motion picture house, the Bijou, at 10166 100 Street. Later there were other Bijous, on 101 Street and on Whyte Avenue, but this was the first, which opened in June, 1907.

The man who got the movies going was Albert R. "Pop" Lawrence, the tall man at the left, who had his usher stand at his right and modestly hide the important part of the sign which announced the ten cents admission charge. Six days a week, Mr. Lawrence put on two afternoon and three evening shows for the price of ten cents; occasionally he charged 25 cents for a big special. Showtime was announced by turning the power onto a string of lights strung across the street.

For a dime, a capacity audience of 240 patrons would get two reels of silent film – first, a few comedy and educational subjects, then the feature film. The show opened with a slide suggesting "Ladies Will Please Remove Their Hats". Because "legitimate theatre" owners made sure there was a law stating that electric motors were illegal, projector operators J. Ellwood and Alex Entwistle (second and third from right) turned the cranks while Mr. Lawrence provided a commentary to explain the action on the silent film. If the show got behind schedule, the projectionist merely turned the crank a little faster to end the show on time. To provide the appropriate mood and to fill the gaps during rewinding, Charles Lynch, seen leaning on the centre post, and his two daughters, dressed in white, provided the musical accompaniment to both the films and audience singalongs during intermission. All this for just ten cents a seat!

[c1910] **O.J. Hallgrimson and S. Swanson** moved their building from 96 Street to this former site of Robertson Hall at Jasper Avenue opposite 97 Street, and set up the 300-seat Dreamland Movie Theatre in 1910. The popular showplace presented two afternoon and three evening screenings a day at modest prices.

In 1920, Alex Entwistle, a projectionist with Edmonton's first Bijou movie house, bought the Dreamland and subsequently became Edmonton's first theatre-chain magnate when, with his sons Clarence and Arnold, he bought the Princess and Monarch Theatres. In 1930, they merged with Famous Players and bought the Empress, Strand and Garneau Theatres.

In 1938, this original Dreamland Theatre was demolished and replaced by a 600-seat, $60,000 new Dreamland Theatre, which stood until it was demolished in March, 1979, to make way for the new Convention Centre.

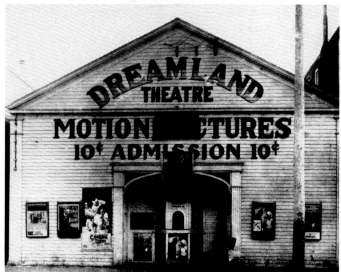

[1908] **What was believed for years** by many Edmontonians to be the first automatic telephone exchange in North America turned out to be, in fact, only the first in Alberta. Although Saskatoon had a small automatic exchange over a year ahead of Edmonton, the Edmonton telephone system, when it went automatic on April 20, 1908, was the first system in Canada to have the potential for extensive expansion, the essential of a truly metropolitan automatic system. By comparison, cities in eastern Canada did not install automatic exchanges until the 1920s.

On January 1, 1905, the city's telephone system came into public ownership after the city bought it from Alberta's first telephone entrepreneur, Alex Taylor. By that time the old manual exchange, located in the top floor of the Gariepy Block at 100 Street and Jasper Avenue, was nearly filled to its capacity of 450 lines.

As soon as the automatic exchange opened with 700 lines, the city ordered 500 more. As this photo shows, only two operators were required to handle long distance calls. By 1912, when the city opened its first two branch exchanges, there were over 6,000 lines in operation and the number of subscribers was increasing rapidly.

[1910] **These attentive operators** worked at the switchboard in Edmonton Telephones' south-side long-distance exchange at 83 Avenue and 104 Street. In the foreground, behind the empty chairs at the rural boards, is the recording desk, where the calls were received and then transferred to the operators at the switchboard. Behind the girls, who are operating the lines to nearby towns, is the chief operator's desk. In 1913, the ladies worked eight hours a day at a monthly wage of $40.

Edmonton Telephones continued, in subsequent decades, to lead the way in customer service. In 1910, it installed emergency call boxes throughout the city. In 1960, these call boxes gave citizens access to police, fire, ambulance and any emergency need. By 1936, Edmonton had twice as many phones per capita as any other city on the continent. (By 1980, the ratio was one phone for every 1.15 persons.) In 1967, Edmonton was the first city in western Canada to have touch-tone dialing.

[October 17, 1907] **An early afternoon fire** on October 17, 1907, damaged the 18-month-old post office block at the northwest corner of 100 Street and 101A Avenue. The blaze raged for three hours, but good hustling by the post office staff and diligent work by the fire brigade resulted in almost no loss of mail. Although the post office block suffered a $20,000 loss, the neighbouring Bijou Theatre had little damage.

In January, 1908, ex-mayor Charles May was awarded the contract for the construction of a large new post office to be located diagonally across this same intersection.

[c1914] **Although the new post office** was completed in 1909, the official opening did not take place until November 7, 1910, because of a delay in getting the clocks in place. For the next 62 years, this elegant 130-foot-high clock tower was a distinctive landmark in downtown Edmonton. In 1930 an addition, to the south, doubled the length of the building along 100 Street.

Thirty years later, the greatly increased volume of mail demanded a much larger building, which the federal government provided on the site of the old Queen's Avenue School. With the opening of the modern Sir Alexander Mackenzie Post Office on July 29, 1966, the old post office closed its doors on August 6, 1966. When the handsome structure was demolished in 1972, the famous clock, made in Derby, England, in 1902 at an original cost of approximately $1000, was preserved and in 1978 installed in a new tower located on the same site at the entrance to the present Westin Hotel.

[November 9, 1908] **On November 9, 1908,** a new sound was heard in the streets of Edmonton. It was the clanging and clattering of two brown wooden streetcars which on that day began to shuttle passengers back and forth along their twelve miles of track. Four more cars were added soon after. The line started here at the new $60,000 Norwood School (which opened formally on February 26, 1909) at 111 Avenue and 95 Street and went south along 95 Street to 106 Avenue, jogged over to 97 Street and south to Jasper Avenue to reach its western terminus at Jasper Avenue and 116 Street.

The name "Edmonton Radial Railway" painted on the side, indicated the original intent of the system to maintain a monopoly development within an 80-mile radius of Edmonton. Although the system never came anywhere near to fulfilling the grandiose dreams of its charter authors, the system did expand to 52 miles of track by 1914 and did have the honour of being North America's most northern electric streetcar line.

[April 28, 1911] **Aviator Hugh Robinson** gave an Edmonton Exhibition crowd of over 600 their first good look at an airplane. With the propellor rotating at 15,000 revolutions per minute, the pusher-type Curtiss bi-plane gracefully rose to a height of about 200 feet, circled the field three times and landed. Later that afternoon, he again fired up the 50-horsepower engine and made two more circuits of the field.

This was not the first flight in Edmonton, however. Alberta's first successful powered flight was achieved by Edmonton carpenter Reginald Hunt, who made a Labor Day flight on September 7, 1909, only six months after James McCurdy made the first Canadian flight of two minutes length at Baddeck Bay, Nova Scotia. Flying his own invention, including the engine that he designed and built himself, Mr. Hunt flew over the houses in Edmonton's west end at a height ranging from 35 to 50 feet and landed safely after being airborne for about 35 minutes. In 1910, he cracked up his mechanical bird while getting it ready for the Exhibition. Happy to be alive, but discouraged with the loss of three years work, the inventive carpenter went north to Athabasca Landing to build river boats. Two years later he moved to Seattle, Washington, where he eventually established Pacific Coast Airways, Inc. Although Hunt built a few more flying machines later, his decision not to rebuild his first successful craft gave Robinson the opportunity to give Edmontonians their first public display of powered flight.

[1910] **In 1909, the city spent** roughly $5,000 on drainage, access roads and a racetrack in order to transform a large slough called East End Park into a new Exhibition Grounds. By August 24, 1910, the many livestock stables and the $25,000, 4,500-seat grandstand were ready, and the four day Edmonton Fair opened for the first time on its permanent site between Borden Park and 118 Avenue. To handle the huge crowds of 20,000 per day (double the size of the previous year down on Ross Flats), the C.N.R. and G.T.P. operated half-hour train service from the downtown Union Station to the Exhibition Grounds. (This transportation preceded by 68 years the Light Rail Transit system, which uses the same tracks today.)

The five race program at the track started with trotters, shown here speeding past the judges stand at the finish line, followed by either a pace or trot, and ended with three races at full gallop. Catering to the desires of the large summer crowds, and adding to the fair's coffers as well, professional bookmakers and outlets for two-percent beer operated conveniently nearby. By 1916, Edmonton boasted that its annual fair was the third largest in North America, behind Toronto and St. Paul, Minnesota.

[1911] **A team of tame moose** provided novel entertainment at the summer Exhibition. They belonged to a northern Alberta homesteader, Billy Day, who captured them as calves, reared them by bottle, and drove them around Edmonton during the Exhibition. The pair behaved well in the parade and were a popular attraction for both young and old folk of the big city.

[June 3, 1908] **Referee Bob McDonald** has Billy Lauder, lightweight champion of Canada (left) and Edmontonian Lyn Truscott, lightweight champion of Australia (right) pose for the press photographer before their June 4, 1908, fight at the Thistle Rink. The 135-pound Scot and 134-pound Canadian "kangaroo" put on one of the fastest exhibitions of boxing skill ever seen in the city. After fifteen rounds of fast-swinging action, referee McDonald declared the bout a draw.

[1904] **These members of the Edmonton** lacrosse team of 1904 were the champions of the Canadian North West.

Lacrosse, the national game of Canada, developed from the game of *baggataway*, which had religious significance among the Algonquin Indians of the St. Lawrence valley. The first mention of the game in Edmonton was in November, 1882. The first Edmonton lacrosse club was organized on March 28, 1883, when seventeen members enrolled for a team on which no person under sixteen years of age was admitted. No further mention of games appeared in the local newspaper until the team was reorganized with 76 members on April 18, 1892, with Rev. C. Cunningham as president and E. Raymer, vice-president. After practicing on the old race track grounds, the Edmonton team accepted a challenge from Calgary and were well-beaten by their southern rivals in their first game held at the beginning of October, 1892. With more practice and game experience, the skills of the Edmonton team improved, culminating with the championship side of 1904.

[c1912] **Long before the turn** of the century and for a decade afterward, the customary sporting way of getting around through deep Edmonton snow was by means of snowshoes. But eight enterprising young Norwegians changed all that when they formed the Edmonton Ski Club on December 19, 1911, and had eight pairs of skis and bindings made in the harness and blacksmith shops of the city. Soon after they started skiing here in January, 1912, these Scandinavian traditionalists challenged a group of local snowshoe advocates to a race from the High Level Bridge to Whitemud Creek. Leaving their embarrassed rivals out of sight after only the first mile, the Norwegian skiers next decided to introduce to their Canadian neighbours the thrills of ski jumping. Later that winter, they staged a jumping demonstration from the 113 Street hill above the Municipal Golf Course. Here seven club members demonstrate the structural safety of their homemade jump.

[1904] **Here, with all its victory prizes,** is the proud Thistle Hockey Club of 1903-04, winners of the Alberta championship.

Their continued successes finally emboldened them to, in the spring of 1908, challenge the Montreal Wanderers for the Stanley Cup. Having just won Lord Stanley's trophy, the confident easterners naturally accepted. Meanwhile, Edmonton businessmen, just to be certain the local team would bring back the coveted cup, reinforced the team by replacing all but three original Thistle players with stars from eastern teams, including two the biggest names in hockey at that time, Lester Patrick and Tom Phillipps of the Montreal Shamrocks. This loaded team easily defeated their Strathcona rivals 21-0 the next winter, and it appeared the star-studded Thistles were ready for the big two-game series at the end of December. After leading the first game 3-2 at half-time, the better conditioned Wanderers, led by the great Art Ross, won the first game 8-3. Although the Montreal team lost the second game 7-6, they kept the Stanley Cup, because it was a total-goal series. The Edmonton team lost the series, its pride and immediately after the games, lost its imports as well.

In 1910, an Edmonton team again challenged the eastern champions. This time Ottawa retained the Stanley Cup by outscoring Edmonton 21-11 in a four game total-goal series. Twice bitten, Edmonton refrained from challenging for the Cup for another dozen years.

6 Amalgamation and Boom (1912 - 1914)

The growing optimism and civic pride that continued after Edmonton became a city and a capital reached its peak in 1912. That year, Strathcona amalgamated with Edmonton and North Edmonton was annexed. The city limits were pushed outward as Canadian immigration increased to a peak in 1913 and as the balance of population in Canada continued to shift from rural to urban centres. Particularly in the West, growth and prosperity continued unabated as city dwellers and their rural neighbours prospered from the wheat boom produced by the new sodbusting farmers.

In Edmonton, as in the other urban centres of western Canada, optimism was unrestrained. Beyond the existing streets, subdivisions were surveyed in every direction as the city swarmed with real estate agents whose brisk business raised land prices to extremes. Jasper Avenue properties were selling at prices of up to $10,000 per lineal foot of frontage. It seemed that everyone was buying property, speculating in land and making money. Since most of the deals involved only small cash down payments, however, the "fortunes" made were only paper profits.

Benefitting greatly from the economic boom that was sweeping the entire country, Edmonton achieved record growth in 1912. The population increased by 63 percent over the previous year, while building permits increased 400 percent. In mid-May, 1912, the time of the famous Hudon's Bay Co. land sale, Edmonton was the only city in Canada to show an increase in bank clearings over the corresponding week of the previous year. Civic pride increased as the Legislative Building and the High Level Bridge were opened, and the new skyscrapers - the Civic Block,

Tegler Building and McLeod Building - were constructed. To accommodate the demand for access to the newly staked out subdivisions, streetcar lines were extended to the Highlands, Inglewood and McKernan Lake areas. The Inter-Urban Railway was built to St. Albert and the Canadian Northern Railway opened a line to Athabasca. Although thousands had to live in tents due to the housing shortage, optimism abounded; the economic boom reached its zenith.

By mid-1913, the onset of a worldwide depression hit over-extended Canadian cities particularly hard. Wheat prices dropped dramatically, money markets collapsed, buying power diminished rapidly while prices rose, the C.N.R. went bankrupt, confidence turned into panic. In just a few months, the boom became a bust. Disillusionment and economic collapse affected both the paper millionaires and the civic administration. It took the city 35 years to pay for all the new facilities and utilities built into the undeveloped new subdivisions. For 40 years a large part of the H.B.C. Reserve remained empty. Although the city's population increased to 72,500 in 1914, many of these belonged to the increasing ranks of the unemployed.

[1913] **Jasper Avenue east** of 101 Street
in 1913 teemed with people and a variety
of modes of conveyance.

The years from 1911 to 1914 were a
time of extensive growth for the city. In
1911, the twin-city population was about
31,000 and the value of building permits
totalled $3,660,327. The next year saw the
amalgamation of Edmonton and Strathcona, on February 1, and the peak of the
real estate and building boom. In 1912,
the population nearly doubled to over
53,000 and the number of buildings in the
city doubled as well. The 3,464 building
permits issued in 1912 totalled
$14,446,819, figures which were not
exceeded until 1946. By 1914, the
population had increased to nearly
73,000, but the boom was over; the
population soon dropped back to 53,000.

[1912] **Along the south side** of Jasper Avenue east from 101 Street, within a half block of the main intersection of the expanding city, twenty-three real estate establishments crowded around the entrance to the Orpheum Theatre. Cadillac cars were waiting to taxi prospective buyers to see the potential for wealth in the outlying farmland and bushland that was now being subdivided. Many eager buyers were not interested in developing the new subdivisions that were popping up all around the perimeter of the city. They were speculators who wanted to buy cheap and sell high. Very little cash changed hands, as the usual deal was ten per cent down and the rest on installments (which usually never materialized). With this system, many became "paper millionaires" in a short time, and when the boom ended, they just as quickly lost their "fortunes".

[c1912] **Here in the offices** of the Western Canada Realty Co., a group of real estate operators devise ways and means of making a handsome profit in the often risky, sometimes lucrative and at times disastrous business of real estate dealings. In 1912 the city swarmed with 32 real estate brokers, 135 financial agencies and 336 real estate agents. By 1914, most of these had vanished from the scene as quickly as they had appeared.

[May 12, 1912] **The longest queue** in the city's early history occurred when well over 1,500 people got in line to draw numbered tickets that would allow them to purchase up to four lots each, when the Hudon's Bay Company put its land for sale on May 13, 1912.

By agreement with the federal government, the trading company owned 3,000 acres of land from the river to 118 Avenue between 101 Street and 121 Street. Although they sold lots on the southern half of their reserve beginning as early as 1881, the H.B.C. decided to wait until May, 1912, before they would sell north of 108 Avenue. The day before the sale, the tickets were drawn, then either kept, traded, sold or used to buy lots in the bush in the center of the city. The H.B.C. made $4.3 million from the sale and kept its promise to build and pave the 100-foot-wide Portage Avenue (now Kingsway) diagonally across the reserve. The City laid out two sets of streetcar tracks down the entire two-mile length of the avenue. But the real estate boom

suddenly burst; no streetcar ever rode those rails and hardly any buildings were ever built along this broadest avenue in the city. Within two years, most people who had crowded the streets to get a lot or two could pay neither the payment installments nor the taxes. Soon the city administration found itself the owner of 75,000 lots, which had reverted for unpaid taxes. The financial crash came even more suddenly than the arrival of the boom itself. This land sale marked the climax of the boom, but unfortunately it also precipitated the bust by taking most of the cash out of circulation.

[c1914] **This view of Jasper Avenue** east of 99 Street shows the old city core with a second wave of buildings which were erected during the first decade of the century. A notable exception is the building housing Kline's jewellery store. It is still the original 1886 building used as a jewellery shop by Emanuel Raymer and later by Jackson Bros. In 1911, Herman Kline opened his jewellery and optometry shop in these premises. This durable little building served various businessmen for over ninety years before it was finally demolished in 1979 to make way for the 16-storey Alberta Gas Trunk Line Building.

[c1914] **This view of Jasper Avenue west** of 100 Street shows the Gariepy Block on the corner and the six-storey C.P.R. office block, which opened in April, 1913. This imposing edifice was given a monumental base of huge two-storey-high Corinthian columns with the intention of the building eventually rising another four stories, an eventuality that never materialized. The completed building, the first all-steel structure to be erected in the city, was built of 700 tons of structural steel and over 9,000 rivets. When it became the headquarters for the N.A.R., it was renamed the Northern Alberta Railways Building. When caretaker Robert Armstrong retired in 1976, it was renamed again as a tribute to the man who lived in its penthouse suite and cared for it so well for thirty years. Built in the boom years for about $350,000, this building was appraised in September, 1980, at $5,500,000.

[c1914] **Across Jasper Avenue** on the southeast corner of 101 Street, the Bank of British North America erected this stone structure in 1913-14. After the boom years, there were far fewer banks and real estate offices in the city, and the Bank of Montreal moved into this stone-faced building in 1918, after they absorbed the business of the B.N.A. Bank.

Between the Allen Theatre (later renamed the Capitol) and the three-storey Union Bank is the six-storey, 25-foot-wide Agency Building, built in 1912. When real estate values were soaring, buildings sometimes had to make the most of a very narrow lot.

The Union Bank, built in 1910, the B.N.A. Bank, and the Canada Permanent Building, built in 1910 at 10130 100 Street (south of the McLeod Building) were fine examples of the talents of local architect Roland Lines, who also designed the Royal Alexandra Hospital and the Exhibition Stock Pavilion (later called the Edmonton Gardens) before he was killed in World War I.

[1914] **Prominent in this view** of Jasper Avenue west of 102 Street are the Hudson's Bay store, with its fourth-floor addition of 1911, and the Brown Block, containing the entrance to the Pantages Theatre and the Shasta Grill.

Tucked away in the basement of the Brown Block was Edmonton's first cafeteria, the popular American Dairy Lunch. In addition to the delicious and abundant food served up by its two Greek owners, George Spillios and Harry Lingas, the cafeteria featured a pool with gold fish swimming beneath a rocky fountain and little carved Czech wine gods holding up the ceiling beams.

In 1912, the Brown Block was intended to be the highest building in the city, at ten stories, but when it was built the next year, it never reached the third floor. The sudden end of the real estate boom and the major recession in the eastern money markets, accompanied by the bankruptcy of the Canadian Northern Railway, brought a sudden halt to local expansion and building activity. Many buildings, such as the proposed ten-storey Royal Alexandra Hotel and the seven-storey Northern Club, were never built.

[May 12, 1913] **Over 1,600 people** filled the house to watch Mayor William Short and Lieutenant-Governor G.H.V. Bulyea open the Pantages Vaudeville Theatre.

Alexander Pantages became the American west coast vaudeville king by joining the Klondike gold rush in 1898. In Dawson, he became romantically involved with "Klondike Kate" Rockwell, who financed his first theatre, a dancehall saloon called the Dawson Orpheum. By 1901, Pantages had made and lost an $800,000 fortune, moved to Seattle, and built the largest independently-owned vaudeville circuit in North America, with theatres in most major western cities from Los Angeles to Vancouver and Winnipeg.

In 1912, another Greek immigrant, George Brown, persuaded Pantages to build this $250,000 theatre on the property he rented at $1,000 a month on the southwest corner of Jasper Avenue and 102 Street. The Pantages Theatre quickly became a long-term success in Edmonton, with a two-a-day schedule of great performers at the reasonable prices of 25, 35 and 50 cents for the evening show and 15 and 25 cents for matinees.

Besides the jugglers, acrobats, chorus girls, animal acts and comedians who maintained the quick, witty vaudeville tempo, there were the "big names" including the Marx brothers, Buster Keaton and his parents, Stan Laurel (later of the Laurel and Hardy comedy duo), Will Rogers, Sarah Bernhardt, Sir Harry Lauder, Eddie Cantor, George Jessel, Walter Winchell, Ethel Barrymore and Edgar Bergen with Charlie McCarthy.

The development of the motion picture industry brought the decline of vaudeville. In September, 1921, the theatre was renamed the Metropolitan and usually played host to touring dramatic companies. In 1929, the theatre closed, but it reopened in 1931 as the Strand Theatre, one of Alexander Entwisle's local chain of cinemas. During the late 1930s, it was from this stage that Premier William Aberhart broadcast his Sunday evening sermons. In May, 1979, the building was dismantled with the intention of being reconstructed at Fort Edmonton Park.

[October 20, 1913] **Using realistic and lively** sidewalk marketing techniques made popular by most other movie houses, the Monarch Theatre succeeded in attracting the largest attendance up to that time in Edmonton. On the first day of a two-day run, nearly 1,500 children crowded the sidewalk on the south side of Jasper Avenue east of 101 Street to see the exciting dramatization of the Sir Walter Scott novel they were studying in school. Admission charges were 15¢ for children and 25¢ for adults.

[1913] **By the boom year of 1912,** the major business hub of the city had shifted to this intersection of Jasper Avenue and 101 Street. Flanking the view north along 101 Street is the 1897 McDougall & Secord block on the left and their 1905 Empire Block on the right. In the right corner, the popcorn vendor's wagon is parked conveniently by the sidewalk where people wait for the policeman to direct traffic from the centre of the intersection.

[October 13, 1916] **John "Mike" Michaels** (left) and Bob Wright (right) brought newspapers outside for the convenience of summertime passersby on Jasper Avenue at 101 Street.

In 1912, Mike came here from New York where he had been a newsboy since the age of ten. Soon he and his original partner John Leary opened this newsstand on the main corner in Edmonton. Business picked up considerably when they added newspapers in seventeen foreign languages to the local and national papers they carried.

Mike's aim was to have the best newsstand in Canada. He soon succeeded. His partner died shortly after the business started, and Mike moved into his Jasper Avenue store west of 100A Street in 1916. In those days before radio, when Edmonton presses produced The *Journal*, The *Bulletin*, and The *Capital*, Mike delivered his papers by horse and buggy. One of the original "horse and buggy boys" was Bob Wright, who was with Mike for forty-four years, while Mike headed the Provincial News Company, which was one of the largest retail and wholesale newspaper and magazine distributors in Canada. He sold his interest in the company when his health began to fail in 1957.

[1913] **Further north along 101 Street,** the ornate 1911 Moser-Ryder Block advertises the new subdivision of the Bronx. Messrs. Moser and Ryder made a sizeable fortune in the real estate business and after only six years in Edmonton, they were able to erect this four-storey office and apartment building and then retire to southern California. The block got a streamlined facelifting after a serious fire in 1944.

The *Journal* offices occupy the 1912 addition to the original 1911 Tegler Building. Robert Tegler eventually finished his huge eight-storey fireproof office addition in 1913. Besides spending part of his fortune on this city's first "skyscraper", millionaire Tegler, who died at the age of 41, initiated a scholarship program to assist worthy high school students with their university education.

North of 102 Avenue, Abe Cristall, the city's first Jewish resident, built the Royal George Hotel in 1910. It was the city's first five-storey building. Born in the Ukraine region of Europe, Mr. Cristall came to Edmonton in 1893 and soon progressed from drayman to liquor store operator to general merchant to owner of a men's clothing store. The successful entrepreneur found himself stranded too far north of the business district when the boom went flat in 1913, so he persuaded Charles Woodward to build his crowd-drawing department store on the corner next to his hotel. Honest Abe's business improved and his $100,000 hotel lasted until October, 1972, when it made way for the immense Edmonton Centre project.

[c1915] **Probably the sturdiest building** in the city is the nine-storey McLeod Building, built from 1912 through 1914 on the southwest corner of 100 Street and 101A Avenue. Local contractor Kenny McLeod, who had walked from Winnipeg to Edmonton in 1881, imported the architect and contractors from Spokane to reproduce the Polson Building of that city. Only Kenny wanted almost everything fifty percent stronger! Over 1,200 tons of steel were used to satisfy the determined Scotsman. The beautifully clean exterior was faced with light buff brick and terra cotta tile, and on the interior, the lobby, washrooms and corridors were sheathed in Italian marble; the only wood used was durable oak. The $600,000 building was opened in January, 1915. Being thirteen feet higher than the Tegler Building, it stood for almost forty years as Edmonton's tallest building. Finally in 1953, the 15-storey addition to the Macdonald Hotel became the first of several buildings that measured higher than the 115-foot-high McLeod Building.

In this photo, the building on the corner, behind the wagon, is the old Post Office which was damaged in the fire of 1907. The white Cheap John's Meat Market was formerly Edmonton's first movie house, the Bijou. It remained as a meat market until it was demolished in the 1950s.

[1915] **North of Jasper Avenue** along 104 Street lies the mushrooming warehouse and wholesaling district. Just south of the Great West Saddlery warehouse is the four-storey Armstrong Block. At the left, west of the Marshall-Wells warehouse along 102 Avenue, is the large six-storey Revillon Building. In the background at the far right is the brick Queen's Avenue School, on the present site of the new 1966 Post Office. The Cecil Hotel, on the northwest corner of 104 Street and Jasper Avenue, opened in October, 1906. In 1910, the northern half of the hotel was added, thereby increasing the capacity from the original 37 rooms to 65.

[1910] **The 1910 addition** to the Cecil Hotel included this fine 300-seat dining room on the main floor. At the time of its opening, the hotel had the distinction of being owned, built and staffed entirely by Edmontonians.

[c1915] **Traffic from the northeast** along the Fort Trail at 127 Avenue was sparce on this particular day, but when the farmers brought their hogs, sheep and cattle to the North Edmonton stockyards, this broad thoroughfare was the centre of activity. The forty-room Transit Hotel, which was built at the same time as the nearby Swift's Packing Plant, was officially opened on September 11, 1908. At that time this community, called Packingtown for obvious reasons, was the first railway stop outside Edmonton. In February, 1910, the area was incorporated as the village of North Edmonton and was annexed to the city in 1912.

In later times, the Transit Hotel had a pair of signs reading "Last Chance" on the near side and "First Chance" on the far side, reminding travellers to and from Fort Saskatchewan and beyond, that this was the last beerparlor, or the first, depending on your direction of travel. On October 8, 1980, the well-worn hotel was declared an historic site by the city.

[c1913] **Shortly before the First World War,** Indians still pitched their teepees on the flats below the McKay Avenue School just as their forefathers had done during the early days of the Hudson's Bay Co. fort. Behind the tents lay the thin line of the Edmonton, Yukon and Pacific Railway. This rail line extended from Strathcona, down Mill Creek, over the Low Level Bridge, west along the flats, and later was extended up Groat Ravine to end at Stony Plain Road and 123 Street. It opened in 1902, ran passenger trains until 1926 and continued in operation over its entire length until 1952.

[c1913] **Careful shoppers survey** the produce and prices at the city market.

In 1912, the city built a covered market building on 101A Avenue between 99 and 100 Streets and then closed its doors two years later when they relocated the market and opened a $100,000 market building at the northeast corner of 101 Street and 107 Avenue. But the expected expansion of the city north of the C.N.R. tracks did not materialize, and the new market location proved as big a mistake as the two lines of streetcar tracks that were laid down Portage Avenue that same year. Within a short time, farmers and city folk were back at the original market location buying and selling eggs at 30 cents a dozen, radishes at 10 cents for 3 bunches, and plants at 15 cents a pot. This old downtown market square remained until the present market opened in 1965 at 97 Street and 102 Avenue.

[c1914] **Overlooking the Market Square** from the corner of 99 Street and 102 Avenue is the six-storey Civic Block, which served as city hall from August, 1913 to March, 1957. All the various departments of civic administration were housed in this one compact structure, built at a cost of $225,000. The staid warehouse appearance of the Civic Block remained until 1961, when an equally unimpressive facade was applied as the building was assigned to the city police department. No attempt was made in the original design to produce an elaborate edifice because it was, in the words of City Architect Jeffers, the "general belief that some day the site will demand a more pretentious structure, and one in harmony with its surroundings."

[1914] **On the third floor** of the Civic Block, Mayor W.S. McNamara and his council sit in their modest 33-by-40-foot council chamber. There was nothing to smile about: the prosperous boom had ended and the world war had begun, the city had spent a fortune expanding streets into the many newly proposed but undeveloped subdivisions, and few property owners could pay their taxes.

[1913] **From their spacious offices** within the Civic Block, city clerks are busy attending to their municipal duties.

[n.d.] **This early law office** of Taylor, Gariepy and Boyle was located in the Gariepy Block at the northwest corner of 100 Street and Jasper Avenue.

The first lawyer to establish a law practice in Edmonton was Henry Y. Bleeker, who came from Belleville, Ontario, in March, 1882. At the end of August, 1882, Bleeker's partner, Charles Hambly, arrived from Winnipeg in three weeks aboard the river steamer *The North West*. By the time their pioneer law firm closed in January, 1884, several other barristers and solicitors had established firms in town.

[1913] **Ready to battle** for law and order amid the problems of prohibited booze, illicit brothels and disorderly gambling houses, the city police force show off their latest vehicles and paddy-wagons.

The town's first constable was appointed in August, 1892, to watch for a suspected arsonist. When the city was inaugurated in 1904, the police force increased from two constables to a chief and four constables, who served double duty as license inspectors. In 1913, when this photo was taken, the total city police force numbered 103, of which 62 were constables. By 1981, the force had increased to 1,300, including 749 constables.

[c1914] **At the No. 7 Firehall** in North Edmonton, the fire department vehicles stand ready for action. At the sound of the alarm, the horses would come out of the stable doors at the left, stand under the harness as the men quickly hitched it in place, and then the crew would gallop through the large double doors to the street outside. In a few seconds, the latest in fire-fighting equipment would be on its way to battle one of man's oldest enemies, the uncontrolled fire.

[c1913] **Surrounded in this photo** by First Presbyterian Church on 105 Street, the Macdonald Hotel, the last remains of the old fort, and the Edmonton, Yukon & Pacific Railway line, the Legislative Building dominates the top of the river bank where Hardisty's Big House once stood. Although the first session of the Alberta legislature held here occurred on November 30, 1911, the building was not completed until minutes before the official opening on September 3, 1912. The Duke of Connaught, then Governor-General of Canada, unlocked the main doors with a key made of Saskatchewan River gold. Since its opening, this structure, with its 178-foot-high dome, has been one of the city's most outstanding landmarks. Like the Big House that preceded it, the Legislative Building, built at a cost of nearly three million dollars, appropriately dominates the view over the site of Edmonton's early beginnings nearly 200 years ago.

[c1913] **Beneath the 48-foot-diameter** dome, the marble sheathed rotunda opens upward to a height of 173 feet from the floor to the ceiling of the cupola. Originally the space also extended downward through the circular well to the lower floor below. This was filled with a fountain and landscaping in 1939. The grand staircase leads from the Renaissance-domed rotunda up to the saucer-domed Legislative Chamber which occupies most of the southern wing of the building.

[1913] **The second session** of the Alberta Legislature held in the Legislative Building pauses for a photograph within the spacious Legislative Chamber. Premier Sifton and his Liberal party (left) are here opposed by Edward Michener, leader of the opposition Independent Conservative party. Above house speaker Hon. Charles Welling-Fisher is the Press Gallery, while the Public Gallery is located above the Premier's backbenchers. Below the Legislative Chamber, on the second floor, is the Provincial Library.

[c1915] **Government House**, which opened in October, 1913, originally cost $350,000. Over the next twelve years, $292,000 was spent on its upkeep and refurnishings. In 1925, a government motion later rescinded, asked for the closure and sale of the building. Two years later, another $10,000 was provided for refurbishing. In 1931, when Lieutenant-Governor W.L. Walsh moved in, $2,400 worth of draperies and carpets were obtained for a July function. To Walsh's request for a fireplace in the reception hall, Premier Brownlee replied that they had got along without one this long and would therefore turn down the request. The maintenance budget that year was $24,845. The deepening depression of 1933 made legislative members more critical of the maintenance costs. A carpet bought for $200 in 1912 was sold for $25 in 1932. In 1934, a resolution was sent to Ottawa to abolish the post of Lieutenant-Governor. In March, 1938, the building was closed and Lieutenant-Governor Bowen moved to a hotel suite.

Wartime needs reopened the house to fliers and mechanics of Northwest Airlines Inc. In October, 1942, a three-day auction sale emptied the house of nearly all of its $300,000 contents, for a return of $19,642. The empty building then served as a war veterans' hospital from 1944 to 1950. In 1951, the federal government purchased the residence for $350,000 and used it until 1964 as a home for disabled war veterans. In 1967, ownership was transferred back to the Alberta government, and the original conservatory (seen at the left) which served as a shower room for troops and a sunroom for convalescent veterans, was removed. In August, 1976, after extensive renovations and furnishings costing $1,700,000, the mansion was again used for special receptions and conferences and opened to the public for weekend tours.

[c1915] **The original Reception Room** and Dining Room of Government House express the heavily patterned interiors typical of the luxuriant Victorian style.

[c1915] **The original State Room** of Government House included Hepplewhite chairs and a fireplace mantel done in the Adams style, which is echoed in details of the walls and ceiling.

[c1915] **Perched on the edge** of the
north river bank, between the Grandview
Hotel and Blowey Henry's furniture store,
is the imposing chateau, Hotel
Macdonald. The seven-storey Grand
Trunk Pacific hotel, faced with Indiana
limestone and roofed with copper, was
built and furnished at a cost of about
$2,250,000. After four years of
construction during the boom period, it
opened on July 5, 1915.

Churning up-river is the *City of
Edmonton*, a paddlewheeler built by John
Walter in 1909. The second deck had a
hardwood floor so the passengers, who
numbered around five hundred at full
capacity, could dance during the weekend
excursion runs to and from Big Island, the
summer resort Mr. Walter developed
eighteen miles up-river. During the war
years, passenger trade dropped off
considerably and the steamboat spent its
remaining years, until 1918, hauling
freight and farm produce to and from
Shandro, 120 miles down-river.

[1915] **Following in the tradition** of the
Frontenac, Laurier, Empress, Banff Springs
and other great railway hotels of Canada,
the Macdonald Hotel was built
luxuriously in the chateau style and
named after a great Canadian personality,
the nation's first prime minister. Taking
over from the local Alberta, Selkirk,
Cecil, King Edward and Royal George
hotels as a hotel of distinction, for over
sixty years the "Mac" stood proudly as
the class hotel of Edmonton.

Here in its original splendor we see the
lounge, with its large Fathers of
Confederation oil painting.

[1915] **The Macdonald's spacious** forty-foot-wide dining terrace along the hotel's southern facade, overlooking the river valley awaits luncheon guests.

[1915] **One of the Macdonald** Hotel's 204 finely-appointed bedrooms features polished brass bedsteads.

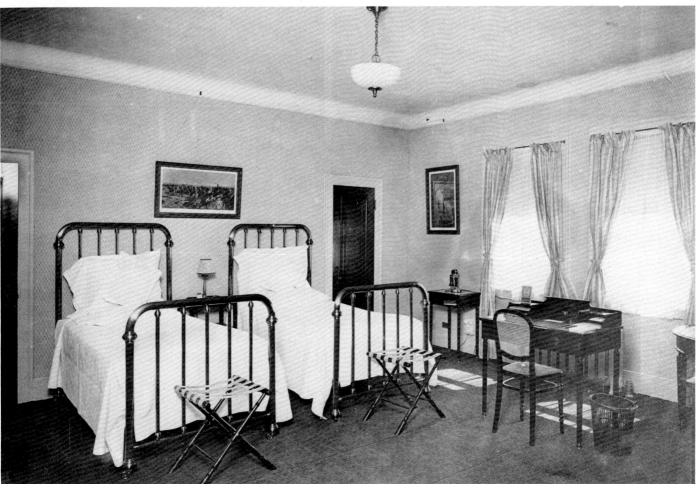

[c1913] **The E.H. Wright home** is representative of many fine new homes built in the west part of the city during the boom period. The July 13, 1912 newspaper remarked that "From the first of the year until the end of June, exactly 144 residential structures are costing owners $2,767,110, which is a remarkable value per house [$19,216]. It is probably the biggest house building year that the city will ever experience." That statement remained true for over three decades, until 1945, when over 1,000 wartime houses were built to meet the pressing need for housing units in the city. Although not as many dwellings were built as in 1912, the 1945 value of residential building permits did finally exceed the 1912 figure of nearly $5.5 million.

[June 2, 1913] **On June 2nd, 1913**, the first special C.P.R. train crossed the High Level Bridge.

Constructed between 1910 and 1913 at a cost of more than $2,000,000, the High Level Bridge was, at the date of its completion, the fourth largest bridge in Canada. It was at that time the only bridge of its kind in the world, a double-deck bridge having two electric streetcar tracks and one railroad track on the upper deck and two sidewalks and a two-lane roadway on the lower deck. The bridge is 2,478 feet long, 43 feet wide, 157 feet high above the high water mark. Construction took the lives of four workmen and used 500,000 cubic feet of concrete, 17,200,000 pounds of steel (500 miles long if placed end to end) and approximately 1,400,000 rivets. Every few years, 5,000 gallons of paint are used to cover the 860,000 square feet of surface area. During very cold winters, the bridge contracts about two feet in comparison to its summer length.

Regular train service across the bridge commenced on June 15, 1913. Streetcars made their first runs over the structure on August 11 and foot passengers had to wait until August 31 before the two seven-foot-wide sidewalks were opened. The 23½-foot-wide roadway, originally paved with wood blocks, was completed for its first vehicles on September 11, 1913, but because the provincial government had not yet paid for its share of the cost, the C.P.R. prohibited the passage of vehicles until the bill was fully paid at the end of the month!

[1919] **In this first aerial photo** of the university, taken by Wop May, standing in a row in the background are the three oldest buildings of the University of Alberta. First came Athabasca Hall (centre) which, when it opened in September, 1911, housed the entire university. Assiniboia Hall (right) opened in 1913 and Pembina Hall (left) opened in 1914. After the Arts Building (foreground) opened on October 6, 1915, as the main

teaching building, the three previous buildings all functioned as residences.

During the first session of the university, the Students' Union was organized, but the first issue of their newspaper, The *Gateway*, did not appear until 1911. The first graduates received their degrees in 1912, the same year the Law Faculty was added to the original Faculty of Arts and Science. In 1913, the faculties of Medicine and Applied Science (renamed Engineering in 1948) were instituted. By 1914, student registration had increased to 439.

[1912] **Just northeast of the university** campus, at 11153 Saskatchewan Drive, this brick mansion was built in 1911 as the residence of the former premier and founder of the university, Alexander C. Rutherford. Behind this $25,000 house, Dr. Rutherford built one of the first brick garages in the city to shelter his red Packard automobile.

Having generous space available in their new house, the Rutherfords invited the graduating class each spring to what came to be called Founder's Day Tea. More than 500 attended the last party held in 1938. In 1940, Rutherford, the Chancellor of the University since 1927, sold his home and furnishings to the Delta Upsilon Fraternity, which resided there until 1969. Through the efforts of the University Women's Club and a $100,000 contribution by the Government of Alberta, the house was restored to its original stately mien and opened to the public on May 11, 1974. Five years later, this second home of Alberta's first premier was officially designated a provincial historic resource.

[c1912] **The first building erected** on the university grounds was not a University of Alberta building, but a Methodist theological college operated as a department of Alberta College. This residence and lecture facility opened on January 3, 1911, a few months before the first university building was ready for students. In 1926, as a result of the union of the Methodist and Presbyterian churches, Alberta College South and Robertson College, the Presbyterian theological school, united to form St. Stephen's College, operated by the United Church of Canada. On November 6, 1927, the Roman Catholic church opened its St. Joseph's College at the western end of the same block. This original St. Stephen's building finally closed as a

theological college in 1972. The United Church sold the building in 1977 for $750,000 to the provincial government, who spent approximately $1,250,000 on restoration and renovations. The historic building now houses the Historic Sites Service of Alberta.

[c1914] **On October 15, 1913**, five instructors and twelve students assembled in the abandoned city streetcar barns on 95 Street to begin the thirty-year history of the Edmonton Technical School. Attendance increased quickly, so that by the end of the term 84 students were receiving from twelve instructors a blend of vocational and academic training very similar to that offered by vocational high schools today. After using these "temporary" quarters for both daytime and evening courses for ten years, the school moved to another city hand-me-

down, the old city market, which previously had a short life at the northeast corner of 107 Avenue and 101 Street. Finally, on June 2, 1943, the school board decided to hand over the facilities to the War Emergency Training Service, and the Techinical School came to an end.

The last principal was Matthew J. Hilton, a mining engineer who joined the staff in 1917 as a science teacher, and who is credited with having written the first textbook ever written and wholly printed in Canada.

[1912] **Collection teams and delivery** wagons crowd the yard of the Edmonton City Dairy.

In 1905, Warren W. Prevey came from Wisconsin and decided that the delivery of milk from open cans into jugs was not adequate in a rapidly growing urban centre. So on May 6, 1906, with one wagon and a staff of six, he set up the Edmonton City Dairy which introduced the first bottled and pasteurized milk in Alberta. Beginning with a 40-pound capacity butter churn, the firm progressed until by 1923 the annual output had reached six million pounds, the largest in Canada at that time.

The enterprise began as a family affair, with Mrs. Prevey using a one-gallon ice cream churn to produce the first commercial ice cream in Edmonton. Additionally, from the family quarters on the second floor of their dairy building, she provided board and room for several of the young men employed by the early firm.

[c1914] **Pushed by French financiers** who held properties in neighboring St. Albert, the Edmonton Inter-Urban Railway was chartered in 1910 with the purpose of constructing an electric railway radiating for over forty miles over the territory north and west of Edmonton and to Vegreville. In September, 1912, the company was formed and on October 11, 1912, a contract was let to build a railway line from the community of Calder (now in northwest Edmonton) to St. Albert. Although never electrified, the line was opened on September 30, 1913, with this one gas electric car making three round trips a day between Edmonton and St.

Albert. By December the service had increased to two cars and five round trips per day from Edmonton. In 1915, fire destroyed the car barn along with the first car, and the next year the Edmonton Radial Railway obtained running rights over the line from 118 Avenue to 127 Avenue. In 1920, the city purchased this part of the line and the E.I.R. disposed of the rest of the steel and ended another big dream that never really materialized.

The only two cars the E.I.R. used were unique in Canada. The first car was a self-propelled Drake "automotrice" of a style used in Hungary since 1905, but only recently introduced to North America. The second car was an English self-propelled hydraulic drive type, which was the first of its kind ever built. From 1914 to 1928, this second car was used on the Lacombe and Blindman Valley Electric Railway (which also never electrified) on their line from Lacombe to Bentley and Rimbey.

[c1914] **The 76-foot-high Livestock Pavilion,** which opened for the annual Edmonton Exhibition fair in August, 1913, was the result of an architectural competition for which the winning designer, Roland Lines, received $350. The building was originally intended to be the finest stock pavilion in western Canada, but a night-time fire which levelled the Thistle Rink a month before the beginning of the 1913 hockey season dramatically altered the original usage of the new exhibition pavilion. Not only did the hockey club need a rink, but the city also was in need of a large assembly building. So this $163,827 building, seating 5,000 with standing room for another 5,000, became The Arena, later the Edmonton Gardens, and even later the Klondike Palace. The first hockey game in The Arena took place on Christmas Day, 1913.

[August, 1914] **Inside the new pavilion,** the horses were finely groomed and the columns and boxes brightly decorated for the horse show which was now the big event of the fair as well as of the spring show. Prestigious box seats, where chairs were provided, separated the cheap seats high behind the columns from the broad wooden promenade just behind the boards surrounding the show area.

[c1912] **Young and old enjoyed** musical concerts at the bandshell in the East End Park, later called Borden Park.

On April 1, 1912, exactly two months after the amalgamation of Edmonton and Strathcona, the city's first Parks Department was formed. Later that year, ten new parks were added to the several that already existed, which included the 100-acre West End Park at the north end of Groat Ravine, the 148-acre East End Park (both established in 1906), and Tipton Park on the north side and Riverside Park (now Queen Elizabeth Park) on the south side. By the next summer as many as seven thousand people visited East End Park on a Sunday to picnic, play and enjoy the band concerts. People complained about the lack of refreshments, which could not be provided on the Lord's Day, but they compensated by bringing their own lunch and using the numerous picnic shelters, cricket pitch, baseball diamond and 100 spectator benches that were placed in this park. The Riverside Park band concerts were also popular and well attended. When the boom days ended, funds for parks became very limited and on August 21, 1914, the Parks Department was abolished, not to reappear for another 33 years!

[c1915] **The roller coaster in Borden Park** at the south end of the Exhibition Grounds was constructed in 1915 and remained as one of the big attractions at the grounds until it was dismantled in 1935. Other attractions which made the old Borden Park a centre of amusement and fun were a merry-go-round and a wooden tunnel of love called "The Old Mill", in which little six-passenger boats floated people through the darkness accompanied by noises and skeletons and ghosts which would suddenly light up and frighten the young folks before they again emerged into the sunshine and safety of the park.

[c1914] **In the early days** of the Exhibition midway on their permanent grounds, the Kline midway shows offered magicians, tumblers, acrobats, wire walkers, daring motorcyclists, wild and tame animal acts and a 19 ½-pound midget songstress called Princess Victoria, who stood only 25 inches high.

[c1915] **Tug-of-war contests** were often one of the main events on May 24, July 1, and Exhibition sports days in early Edmonton. As early as 1884, the local paper began recording these popular struggles of strength.

[1913] **At the Exhibition foot-races,** neither uniform nor style mattered, just as long as there was a suitable challenge.

[c1914] **Two hilarious novelty races** featured at the Exhibition track were the barrel race and...

...the greased pig race. Again, neither dress nor technique mattered, as long as you brought home the bacon.

[1912] **Despite the fact** that the new racetrack was built on a soggy marsh, the track was a good one. On this course in 1911, the thoroughbred Bland S. set a Canadian record of 2 minutes 5¼ seconds for the half-mile.

To add novelty to the regular horseracing of thoroughbreds and standardbreds in harness, one year the Exhibition added this harness race between mules. In this photo it appears that the sulky mules are more ready for a race than their inattentive drivers. Or is the consternation of the drivers due to the stubborn beasts' refusal to run?

[c1914] **The equestrian sport** of show jumping was another amusement at the racetrack infield. Here the rider is more camera-shy than the jumpers. In addition to regular show jumping, there was featured the high jumping event in which the horses cleared over six feet.

[c1912] **In Diamond Park,** down the hill on Ross Flats, the gentlemanly game of cricket continues to be a popular summer pastime. Here the Edmonton team matches skills with a team from Australia.

On top of the river bank can be seen, from left, the white former residence of Matt McCauley, the Edmonton Club, the Grandview Hotel, and Blowey Henry's furniture store. Over the fence at the right is the Edmonton Brewing and Malting Co. brewery at 9843 100 Street, built in 1894 for Yellowhead Brewing.

[October, 1912] **With tousled hair flying** in the chilly fall air, the Edmonton Eskimos play a tough game of rugby football against the Calgary Tigers.

Although the Fort Saskatchewan team, playing for Edmonton, won the Alberta Rugby Football championship against Calgary in 1895, Edmonton's football story begins in 1896 when teams from Edmonton, Strathcona and Fort Saskatchewan formed a league. By 1908, the Edmonton-Calgary rivalry had increased to the point where they were playing for the Alberta championship. Prior to the November game, a Calgary *Herald* sportswriter disparaged that,

unlike the Carlyle Indian school that had one Eskimo on its team, "a full team of Eskimos will be down from Edmonton on Sunday to play against the Calgary Tigers". The Edmonton rugby team won the championship game 7-1, and the nickname stuck. Some days later, the Edmonton *Bulletin* referred to the team as the Eskimos and the Calgary *Albertan* called them the Esquimous. In 1910, the name "Eskimos" became official and became synonymous with and unique to only Edmonton sports teams. In the 1920s, "Eskimos" was the name for the football, hockey and baseball teams, to say nothing of the occasional ping-pong

or snooker teams. By mid-October, 1922, the football team, under the sponsorship of the Elks Club, decided to rename itself the "Elks" in order to rid itself of the over-used title, which it felt gave eastern Canadians a false idea of the city's location. However, the former name was too strongly entrenched and only one of the local papers used the new name during its month-long existance.

Not only did the old name stay, but so did the inter-city rivalry. In the boom years prior to World War I, it reached a peak of intensity that was not again reached until the re-emergence of the football Eskimos after World War II.

[1915] **Speed and timing** are essential for a successful dry run in this exciting and ususally hilarious event held at the Victoria Park sports day. The object of this race was to flip up the pole and run through faster than the water would spill from the bucket overhead. In the early days, the lack of sophisticated sports equipment was more than compensated for by enthusiasm and ingenuity.

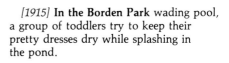

[1915] **In the Borden Park** wading pool, a group of toddlers try to keep their pretty dresses dry while splashing in the pond.

[1915] **At this city playground** in the
Boyle Street area near 95 Street, a new
generation of young Edmontonians enjoy
the pleasures of summertime amusements.
A few years later, in 1922, the Gyro Club
of Edmonton furnished, in a similar
manner, the first of several Gyro
playgrounds throughout the city.

[1915] **In another corner** of the
playground, the older sisters of the young
tots enjoy a serious game of baseball.

[February 22, 1913] **Because of the strong** wish of Norwegian members of the Edmonton Ski Club to have proper facilities to accommodate their love for ski jumping, a seventy-foot-high slide was erected in 1912 atop Connor's Hill (just above the present Muttart Conservatory). After many exciting seasons of spectacular jumping, including night jumping with torches and jumping through flaming hoops, the structure was condemned as unsafe and dismantled in 1925. In 1934, a new jump was erected on Connor's Hill, and this was extended even higher in 1947. Finally, to rid the city of a declared eyesore before the Commonwealth Games in the summer of 1978, the deteriorating wooden structure was again removed.

[c1913] **Three thousand eager** spectators crowded along the run to view the new local attraction of ski jumping.

The first ski tournament was held on February 24, 1912, the same day that ski jumping enthusiasts from Camrose and the Edmonton Ski Club formed a National Ski Club for Western Canada, with plans for holding annual tournaments. The local jumping star was John Haugen, who set a Canadian record of 109 feet at the second annual tournament in February, 1913, and increased it to 112 feet the following year. Although the jumping style was far different from that used sixty years later, the challenge and the thrill of the sport remains the same.

[1913] **Spacious McKernan Lake** south of 76 Avenue at 111 Street was a favourite winter recreation spot with plenty of room for outdoor curling and hockey matches as well as recreational skating and tobogganing. To come to this thirty or more acres of winter playground, everyone took the "Toonerville Trolley", the single streetcar that reeled and rolled along the single track from Whyte Avenue and 104 Street, past the bush, marshes and a mile of empty lots, before finally arriving at the spot for fun and games. In summertime, the lakeside was a favourite picnic ground for both family and Sunday School groups.

[n.d.] **On an early winter day,** some pioneer families enjoy a stroll with their children past the gazebo in Riverside Park on the south bank of the river opposite the power plant. Through the efforts of the civic government and landscape architect T.B. Morrow, boardwalks, benches, a bandstand and roads were added to enhance the facilities of the park for the pleasure of the townsfolk who liked to enjoy a picnic or a stroll through the natural amenities of the river valley. The park opened in 1910 and soon became one of the city's favourite beauty spots.

[August, 1914] **At the northwest corner** of 101 Street and Jasper Avenue, crowds gather to read the latest news posted as soon as it arrives on the telegraph facilities. The news is not good. World War I has been declared. The boom era of the young city is over.

7 War, Women and Wings (1915 – 1929)

Edmonton events for the decade-and-a-half following the outbreak of World War I could be arranged under the following topics: war, water, wine, women, wings, wireless, winners, and woe on the money market.

Soon after the first local men had left to fight in the Great War, the concern of Edmontonians was in their own front yard, as heavy rainfall in the summer of 1915 caused the most serious river flooding in the city's recorded history. Although the flood caused nearly a million dollars damage, the rains benefitted farmers greatly. That fall they reaped the most bountiful bumper crop of wheat in Alberta history.

In 1915, women began to be more involved outside the home. The growing manpower shortage, the rapid growth of the munitions industry and emergence of several women's organizations brought about many changes in both the lives of Canadian women and the attitudes of the entire populace. Many women entered the work force in jobs that were considered inappropriate for women prior to the war. They banded together to campaign successfully to bring in Prohibition, which reduced alcohol consumption by as much as 80 percent, and caused family savings to double. The suffragettes in Alberta were the first in all Canada to vote in municipal and civic elections in 1916. Within a year, the province enacted suffrage legislation for provincial voting. Also in 1916, Edmonton author Emily Murphy was appointed the first female police magistrate in the entire British Empire. In 1915, the Commercial Grads basketball team was formed, and continued to keep Edmonton women in the national and international spotlight for the next quarter of a century.

With the men flying in the war, Katherine Stinson came to Edmonton to demonstrate the agility and capabilities of biplane aircraft. She also brought in the first airmail from Calgary in 1918. But the real air age did not begin here until the return of war pilots like Wop May, Roy Brown and Punch Dickins, who began barnstorming and bush flying from Edmonton. In spite of these illustrious aviators, commercial flying in Edmonton was much slower than other Canadian cities in getting started, due largely to the reluctance of the city fathers to spend the few hundred dollars necessary to upgrade the air strip, which became known as Blatchford Field. It wasn't until May and Horner made their dramatic mercy flight to Fort Vermilion in 1929 that the city developed an adequate airport and allowed Edmonton, as the most northerly city in Canada, to take its rightful place as one of the prime centres along the bush-flying frontier.

Another technological advance which opened up the north and broke down the isolation of rural centres across Canada was radio, the great invention of the twenties. By the end of 1922,

the year Edmonton opened its first station, there were over thirty radio stations in operation across Canada, and in three years the number tripled. Radio brought Canadians closer to the life styles of their American neighbors. In came the fast new music of jazz, along with the Charleston and the Black Bottom. Toward the end of the twenties, the "talkies" brought in the age of the Hollywood screen stars.

The twenties were also Canada's Golden Age of Sport, and leading the parade of national athletes along the victorious international trail were the Edmonton Grads, who won nearly every basketball game they played. In 1921 and 1922, the Edmonton Eskimos football team played for the Grey Cup, the first western team to do so. In 1923, the Edmonton Eskimos hockey team played for the Stanley Cup. Sports had become big-time and exciting.

The end of the Great War coincided with the worst epidemic to hit the world since the Black Death of the fourteenth century. Spanish influenza brought quick death to about 450 Edmontonians. The return of peace and of the soldiers was accompanied by widespread unemployment and rising prices. The shortage of peace-time goods around the world led to inflation that saw the 1919 cost of living in Edmonton rise 58 percent above the 1914 standard. Prairie droughts in the later war years and smaller-than-normal wheat crops in the early twenties reduced farmers' incomes by about 40 percent. By mid-decade, however, the world economic climate improved and western Canadian grain growers enjoyed successive bumper crops. World wheat prices rose, and in 1927 Alberta farmers attained an income that was not surpassed for almost another twenty years.

An economy that was booming once again, and intense oil speculation in southern Alberta brought a buoyant mood and good times to the entire nation. Since people were now required to spend only half their income on the necessities, they bought electrical appliances, radios and cars, went to movies, and followed the fads of mah-jong, crossword puzzles, contract bridge, table tennis, the new dances and jazz. By mid-decade, most provinces had voted back public liquor, and segregated beer parlours were opened for men and women. In 1929, Alberta's Famous Five, led by Emily Murphy, won their case to have women recognized as "persons" who could not only vote, but also sit in the Senate.

The great binge of installment buying came to an abrupt end in October, 1929, when bumper crops around the globe put a glut on the wheat markets of the world. The sudden Great Crash on Wall Street put an end to the good times of the late twenties. Depression and hard times were back again.

[October 12, 1915] **After sitting peacefully** on the high north
river bank for three-quarters of a century, the old fort finally
disappeared from its location below the Legislative Building. This
demolition photo reveals the method of log construction using
slotted posts to hold the horizontal logs in place along the length
of the wall. After years of service, the timbers of old Edmonton
House were torn down with the intention that they would be
rebuilt one day on another permanent site.

[June 29, 1915] **The waters of the North Saskatchewan** River rose 34 feet in approximately 48 hours to reach a crest 4 feet higher than the flood of 1899. All the flats on both sides of the river were entirely flooded: 700 residences were inundated, 60 houses were carried away and 2,400 people were forced to leave their homes. Damage was estimated at nearly $1,000,000, with John Walter's mill alone losing about $50,000.

Here the flood waters almost reach the nearest dry refuge, Donald Ross's old Edmonton Hotel. Behind the large billboards, Diamond Park is covered with the muddy flood waters.

[June 29, 1915] Flood waters and the wreckage of houses, barns, chicken coops, woodsheds, outhouses, and thousands of board feet of dressed lumber and rough logs from John Walter's sawmill threaten the Low Level Bridge. To prevent losing Edmonton's first bridge, a 14-car freight train loaded with ballast was parked on the bridge for deadweight. The technique proved successful as the water level dropped rapidly after cresting overnight to 45 feet above the low water mark. On the river bank from left to right are the College Avenue School, the Edmonton Club, the Macdonald Hotel and Blowey-Henry's furniture store.

[June 29, 1915] **Punting became a prerequisite** rather than a pastime as flood waters sent the residents of Ross Flats to higher ground. The building on the left is the first public school, used as a residence after it was moved down from the original McKay Avenue school site. The flood waters subsided almost as quickly as they came and the inhabitants of the flats were soon back cleaning their houses. But the sawmills, sash and door factory, brick yard and tannery never reopened.

[July 19, 1915] **Women, led by Mrs. Nellie McClung** and Mrs. Wesley Howard, form a large part of a three-mile-long procession of concerned citizens who participated in one of the largest demonstrations ever seen in Edmonton. Beginning here at 96 Street and Jasper Avenue, an estimated ten to twelve thousand persons, along with 320 autos and wagons, paraded down Jasper Avenue, over the High Level Bridge and down Whyte Avenue to urge the populace to "Vote Dry", "Vote for Prohibition" on July 21, 1915. They were successful, as over 7,900 voted "Dry" as compared to almost 4,500 who voted for continued legal sale of alcoholic beverages. Prohibition lasted until 1923, when Alberta voted back lawful liquor sales.

[1918] **Judge Emily Murphy** (1868-1933), second from the right, is presiding over Edmonton's Juvenile Court.

She became the first woman in the British Empire to be appointed to such a position, when in 1916 she took office as magistrate of Edmonton's newly formed Women's Court and judge of the Juvenile Court, positions she held until her retirement in 1931. Without formal legal training, she was a self-taught expert on laws relating to women and children. Coming from a family of lawyers, she began reading legal books during her campaign for an effective Dower Act to guarantee property rights for wives and widows. Later she helped prepare the Children's Protection Act, one of the statutes governing juvenile courts. As judge, Murphy felt responsible for those she sentenced, visited them in prison and helped them find jobs when they were released. She also fought for improved conditions in jails, hospitals and mental institutions and for changes in the laws relating to narcotics and drug addiction, which so often contributed to crime and suffering.

However, one objection to her role as judge kept recurring: as a woman, she was accused of being ineligible to hold public office according to the current interpretation of the B.N.A. Act. Such an accusation was bound to offend her keen sense of social justice and led eventually to the "Famous Five" Alberta women challenging this interpretation in the highest courts, until in 1929 Canadian women were declared "persons" and eligible for public office, including the Senate. Although women's groups across Canada petitioned the federal government many times to have Mrs. Murphy become Canada's first woman senator, none of the Famous Five was ever granted that honour.

[June 13, 1916] **The leader of the militant** British suffragist movement, Mrs. Emmeline Pankhurst, is standing in the centre (with the bouquet of flowers) between Nellie McClung (left) and Emily Murphy (right). The occasion was a reception at the McClung home, at 11229 100 Avenue, given by the Edmonton Equal Franchise League, who were sponsoring Mrs. Pankhurst's fund-raising lectures urging wholehearted support for the war effort. Mrs. Pankhurst also complimented the people of Alberta for granting women the franchise quickly, while British women were still waiting for that victory. The next morning, the *Bulletin* gave front page coverage of Mrs. Pankhurst's lecture and also announced the appointment of Emily Murphy as police magistrate for the city.

[c1910-18] **Another of the "Famous Five"** was Nellie McClung (1873-1951), who was already well-known as a writer and vigorous advocate of temperance and women's suffrage when she moved to Edmonton with her husband in 1914. Her remarkable talent for public speaking gained nationwide attention when the Political Equality League in Winnipeg held a mock parliament, composed entirely of women, in which Nellie impersonated the premier of Manitoba as she enunciated reasons why it would be foolhardy to allow men the vote. In Edmonton, she continued to apply her ready wit to her wholehearted campaign for prohibition and votes for women until success was achieved on both fronts in 1916.

In the 1921 provincial election, when the United Farmers of Alberta were swept into power, Nellie was elected to represent Edmonton as a Liberal. As M.L.A. she worked diligently for social reforms and supported legislation for better working conditions, minimum wages, women's property rights, mothers' allowances and free medical care for school children, sometimes crossing party lines to do so. In 1926, she was defeated in her campaign for re-election and for the return of prohibition, which had been voted out in 1923.

She continued to pour her energy into writing, publishing altogether sixteen books and numerous articles. From 1936 to 1942, she was the first woman to serve on the C.B.C. Board of Governors and in 1938 she was appointed one of Canada's delegates to the League of Nations, where she continued to work for social reforms.

[November 11, 1918] **Jubilant Edmontonians crowded the streets** on this declared public holiday to celebrate the recent news of the Armistice. From early morn until the "wee sma' hours", the streets were filled with cheers and song. At one o'clock, a huge Victory Loan procession wound its way down Jasper Avenue. There was double reason to celebrate. Just two days before, Edmonton set a single day's record for the victory bond campaign, as people, imbued by the spirit of victory that filled the air, subscribed a total of $147,357. At eight o'clock a torchlight parade followed the Journal Newsboys' Band, playing such patriotic marches as "The Marseillaise", "Rule Britannia", "God Save the King", and the appropriate favourite "Pack Up Your Troubles in Your Old Kit Bag and Smile".

But jubilation was mixed with apprehension. Already, since the beginning of October, 262 local people had died from the Spanish Flu epidemic. By the end of the year, the death toll reached 445. The enthusiastic crowd had to whoop and holler behind the protection of face masks and warm woollen overcoats.

[March 22, 1919] **After an absence of four years,** two trainloads of soldiers (500 men) of the 49th Battalion arrived at the C.P.R. station at 109 Street and Jasper Avenue. Thirty thousand citizens lined Jasper Avenue and packed the station square to watch the veterans parade home. The building with the three dormers, sitting in the middle of the street, is a float depicting the newly proposed Memorial Hall. The Edmonton Journal Newsboys' Band led the parade of homecoming soldiers down Jasper Avenue through a welcome arch erected at 101 Street, past the site of the proposed Memorial Hall (between Alberta College and the Macdonald Hotel) to eventually come to their final maneuvres at the armories at 104 Street and 108 Avenue.

[September 13, 1919] **Outside the Arts Building** on the university campus, the Prince of Wales is escorted by Dr. Henry Marshall Tory, the first president of the University of Alberta. At a special convocation held in Convocation Hall, an honorary Doctor of Laws degree was conferred upon the Prince, who in 1936 became King Edward VIII of England.

Dr. Tory was a McGill University graduate and professor of mathematics, who in 1907 accepted the invitation of Premier A.C. Rutherford to assume the presidency of the provincial university. In 1923, he became the first president of the newly founded Canadian National Research Council and consequently resigned from the University of Alberta in 1928 to take up residence in Ottawa. Later he became the president of the new Carleton University in Ottawa.

[August, 1920] **During prohibition, the old** Strathcona Hotel exchanged beer mugs for flower boxes and railroaders for girls and became an institution of eduaction, culture and refinement behind a door now closed to railway passengers and weather-beaten travellers. The Westminster Ladies' College, formerly the Alberta Ladies' College of Red Deer under the authority of the Presbyterian Church of Canada, operated a residence and school from this building from 1920 until 1929, when it again became the Strathcona Hotel, complete with a licensed beverage room.

[c1919] **Taxi vehicles parked outside** the Macdonald Hotel are equipped with wheel chains and high running boards in order to cope with the muddy streets, which were unpaved except for Jasper Avenue, 101 Street and a few adjacent streets.

The first taxi services in Edmonton were established in May, 1913, by Robert M. Tryon of Calgary, who used the King Edward Hotel as headquarters for his fleet of specially designed Laudaulet-type Fords, fully equipped with cigar lighters, flower cases and taxi-meter system. The uniformed drivers charged 60 cents for a half mile and 10 cents for each additional quarter mile. By 1914, there were four taxi companies in business in the city.

[c1926] **Alex McNeill** (left) helps carry out his father's taxi and transfer business at 10079 Jasper Avenue. The taxi company invented a neat slogan, but it didn't work, because people wanted to hire a shiny black cab – not a yellow one.

John McNeill came to Edmonton in 1910 and started in the transportation business with two dray wagons. By 1912, the facilities had expanded to 75 horses. In the days when there were no license fees, gasoline tax or business tax to eat up the profits, it was relatively easy to expand such a business. In 1914, the company motorized its fleet by converting a number of used Cadillac touring cars into trucks. To improve their taxi business, and to help the thousands of new immigrants in the city, McNeill employed people who could translate the major languages spoken by the European and Asian immigrants. After automobile agents opened outlets in Edmonton, McLaughlin, Ford, Terraplane, Cadillac and Studebaker taxis replaced the second-hand vehicles previously used.

Shortly after World War II, the taxi business was sold to "Pop" Miller who changed the name to Yellow Cab. McNeill Van and Storage continued until it was sold in 1955 to Hill the Mover.

John McNeill also started the city's first private ambulance service in 1934, with Max Smith as the first driver. McNeill's Ambulance later became the Smith Ambulance service.

[1920] **In July, 1920,** the Edmonton Radial Railway, now the Edmonton Transit System, began operating this open passenger streetcar. The observation car was built locally, at the street railway barns, and during the summer season it made hourly sightseeing trips for a 25¢ fare, to various parts of the city from its departure point at 101 Street and Jasper Avenue.

145

[June, 1920] **Horse-drawn dray wagons** were slowly being replaced by trucks powered by gasoline engines. These new Model-T Ford trucks are parked on 99 Street south of the Queen's Avenue School (seen in the background). In 1922, they were the only padded moving vans in the city.

The Big 4 Transfer and Storage Co. started business in Edmonton about 1903 and in two decades expanded to become one of the largest storage and warehouse companies in western Canada. In 1924, the company moved into the old Alberta Penitentiary buildings, which had been vacant since the maximum security cells were emptied on March 31, 1921.

[c1920 s] **In the market square** as seen from the Civic Block, horse-drawn wagons were largely replaced with "Tin Lizzies", Model-T Fords and other gas-guzzling vehicles. City still met country here but the hay wagons and oat buckets were almost gone forever.

The tall building in the center is the McLeod Building. The clock tower identifies the Post Office, and the chateau style characterizes the Macdonald Hotel at the extreme left.

[c1918] **The McLaughlin Motors'** showroom at 10048 104 Street displays the new horseless carriages that began to take over the streets and roads of Alberta during the First World War. For $2,150 in the summer of 1915, a progressive Edmontonian could buy a seven-passenger, six-cylinder, 50-horsepower McLaughlin Touring car with 4½-inch tires on its 130-inch wheelbase. A five-passenger, 30-horsepower model with 3½-inch tires and 110-inch wheelbase cost $1085. In 1923, a seven-passenger McLaughlin-Buick sedan cost $3,095, while a five-passenger touring car sold for $1,235.

To promote the 1923 four-cylinder McLaughlin-Buick stock cars, on Sunday, November 5, 1922, the dealer's service manager, Paul Welch, set a new world dirt-road record by driving the 416 miles from Edmonton to Calgary and return in 9 hours, 26 minutes, 55 seconds, averaging 43½ miles per hour. He reached Leduc in 23½ minutes, Red Deer in 2 hours 15 minutes, Calgary in 4 hours 32 minutes. After a three-minute stop in Calgary for refuelling and a quick coffee, he started the return trip, got lost on the wrong road (losing 15 minutes while finding his way back to the Edmonton Trail) changed a flat tire and after speeding up to 60 miles per hour between Innisfail and Carstairs, arrived back at the corner of 101 Street and Whyte Avenue to the cheers of about 1,000 interested spectators.

[June, 1923] **The new "mounts" ate** gasoline instead of oats and required more sophisticated maintenance than the old wagons, buggies and stage coaches. Blacksmith shops were no longer adequate, so new motor car garages were provided to keep the horseless carriages in good working condition. The simple life had passed away. Here are mechanics endeavoring to make some McLaughlin-Buicks roadworthy and reliable. In 1916, a new front axle could be installed for $12, any fender cost $4, a new radiator sold for $15, while a complete engine could be purchased for $25.

[July, 1916] **Edmontonians momentarily left** their concern for their men at war and came to view the daring loops, dives and spirals of the twenty-year-old American aviatrix Katherine Stinson. She flew in from Texas to give the Exhibition crowds their first glimpse of a 1913 Martin bi-plane. In following years, she set distance and flight endurance records for women aviators and returned to Canada to train fliers for the Royal Air Force.

After the war, air shows at the Fair were far more carefree. In July, 1919, while the British dirigible R-34 was making the first air crossing of the Atlantic, returned war pilots George Gorman and Wop May put on such a daring display of loops and dives that John Philip Sousa's Band, the Fair's main

attraction, decided to retire to safer quarters. The next year the crowds again gasped as daring aviator Ormer Locklear added a little spice to his act by leaping from one plane to another without the aid of a rope ladder. Then the crowds held their breath as Pete Derbyshire dropped 300 feet before opening his parachute. Parachutes were just as new to Pete, since the small bi-planes of World War I were not equipped with such safety devices.

[June 7, 1919] **A Sunday crowd gathered** at the Walter Sproule farm airport, west of the St. Albert Trail at about 124 Avenue, to watch the landing of a Curtiss JN 4 (known as the "Curtiss Jenny" by all airmen of the day). In recognition of Edmonton's contribution of money for war planes, the Royal Air Force donated this plane to the city and named it the "Edmonton". In 1919, Wop May and his brother Court organized May Airlines Ltd. with a capital of $20,000 and rented the bi-plane from the city at $25 per month. They took the plane barnstorming around Alberta and sold rides at a top speed of 80 miles per hour for a fee of $15 for a five-minute flight.

[July 10, 1918] **Katherine Stinson arrived again** at the Exhibition grandstand, this time with the first air mail delivery in western Canada. Postmaster George Armstrong smiled proudly as Exhibition Manager W. J. Stark received the mail bag containing 259 letters. This was only the second mail pouch carried by airplane in the entire Dominion. After engine failure seven miles north of Calgary caused a lengthy delay, Katherine restarted her trip from Calgary and flew non-stop along the C & E rail line to Edmonton, making the 196-mile trip in 125 minutes.

[June 7, 1919] **As Court May readies** the *Edmonton* on the grass of Sproule's farm, returned war pilot George Gorman shakes hands with Edmonton *Journal* publisher M. R. Jennings before they start the first commercial air flight from Edmonton. Accompanied by mechanic Pete Derbyshire, a full load of gasoline and 75 pounds of freight consisting of two large bags of the noon edition of the Edmonton *Journal,* the crew followed the railway tracks at a height of 500-600 feet and delivered the papers to the newspaper's Wetaskiwin agent by dropping them from the bomb-rack at the side of the plane. Aided by a 30-mph tailwind, they made the 42-mile trip to Wetaskiwin in 30 minutes, averaging just under 90 mph.

[1925] **At his desk in** the Civic Block, Mayor Kenneth A. Blatchford discusses city business with City Solicitor Dr. J. C. F. Bowen (left) and Commissioner David Mitchell.

Blatchford's interest in a better "air harbour" resulted in the City investing $400 in 1926 to upgrade the airfield to the standard required for obtaining a license. On June 16, 1926, the federal government's newly formed Civil Aviation Board certified the McNeill airstrip on Hagmann's farm as the first municipal airport in Canada. On November 22, 1926, City Council suggested the air harbour be named "Blatchford Field" in honour of the past mayor, who did much to promote the importance of the air field. A few days later, the Department of National Defence in Ottawa acknowledged the new name. Blatchford Field was officially opened on January 8, 1927.

[1929] **In 1919 John McNeill,** a key figure in Edmonton's taxi and moving business, incorporated an air taxi service known as the Edmonton Airline Company. He erected this rough hangar near the west end of Portage Avenue (now Kingsway) on a site cleared in 1900 by John Hagmann for his farm. In 1929, parked in front of the original hangar, are four DeHaviland Moth bi-planes and a single-winged Lockheed Vega.

The Moths belonged to the Edmonton Flying Club, which was organized on October 14, 1927, with Wop May as president. The club soon became one of the most active pilot-training clubs in Canada. Out of this flying club, in 1928, grew Commercial Airways, which owned the Vega. The Edmonton club increased the pace of training pilots so that in 1930 it led all clubs in the Dominion in most flying hours and the greatest number of graduating licensed pilots, including the ambitious Grant McConachie.

Dressed in the leather windbreaker and motorcycle pants of the daring bush pilots of the 1920s, stands the confident Clennel H. "Punch" Dickins, winner of the McKee Trophy for 1928. His chief claim to the trophy was the first flight made across the Barren Lands from Winnipeg to Chesterfield Inlet and to Fort Smith on the Slave River. This September flight covered a distance of about 1,750 miles each way.

In 1929, Punch made front page headlines when courageously searching for the Colonel MacAlpine party whose plane went down in the Arctic. In that year, while flying for Western Canada Airways of Winnipeg, he started regular air service between Fort McMurray and the northern outposts, Fort Chipewyan, Fort Smith, Fort Resolution, Hay River, Fort Providence, Fort Simpson and Aklavik.

[1931] **Wilfred Reid "Wop" May,** the quiet, Edmonton-raised bush pilot, first achieved fame when he daringly led the German "Red Baron" to his death in World War I. Back at home, he next received national acclaim when he and Vic Horner undertook the first mercy flight on record, for which brave service he was awarded the Order of the British Empire in 1935. Also in 1929, he made the first air-mail flight to Aklavik and was awarded the McKee Trophy for "most meritorious service for the advancement of Canadian aviation". Three years later, he again made headlines when he hunted

The following year, he again made aviation history when in March, 1930, he piloted his Fokker super-universal monoplane over 4,500 miles of barren northland from Edmonton to Fort Hearn at the mouth of the Coppermine River and to Aklavik, where the Mackenzie River empties into the Arctic Ocean. It was the first time a battery-powered shortwave radio set for transmitting and receiving was carried on a northern flight.

Punch Dickins, who like Wop May got his nickname from a relative, was so well known and respected throughout the north, that an Inuit, who was trying to convey to a court in Aklavik that he had seen an airplane but was unable to find a word for it, lifted his eyes and said "Punch Dickins". Everyone understood.

[January 2, 1929] **While Vic Horner readies** the plane, Mayor A.U.C. Bury watches Deputy Minister of Health Dr. M.R. Bow give pilot Wop May the carefully wrapped package containing 600,000 units of diphtheria anti-toxin for treating the epidemic at Little Red River, near Fort Vermilion, Alberta. Despite the -33° Fahrenheit temperature and the open cockpit, the two bush pilots risked their lives to fly the 75-horsepower single-engined Avro Avian without the benefit of an on-board radio. Stopping at McLennan and Peace River, the frost-

the "Mad Trapper of Rat River". This was the first instance on record of aircraft being used in a manhunt of a dangerous criminal. At the beginning of World War II, in 1939, May was placed in charge of No. 2 Air Observers School in Edmonton and he pioneered the formation of the first search-and-rescue units for the Canadian and American Air Forces. For this he was awarded the American Medal of Freedom in 1945. Probably one of the finest natural fliers in the history of aviation anywhere in the world, Captain May got his nick-name "Wop" early, when his young cousin was unable to pronounce his name Wilfred.

bitten fliers returned from their 840-mile mercy flight to a warm, city-wide heroes' welcome. The 10,000 residents who flocked to Blatchford Field to await the return of the silvery little craft were well aware of the epic three-day flight. Radio station CJCA had diligently kept Edmonton and all of northern Alberta informed of the progress of this first mercy flight in Canadian history.

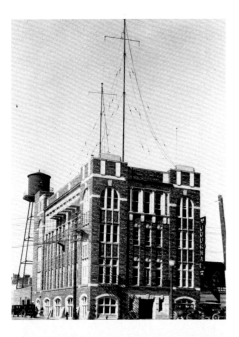

[1926] **Two years after the world's** oldest broadcasting station first went on the air in Montreal, Edmonton was buzzing with excitement as the 75-foot-high masts, stays and antenna atop the Journal Building signalled the beginning of radio broadcasting in Alberta. On May 1, 1922, Mayor D.M. Duggan officially opened CJCA from a microphone in one corner of the *Journal* newsroom. After the mayor's brief opening message, the Metropolitan Theatre Orchestra played rousing musical selections under the direction of Edgar Williams. The broadcast was heard in Edmonton, Calgary and High River. Three weeks later, the Edmonton *Journal* reported that there were two hundred radio sets in the city. Radio had quickly caught on and was here to stay.

[c1920s] **CJCA's first studio** was located just beneath the linotype machines in a cramped corner of the *Journal's* newsroom. Every time the machines started operating, the radio broadcasting became inaudible. The studio space was fitted with cloth wall hangings to dampen echoes and the doors and windows were kept closed, even on hot summer evenings, to improve the acoustics. The equipment was rudimentary also. When the microphone made from a telephone

transmitter failed, another one had to be made. The telephone lines used to transmit remote-control broadcasts also caused problems. Often, while the station was on the air, an operator would cut in and say, "Number please".

By 1926, three radio stations were operating in Edmonton: CJCA operated by the Edmonton *Journal,* CFCK operated by Radio Supply Company Ltd., and CHCY operated by the International Bible

Students' Association (later called Jehovah's Witnesses). For a time, all three had to share the same frequency. One night two stations went on the air at the same time! Nothing was dull about the early days of radio.

In 1927, CJCA helped celebrate Canada's Diamond Jubilee by participating in the first Canadian coast-to-coast radio program, which featured the opening of Ottawa's Peace Tower and the sounds of its new carillon.

[c1923] **George Richard Agar Rice,** popularly known as Dick, operated at the microphone in Alberta's first radio control room. In the early days of CJCA in Edmonton, Dick Rice was manager, announcer, news reporter, engineer and even janitor. He got into the radio business in 1916, when, at the age of 15, he joined the Marconi Company in his native England. While visiting Edmonton in 1922, he was invited by the Journal to operate CJCA. He started in a cramped studio in the corner of the *Journal's* second-floor newsroom. In 1924, he began broadcasting to the far North twice a week after midnight. In 1927, his wife began broadcasting with him, becoming one of North America's pioneer women broadcasters. She was known as Susan Agar, "the chatelaine of the air".

In 1934, Mr. Rice and his partner Hans Neilson formed the Sunwapta Broadcasting Company and bought local radio station CFTP, that had been broadcasting from a small studio on the top floor of the Royal George Hotel. They changed the call letters to CFRN (R for Rice and N for Neilson) and began the new station with a staff of seven, broadcasting thirteen hours daily on a 100-watt Marconi unit. The following year, CFRN moved to new studios on the second floor of the C.P.R. Building and in 1941 increased its power to 1,000 watts. Its power continued to increase until in 1961 it was operating on 50,000 watts. In 1951, the FM station was added and in 1954 the Sunwapta Broadcasting Company began television broadcasting.

[1922] **At the other end** of the radio waves, amateur radio enthusiasts eagerly donned their earphones to hear the new phenomenon.

Often their receivers were crystal sets, consisting of headsets connected to a cylindrical Quaker Oats box wound with 120 turns of fine copper wire and connected to a stiff moveable wire called a "cat's whisker", which was manipulated to find the most sensitive spot along the surface of a small piece of crystal. Prior to the opening of its station, the Edmonton *Journal* carried a series of articles on how radio buffs could build these sets for three dollars worth of simple materials. Since the crystal had the unusual property of converting radio waves into a form that would produce sounds that were audible in the earphones, no electricity, tubes or transistors were required. After the invention of the vacuum tube, radios became much more powerful and loudspeakers replaced the restrictive earphones.

[1926] **Lined with burlap soundproofing**, a radio studio at the University of Alberta broadcast from a corner of the Department of Extension through the facilities of CJCA at the Journal Building.

Meanwhile, Harry P. Brown, head of the university's Visual Aids Department, finalized preparations for the university's own radio station. With help from W.W. Grant, radio engineer and owner of

station CFCN, Calgary, and a few electrical engineering students, Brown erected 25-foot-long poles atop two 75-foot-high windmill towers to carry the antenna. He also outfitted a burlap-lined studio in a small shack south of Athabasca Hall. At a cost of less than $4,000, the station was ready for business – except it had no license. The University of Alberta radio pioneers promptly raised $600, bought local station CFCK and adopted the new call letters CKUA.

On November 21, 1927, CKUA made its debut and started with a ball of fire! Harry Brown brought his camera and magnesium flash from the Visual Aids Department to photograph the inauguration. The flash set the burlap drapery on fire and had to be quickly extinguished to save the day. Then the equipment was not able to generate up to its own frequency. The problem was solved when engineer Grant shut his Calgary station off the air so CKUA could use that nearby frequency. After that exciting start, Brown continued as announcer, disc jockey, lecturer and mechanic while working 18 hours a day to keep everything on schedule for the eight-hours-per-week broadcasts.

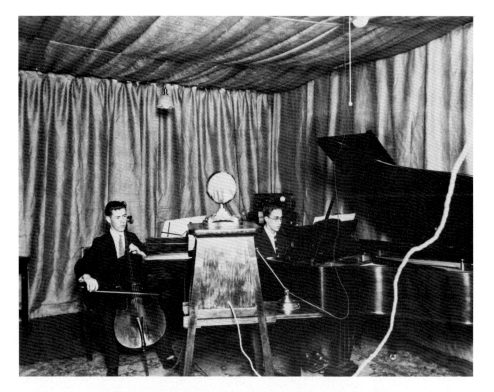

The varsity station also pioneered several other radio firsts in Alberta, such as its own dramatic radio players, its own lecturers, concerts from one of the nation's finest pipe organs in Convocation Hall, the first broadcast of French lessons in 1928, the first live broadcasts in Western Canada direct from the press gallery of the legislature, first live play-by-play broadcast of football games in Canada in 1928 and the first traffic and road information in the early 1950s. On May 23, 1929, the first school broadcast in Canada took place from CKUA. In 1930, the first Canadian National Railway network broadcast from Edmonton originated in CKUA's studios with a program by Vernon Barford's choir. The first football game was broadcast on October 13, 1928, when the U. of A. Golden Bears played against the old Edmonton Eskimos.

In 1941, a 1,000-watt transmitter was opened along the Calgary highway. In 1960, CKUA increased its power to 10,000 watts and became Canada's first full-time non-commercial AM radio station with that size of broadcasting power. Quite a change from the original 500-watt signal of fifty years ago.

[1927] **Here the University of Alberta's** radio orchestra pose around the large circular microphone. The orchestra was organized and conducted by Mrs. Carmichael (front centre). While CJCA would bring Edgar Williams and his Pantages Theatre Orchestra up to its studio to perform, radio station CKUA was the first to have its own resident orchestra.

[November, 1920] **The New Empire Theatre,** which opened on December 23, 1920, was the last of the local theatre houses to be built in the grand manner. Erected in just five months at a cost of $300,000, this 1,477-seat theatre was the first in Canada to have all the decorations and furnishings, with few exceptions, designed and executed within the city it served. Notable exceptions were murals painted by Italian artists and the custom-made brocade wall coverings imported from France.

The first Empire Theatre was erected in 1906 on the west side of 100 Street just a few doors north of 101A Avenue. After only a few months, it closed and later re-opened as the Bijou movie house. Also in 1906, the Edmonton Opera House was built at the northwest corner of Jasper Avenue and 103 Street. In 1910, its name changed to the Lyceum Theatre, the only theatre in Edmonton that supported its own stock company all year round. In 1912, Edmontonians spent about $1,700 per week attending performances at the Lyceum where the highest price seats sold at 50 cents each. In December, 1914, the theatre was destroyed by fire. By this time, however, the second Empire Theatre (Old Empire Theatre) was in existence. In 1909, a dance hall on 103 Street north of the Hudson's Bay store had been renovated to serve as a theatre and opera house until it was torn down in 1920, when the Bay expanded its store northward and forced the construction of the New Empire Theatre.

After the Old Empire Theatre joined the Orpheum vaudeville circuit in 1912, the Old and later the New Empire Theatres presented some of the continent's finest performers, including George Jessel, Eddie Cantor, Will Rogers, Sarah Bernhardt, Fred and Adele Astaire, Charlie Chaplin, Harry Lauder, Sir Johnstone Forbes-Robertson, Lawrence Irving, Ethel Barrymore, Mischa-Elman, Ignace Paderewski, John McCormack and many others. The depression of the 1930s put an end to all but the occasional road show. After it closed as a theatre during World War II, the New Empire Theatre re-opened as the Trocadero Ballroom on New Year's Eve, 1946. Thirty-five years later, the building was demolished in January, 1981. Like the Pantages, another fine theatre house was gone.

[n.d.] **The original Edmonton Symphony** Orchestra performed in the New Empire Theatre under the baton of Albert Weaver-Winston.

Forerunners of the original Edmonton Symphony Orchestra were the Edmonton Philharmonic of the 1890s and the Edmonton Orchestral Society after the turn of the century, with Albert Weaver-Winston as conductor and players drawn largely from the musicians of the Pantages Theatre, where the Orchestral Society's Sunday-evening concerts were held.

It was from this nucleus of vaudeville musicians that the Edmonton Symphony Orchestra emerged in 1920 with Weaver-Winston continuing to conduct the 53-piece orchestra in concerts in the Pantages Theatre. Later these performances were moved to the new, larger Empire Theatre. During the Depression, financing the symphony – never an easy task – became impossible and the orchestra disbanded in 1932.

During World War II the Edmonton Philharmonic Orchestra was launched under the leadership of Abe Fratkin, who had been associate conductor with the earlier Symphony Orchestra and for several seasons it gave concerts in the Strand Theatre. In 1947, the Edmonton Pops Orchestra began giving summer concerts conducted by a young Edmontonian, Lee Hepner, who spent his winter months studying conducting in Toronto and in the United States.

In 1952, Mrs. Marion Mills took the initiative to mould all these talents into a revived Edmonton Symphony Orchestra and on the evening of November 30, 1952, Lee Hepner raised his baton for the 60-piece orchestra's debut performance in the Capitol Theatre. The ESO has carried on ever since.

[October 27, 1921] **Before a final rehearsal**, the singers and dancers of the Rotary Minstrel Revue pose for their photograph on the stage of the Old Empire Theatre.

The Rotary Club, a businessmen's community service club organized in March, 1916, sponsored an annual minstrel show as their major fund-raising activity. The first one was held in November, 1917, at the Empire Theatre. Tickets sold from 50 cents to one dollar. The black-faced cast was made up of local club members and men and women from outside the city. Conducting the large cast each year was Vernon Barford. The last of these shows was put on in 1932. The onset of the depression and the ever-increasing work of preparing the show led to its discontinuance. For some fifteen years, though, the show gave great entertainment to local folk and produced between $1,000 and $2,000 annually for community service. In the late 1960s, the Edmonton Rotary Club played a major role in the conception and development of Fort Edmonton Park.

[December, 1920] **The Edmonton Mendelssohn Choir** assemble under the direction of Vernon Barford in front of the organ of McDougall Church, ready to present Handel's oratorio *The Messiah.*

The one-hundred-voice choir was organized in September, 1918, having no affiliation with a church or other organization. The self-supported group put on winter concerts from 1918 until 1924. It was revived in January, 1952, under director Ernest A. Moore, and in December, 1954, the group again presented *The Messiah* from First Presbyterian Church.

[1919] **When Mrs. J. B. Carmichael** first came to Edmonton in October, 1919, she was Beatrice van Loon, a musically talented young American in charge of a 5-piece all-girl orchestra which came to fulfill an 8-week engagement at the Macdonald Hotel. By this time, she had already made her public singing debut at the age of 4, conducted her first operetta (with 100 children in the company and 50 in the orchestra) at the age of 16, won a gold medal over all the men in a singing competition in Chicago at the age of 17, appeared as the guest vocalist with a 100-piece symphonic orchestra for several seasons and studied violin, piano, voice and conducting while earning her degree of Bachelor of Music at Chicago. Her Edmonton debut was so successful that the Macdonald Hotel extended her contract.

The next year she married local dentist, Dr. James Carmichael. "Auntie Van", as she was affectionately called, stayed in Edmonton, taught singing and violin and conducted the Women's Musical Club choirs as well as an amateur orchestra which produced regular monthly programs over radio station CKUA. For

12 years, she conducted the 45-piece University of Alberta Orchestra which produced one light opera each year. In addition, she played first violin with the original Edmonton Symphony Orchestra and appeared as their vocal soloist and guest conductor.

In January, 1935, she invited a number of her musical friends to her living room, where they formed the Edmonton Civic Opera Society. This strictly amateur and largely local group produced and conducted by Mrs. Carmichael gave Edmonton over 40 presentations of grand opera and Broadway musicals. After 28 years as musical director of the E.C.O.S., Mrs. Carmichael presented her last production, *The Music Man,* in 1962, two years before her death. Although the E.C.O.S. continued until 1967, when it was renamed the Civic Musical Theatre, the retirement of Mrs. Carmichael ended an era which established the E.C.O.S. as the only opera society in the country with a 28-year record of uninterrupted annual performance.

[c1929] **A queue forms for** the latest movie at the Capitol Theatre, 10065 Jasper Avenue. The theatre first opened on December 2, 1918, as a silent movie house, with a pipe shop and H.B. Kline's jewellery shop flanking the central box office. At first it was called the Allen Theatre, after the family who owned 32 theatres across Canada, and managed by Max Allen, who also managed the Monarch Theatre next door.

In 1929, the owners spent $50,000 to install sound equipment in the form of record players that had to be synchronized with the film. At that time, the old organ that used to accompany the silent movies was removed and a balcony was added to increase the seating capacity from its original 1,000 to over 1,600. The theatre received another major overhaul in 1938 when the largest theatre marquee in the British Empire was added. Its 2,000 60-watt bulbs were so bright and so hot that they melted the snow from the sidewalk underneath.

The building was demolished in November, 1972, and replaced with the 20-storey, $10.5 million Capitol Square office building which contains four small movie theatres with seating capacities ranging from 217 to 466, totalling 1,401, plus shops, restaurants and 14 floors of office space.

[July 1, 1927] **The 150-member Edmonton Newsboys' Band** pause for their photo before leading the Confederation Day parade down Jasper Avenue to celebrate Canada's Diamond Jubilee. The girl standing by bandmaster F. G. Aldridge is Audrey Michaels, the daughter of newstand operator and one-time newspaper boy John "Mike" Michaels.

In 1913, Mike and Edmonton *Journal* editor and managing director, Milton Jennings, founded the Edmonton Journal Newsboys' Band as a measure to combat juvenile delinquency. No previous musical training was necessary; the sole prerequisite for joining the band was that the boy had to be a paper carrier. The

lads raised money for instruments by selling flowers as well as papers in the streets. Under the direction of Mrs. Ruth Michaels as the first bandmaster, the first several dozen "newsies" were ready for their first performance on June 11, 1914. After giving several concerts in local parks and theatres for the first few seasons, they made their first tour to Buffalo and Detroit in 1916.

In 1924, the band accepted an invitation to appear for a four-week engagement at the British Empire Exhibition at Wembley, England. For this the 54 boys, aged 9 to 22, practiced twice a day under conductor R.A. Bullock. After a local sendoff by 5,000 admirers at the C.N.R. station, the

band took time to give two concerts in several major Canadian cities enroute to England. At Wembley the band, with a repertoire of 300 selections, was able to provide a complete change of program for each concert. Since each boy had only one uniform, Mrs. Michaels, assistant bandmaster and cornet soloist, spent her nights ironing the suits for presentable readiness the following day. While in England, the band opened the largest ballroom in the country, with a capacity of 10,000 couples, and they drew their largest crowd of 35,000 people at Edmonton, England.

When many experienced members left in 1926, the group was reorganized under the name Edmonton Newsboys' Band to allow all city newsboys to be included. In 1927, a complete set of 101 instruments, costing $7,000, was purchased through public subscription. After receiving acclaim as one of the finest bands in the world and the largest in Canada, the band's concerts were brought to an end by the Depression in 1929. Nine years later, their instruments and uniforms provided the equipment for the newly formed Edmonton Schoolboys' Band.

[May 10, 1919] **Mayor Joe Clarke had assistance** from Cliff Dunham and John Michaels in starting the annual Edmonton Journal bicycle race for boys aged 15 and under. Five thousand onlookers crowded around to see a field of 66 eager bikers start the 6½-mile race that followed a course from the Journal office on 101 Street west on Jasper Avenue to 124 Street, swinging north to return along Portage Avenue and 101 Street to the Journal Building. After whizzing along Portage Avenue at speeds of between 30-45 mph, young Dan Carrigan finished first in 22 minutes and 2 seconds. His prize was a new bike.

The first velocipede was brought into Edmonton in May, 1890, by Hudson's Bay Company employee, Mr. E. Taylor. In June, 1893, the first bicycle club was formed with banker George Kirkpatrick as honorary president.

[September 13, 1922] **Exhibition grand-stand entertainment** provided for the Governor-General of Canada, His Excellency Lord Byng, pitted the old era against the new as Miss Dorothy Wood put her horse Sir Aran through a series of jumps over this 4 cylinder Grey-Dort car. Horses and haywagons were rapidly becoming an uncommon sight in the city as gas-guzzlers rattled along in their place. In this confrontation the horse won, but in reality the horse had gone to pasture.

[May 22, 1920] **Early summer crowds filled** Diamond Park, in the flats below the Macdonald Hotel, to attend the first game of the season of the local amateur baseball league.

More spectacular was the first game of the 1920 professional season. For that game on May 6, a record 4,500 fans filled

every square inch of grandstand and bleachers and the overflow crowd extended around the baselines. Because of this, the game had to be played under ground rules, whereby a ball hit into the crowd went for two bases. The Edmonton Eskimos Baseball Team disappointed their fans by allowing the rival Calgary Bronks to score eight runs in the third inning and thereby win the game 11 - 4. But the good news was, that with the baseball season in full swing, another good ol' summertime had arrived in Edmonton.

Professional baseball made its appearance in Edmonton in 1906 under the leadership of Deacon White. This outstanding sports organizer and coach also headed the football and hockey teams here in the early years of this century. In 1966, he was named to the Edmonton Sports Hall of Fame.

[October 1, 1921] **On this bright Saturday** afternoon, fans filled the stands of Diamond Park to watch the Edmonton Eskimos football team run roughshod over the Calgary Tigers to open the Alberta rugby season. With 130-pound quarterback Bill Rankin (who represented Canada in the international boxing championships in Antwerp the year before) calling the signals and 172-pound halfback "Curly" Dorman scoring three touchdowns in the first half, the blue and white troops of coach and organizer Deacon White rolled up a score of 29 - 2 by half-time. The game continued with Rankin's two touchdowns (5 points each in those days), two more by 200-pound middle-wing Yancey (only one other player weighed over 199 pounds), and another by captain and rover Jimmy Enright, a 177-pound line-smasher who was discovered playing baseball in Edmonton's city league. With the score 51 - 2 at three-quarter time, and the fans yelling "Make it a hundred!", 165-pound halfback, punter and drop-kicker Jack Fraser scored three more touchdowns (the

Esks scored a total of 13) before the game ended with the score reading 72 - 2.

That fall the Eskimos won the Alberta championship and in mid-November they beat the Winnipeg Victorias on a snow-covered field to become champions of the Western Canada Rugby Union. On December 3, 1921, the Eskimos met the undefeated Toronto Argonauts in the first Grey Cup game between East and West.

Fumbles, penalties and predictable line plunges by the Esks contrasted with the end runs, balanced play selection and solid line play by the Argos. With Lionel "Big Train" Connacher (chosen in 1950 as Canada's athlete of the half century) scoring three touchdowns, a drop-kick and a single, the Argonauts won the game 23 - 0. The following year, the Eskimos again lost the Grey Cup game 13 - 1 to Queen's University and then did not play in the national final for another thirty years.

The first forward passes ever attempted in Canada in a regularly scheduled football game were thrown in Edmonton on September 21, 1929. Halfback Jerry Sieberling of the Calgary Tigers threw the first pass, which went incomplete. Then Eskimo quarterback Cook tried the next pass, which also went unreceived. On the first play of the fourth quarter, Sieberling threw a 15-yard forward pass to halfback Mackenzie and the first pass reception went into the record books. Calgary won the game 33 – 8, but Edmonton fans had the honour of seeing the beginning of a new era in Canadian football.

[March 10, 1923] **These west-end skaters** took advantage of the warm weather and excellent ice conditions to enjoy a social skate at the Glenora Rink, opposite the Government House grounds. After displaying many fancy maneuvers for photographer Joe Tyrell of McDermid Studios, the group began a leisurely waltz on ice, caught here.

[1916] **On the outdoor rink** in Ross Flats, the ladies get some playing tips from their coach as they practice for their scrappy games against their Strathcona rivals. As early as 1899, the women donned their flat blades and turtleneck sweaters to demonstrate their skill and ability to chase the puck up and down the rink to the enthusiastic applause of their husbands and loyal supporters.

[1921] **In this earliest photo** of hockey in the building, members of the Edmonton Eskimos hockey club take their positions at the start of another hockey game at the Edmonton Exhibition Arena, the great stock pavilion that became the Edmonton Gardens in later times. In the early days of hockey, and even in the roaring twenties, the intrepid goal judges stood on the ice behind the net. The eight-foot-wide promenade around the rink is filled with fans eager to get a good piece of the action as it streaks by the boards. The box seats above and just behind give a royal view of the action to those who could not afford the $1.00 promenade seats below.

In 1923, the Eskimos won the Western Canadian Hockey League championship over the plucky Regina Capitals, when team captain Duke Keats scored on a penalty shot midway through the second overtime period. The triumphant green and white team then met the tough Ottawa Senators of the National Hockey League to challenge for the Stanley Cup. After being outplayed for fifty minutes,

the Easterners won the first game on an overtime goal. They took the coveted cup after winning the second game 1 - 0 by keeping all their players behind the blue line after scoring the lone goal midway through the first period. For their efforts in playing in the finals, each Eskimo player received $116. Earlier, in 1910, an Edmonton Eskimo hockey team was like-wise beaten by a rough and overpowering Ottawa club in the Stanley Cup finals.

[c1923] **"The finest basketball team** that ever stepped on a floor", declared the inventor of basketball, Canadian Dr. James Naismith, after he saw the Edmonton Commercial High School Grads play in 1925. By then the young ladies were already world champions.

The beginnings of this amazing team go back to 1914, when John Percy Page, principal of McDougall Commercial High School, began to teach physical education to the girls. From 60 girls, he formed a basketball team that played girls' rules on an outdoor cinder court. Much to everyone's surprise, they won the City High School Championship that year. The next year, they won the provincial title and upon graduation the girls asked Mr. Page to continue coaching them. On June 15, 1915, the Commercial Graduates Basketball Club was formed and a legend began.

Coach Page and his assistant, Bill Tate, soon developed a McDougall School basketball farm system, whereby girls developed their skills under their direction while playing for the junior girls' team, the senior girls' team, then the Gradettes (who could be either students or graduates), finally joining the Grads when there was an opening because of retirement. In 1922, the coach took only six players east to challenge the London Shamrocks in the first Dominion women's basketball championship. The Grads won that series and held the Canadian championship until they disbanded in 1940. Since 1922, the Grads followed the practice of the eastern teams who played only under boys' rules.

In 1923, the Grads challenged the top amateur American team, who wore the words "World Champs" on their trim shorts. Playing before a crowd of 5,000 in the first basketball game ever held in the Edmonton Exhibition Arena, on June 12, 1923, the Grads came out in their usual heavy woolen stockings, knobby knee-pads, voluminous knee-length bloomers (made of three yards of British serge), loose sailors' middies that were cut like flour sacks, and black and gold head bands tying down their long hair. The Grads won both games and took the Underwood Trophy in their first try at international competition. This was the first time Edmonton could proudly boast of having a world champion team. After successfully retaining the trophy 25 times, it was donated permanently to them when they retired.

The Grads appeared in the first of four successive Olympics in 1924. Although women's basketball was not an official Olympic sport then, the Grads were never defeated in 27 exhibition games against international opponents. The Grads were officially awarded the title "World's Basketball Champions" at the annual meeting of the *Federation Sportive Feminine Internationale*, in Paris, July 30, 1924. No other team was able to rightfully claim that title during the next 16 years while the Grads continued in competition!

[March 17, 1928] **Ten thousand citizens sauntered** to the Queen's Avenue School site to attend the official opening of the new Canadian National Railway Station at the north end of 100 Street. That evening, 4,000 railway employees and friends jammed into the central concourse and adjacent corridors to celebrate the opening by dancing to two orchestras, including one from the prestigious railway hotel, the Macdonald.

Early the next morning, the eastbound Continental picked up the first passengers from the new depot. That year, forty trains a day were passing through Edmonton, as compared to only one train when the C.N.R. first came to the city in 1905.

In one month in 1927, the old Edmonton depot handled 85,000 passengers. The need for larger and better station facilities was satisfied by the new depot for twenty years, but in 1948 a third storey had to be added to keep pace with increasing railway business. Sixteen years later, on February 12, 1964, the station serviced its last train. That summer, the building was demolished to make way for the 26-storey CN Tower.

[March 17, 1928] **The 34-by-90-foot central** skylit concourse of the Canadian National Railway Station preserved the tradition of earlier large stations across the country. To accommodate the large crowds attending the official opening, the wooden benches were removed and a temporary podium was erected on the right. Beyond the windows and through the door on the right was a long, up-to-date restaurant and dining room. The spaces to the left accommodated news and ticket facilities. The second floor contained railway offices. The steps at the rear of the concourse led to the station platform north of the station.

Unlike most railway stations which faced parallel with the track, the Edmonton depot was designed at right angles to the track to provide, as CN's chief architect stated in a speech at the opening, "a smooth and convenient flow of passengers through the building."

[c1929] **The store in the Tegler Building** at the southeast corner of 101 Street and 102 Avenue that James Ramsay opened in 1911 was taken over by the T. Eaton Company in January, 1929. Eaton's Department Store remained at this location until their own building across the intersection was ready in August, 1939.

The nation-wide chain of department stores was started by Timothy Eaton in 1869, when he opened his first store in Toronto. In 1884, the first Eaton's catalogue was printed and the mail-order business began. Particularly on the prairies, the semi-annual Eaton's mail-order catalogues were a vital part of daily life. They built the dreams of young and old of having the latest styles and newest equipment. Through the years, they chronicled the change in life style from hand power to machine power, coal oil lamps to fluorescent lights, whalebone corsets to pantyhose, clammy calcimine to prepasted flock wallpaper, leather harness to vinyl seat covers, threshing machine belts to television sets, manure forks to electronic calculators. As these large volumes slowly disappeared each year in out-houses across the prairies, city dwellers kept pace with changes on the farm and farmers learned of the latest fads and fashions followed by their urban cousins. This multi-purpose service from Eaton's mail-order department passed out of existence with the Spring / Summer issue of 1976.

[n.d.] **A gentlemanly game of bowls** is being played on the lawn of the Magrath Mansion at 6240 Ada Boulevard.

Whereas John A. McDougall and Richard Secord had purchased their properties much earlier and could build their impressive mansions in the central downtown area, real estate magnate William J. Magrath built this palatial residence in 1912 in the new Highlands subdivision. To enhance the attractiveness of this area out in the bush overlooking the North Saskatchewan River at the east end of Jasper Avenue, he and his real estate partner Bidwell A. Holgate built their huge houses side by side and arranged for the street car line to be extended to the new subdivision, much of which they owned.

Magrath's mansion had 14 rooms, including a large ballroom and billiards room on the top floor and a swimming pool in the basement, and was built at a cost of $85,000 (in 1912, remember!). Holgate's 20-room house to the east had 8 bedrooms, 3 fireplaces and ceilings decorated with painted frescoes. Workmen were brought in from Ontario and England.

While their houses were still under construction, the two men retired when the building and real estate boom abruptly ended. This sudden collapse of the real estate boom and subsequent depression left both families destitute. In 1921, Holgate lost his house to the city of Edmonton when he could not pay $5,000 in taxes; in 1931, the sheriff seized Magrath's properties for the same reason.

Unlike McDougall's and Secord's mansions, however, the houses of Magrath and Hogate still remain. In 1975, the Magrath mansion was classified by the Province of Alberta as an historic site.

8 Depression and War Again (1930 - 1946)

Canadians entered the decade of the 1930s amid optimism and prosperity. They enjoyed the second highest standard of living in the world and believed the experts who said the financial problems caused by the 1929 stock crash would be temporary. Within a few months, a stagnant world economy and drought on the Canadian prairies changed all that with a dramatic suddenness that surprised and affected everyone.

The prosperity of the late twenties was based on easy credit, rampant optimism and a dependence upon an export market to a Europe that was recovering from the effects of the Great War. By 1929, Canadian agriculture and industry had over-expanded at a time when glutted world markets caused world trade to decline by more than fifty percent. Because Canada was so dependent on foreign trade and wheat export, Canadians, and especially the western farmers, were severely affected.

The dramatic decrease in rain on the prairies after 1927 caused the dust bowls of the thirties. As the top soil blew away, grasshoppers and Russian thistle moved in. The drought and the 40 percent drop in wheat price practically wiped out farm incomes. Between 1931 and 1937, 21,000 people left Alberta.

The effect of the Depression on cities like Edmonton, supported by an agricultural economy, was dramatic. Thousands lost their jobs, without severance pay or unemployment insurance. In 1933, over a quarter of all wage-earners were unemployed. Three years later, only one-third of the young people entering the work force could find a job. By 1934, the City of Edmonton owed the Imperial Bank $2.5 million. The provincial government was broke. In 1935, William Aberhart brought in a Social Credit government. The next year he introduced Prosperity Certificates, popularly called "funny money". Throughout the Depression, the federal government disbursed $813 million in relief. Hard times, unemployment, the dole and relief were signs of the times.

Movies, radio and magazines helped lighten the desperate decade. Movie-goers witnessed the tremendous development of sound movies. The radio replaced the piano and the phonograph as the centre of home entertainment. The *Reader's Digest* led the vast array of American magazines that emphasized amusement and optimistic assurance instead of the miserable reality of the Depression. At the same time, these mass media gradually shaped the Canadian way of life to be more like that of our southern neighbours. To counteract this subtle Americanization, Prime Minister Bennett started the Canadian Radio Broadcasting Commission, later called the C.B.C., which soon became a powerful force in unifying the nation and solidifying a Canadian identity.

Despite the Depression, Edmonton continued to establish itself as an important air centre in the world. Globe-girdling aviators made Edmonton a refuelling stop and the bush pilots made it the air gateway to the north. The discovery of gold and silver in the Arctic created a tremendous increase in air traffic to the isolated northern settlements. The air supply business to the north was so extensive, that by 1935 Edmonton's air freight of 13,000 tons amounted to more than all the air freight carried by the United States, Great Britain, France and Germany together.

The return of rain and a record harvest in 1939 ended the drought and the declaration of war created a sudden demand for new materials, munitions, equipment and supplies. Prices rose as the war effort took care of a backlog of over-production. The Depression was over; the war boom was on.

Suddenly Blatchford Field became "the crossroads of the world", the busiest airport on the continent. The British Commonwealth Air Training Plan had one of its schools in Edmonton. The construction of the Alaska Highway and the Canol Pipeline created tremendous business for the highways and railroads north from Edmonton. Thousands of American war-related workers flooded into the city. By 1941, Edmonton's population had finally surpassed Calgary's.

Problems also accompanied the boom. Within two years, the cost of living increased 17 percent and money was still scarce. In 1941, Canada became the first democratic nation to implement almost total control of the economy. Rationing was imposed on the sale of butter, meat, tea, coffee and sugar, as well as gasoline and liquor.

At the war's end, Canada emerged as one of the major industrial nations of the world, and the government provided aid to the returning soldiers and their families, including a monthly "Baby Bonus". During the last few years on the 1940s, the Canadian birth rate was the highest of any developed country in the western world.

The return of the military personnel and their families was soon followed by thousands of displaced persons from all over Europe. As a result, Edmonton's population swelled to over 113,000 by 1946. That year, the wartime housing assistance program, finally pushed Edmonton's building permit values past the 1912 record. Just when the war boom ended and the economy was beginning to level off, oil was discovered at Leduc in February, 1947. Another boom time for Edmonton was on its way.

[c1929] **This night view of Jasper Avenue** east from 102 Street reveals little change from the bustling boom days of 1912. The five-storey Canadian Bank of Commerce building opened on July 2, 1929, replacing the old Purvis Block which McDougall and Secord had erected for their store in 1897.

Otherwise it was primarily the vehicles that changed the appearance of the city's streets. Except for the early morning milk wagons, horses were seldom seen on the city pavement. In 1933, it became necessary to install the first traffic light at Jasper Avenue and 101 Street (coincidentally the same intersection where the first serious traffic accident occurred 40 years earlier, on April 27, 1893, before the days of automobiles). By 1950, seventeen sets of traffic lights helped organize traffic at the busiest intersections of the city.

The introduction of neon advertising lights in 1929 helped add some colour and freshness to the prolonged familiarity of the city's business establishments.

Throughout most of the 1930s and 1940s the city physically seemed to be asleep. But within the aging buildings and the tranquil streets life went on and at times even became exciting.

[1931] **One of the most spectacular** rides for generations of Edmontonians was that on the streetcar which carried them over the top deck of the High Level Bridge. The prospect of such an unnerving ride atop such a high bridge was said to have dissuaded many people from even making the crossing. As a safety precaution, the streetcars travelled on the left-hand set of tracks so that in an emergency the passengers could alight onto the centre of the bridge instead of the water 160 feet below.

[1928] **Airplane passengers can see** the Macdonald Hotel, McLeod Building, Tegler Building and Civic Block towering above the collection of 2-and-3-storey buildings spreading around the Market Square. Since the boom burst just prior to World War I, few buildings were added to or subtracted from the city's architectural fabric. The depression years, following the stock crash of October 29, 1929, saw this stagnant pace continue for another decade, only to be followed by another global war and another decade devoid of significant construction activity.

[1931] **On a site very near** where Rev. George McDougall built his house in 1871, stood the city's first permanent public library.

Edmonton's first library committee came into being on the first day of the twentieth century. The first reading room was opened on January 17, 1901, in a building located a few doors west of 101 Street on Jasper Avenue. In March, 1902, the society was organized into a Public Library and Mechanics' Institute. In August, 1902, with a membership of 85, who paid $3 apiece to have the privilege of access to 100 volumes, 16 newspapers and several national and foreign magazines, the library opened two rooms two days a week in the McLeod Block.

After the provincial Legislature passed a Public Libraries Act in 1907, Edmonton appointed a library board in November, 1909. On March 27, 1913, the library began circulating books from 1,850 sq. ft. of temporary quarters in the Chisholm Block on the southeast corner of Jasper Avenue and 104 Street. On March 13, 1913, the Strathcona Library was formally opened and became the first branch library. Because the expanding library needed more space, it moved to the Roberts Block on 102 Street in October, 1914. For the sake of economy in war time, the library moved to the Civic Block in September, 1917.

In 1922, the City and the Carnegie Corporation of New York jointly agreed to finance a permanent city library on the site west of the Edmonton Club that was secured in 1910 for that purpose. On August 30, 1923, this new neo-French-Renaissance building costing $150,000 was formally opened. This fine building was the first project erected by Poole Construction. Forty-six years later, the same company, headed by E.E. Poole's son John, tore the building down to make way for the 33-storey, $19,000,000 A.G.T. Tower, also erected by Poole Construction.

On September 30, 1967, the library officially opened a new building facing Sir Winston Churchill Square, a $4,000,000, six-storey structure jointly funded by federal, provincial, and municipal governments as a Centennial project.

[September, 1932] **At the southeast corner** of 106 Street and Jasper Avenue, the Loveseth Service Station provided complete automotive care. The red-tiled hip roofs and the white stucco quasi-Rococo facades afforded a touch of charm and elegance to the surrounding residential neighborhood.

The convenient and popular service station served changing styles of automobiles from 1923 to 1977. During the Depression, Enoch Loveseth lost title to the station because he was unable to pay his taxes, and thereafter he leased the premises from Imperial Oil Ltd. In 1931, his 12-year-old son Loyd began working

his way up the family business by pumping gas. The next year Mr. Loveseth began a small automotive parts business in a space across the street. From this two-man operation, Loveseth's grew to become a leader in the auto parts business with its main office and plant at 102 Avenue and 105 Street and 5 other branches in the city, staffed by 185 people in 1973, when it celebrated its 50th anniversary under the direction of grandson Ted.

Another aspect of the automobile repair business that Loveseth's pioneered, before trade schools were set up, was training courses for automobile mechanics.

[*March 3, 1930*] **A Chevrolet mail truck** and Fokker F-14 airplane meet to inaugurate the Edmonton-to-Regina leg of the Prairie Air Mail Service that gave 24-hour service daily to Edmonton, Calgary, Saskatoon, Regina, Moose Jaw and Winnipeg. In order to make such rapid service possible, the airport had new lights installed a few days before to allow for night flying.

[*July 29, 1931*] **As 30,000 people crowd** every side of the airfield, daring and imaginative pilots bring the first Trans-Canada Air Pageant to Edmonton, under the direction of John "Mike" Michaels. The large plane parked in the foreground is the 16-passenger Saro-Cloud amphibian, powered by two high radial engines. Flying from left to right are a tri-motored Ford, a Pitcairn autogyro (this first commercial helicopter to visit Canada had four 22-foot rotor blades and was referred to as the "flying egg-beater"), a Siskin fighter flying over the No. 1 hangar, three silver Siskin fighters looping in perfect formation, and a DeHaviland Puss Moth

bi-plane piloted by Major-General Geoffrey O'Brian, the chief test pilot for the DeHaviland company.

For his air trick of the day, pilot O'Brian stepped into his company's smart new Puss Moth accompanied by an 18-year-old aviatrix named Clara Hooker. They entered the tiny plane dressed in old farm togs, but after a brief spin around the sky bowl, they stepped out dressed in the latest 1931 fashions. Leading off the show were five of the Edmonton Flying Club's Moths that gave a competent display of banking and turning, looping and diving and a mock bombing of a fake fort in the centre of the airfield.

[*July 1, 1931*] **Crews at the aerodrome** hurry to service the high-winged Lockheed-Vega monoplane of Wiley Post and his navigator Harold Gatty as they race around the world in 8 days, 15 hours and 51 minutes, beating the Graf Zeppelin's circumnavigation record of 21 days. Unable to get off the muddy runway of Blatchford Field, they departed at dawn the next day from the two-mile strip of concrete called Portage Avenue. On July 22, 1933, Wiley Post landed his "Winnie Mae" here again in his solo flight around the world.

[c1938] **A quarter century after** the Hudson's Bay Company land sale, there are still few buildings to be seen on the entire northern half of the old Reserve. Stretching for two miles southwest into the distance is the broad concrete street called Portage Avenue. Paved by the H.B.C. in 1912, the thoroughfare remained free of frontage buildings for over thirty years. No wonder visiting aviators occasionally mistook Portage Avenue for one of the airport's runways!

The X-shaped strips at the left are the runways of Blatchford Field. Running diagonally to the bottom right corner is 118 Avenue. At the intersection of Portage and 118 Avenue, a train proceeds along the rail line at the approximate location of 121 Street. Beside the tracks at the left are Hangar No. 1 (built 1929) and Hangar No. 2 (built 1938), the farthest to the left. The airport building, which seems to be in the centre of 118 Avenue, is the new Trans-Canada Air Lines hangar.

[1950] **Another of Edmonton's many** great bush pilots was Grant McConachie, shown here with Wop May (left) and Punch Dickins (right).

The Grant McConachie (1909-1965) success story is a classic one of determination, disappointments, hard work and raw courage. After only 5½ hours of instruction, he began flying solo and was soon giving people rides at $10 apiece to pay his plane rental. On February 20, 1931, he received his first pilot's licence, which authorized him to fly a DeHaviland Moth 60 bi-plane. Grant then got his uncle to buy a used Fokker monoplane and they set up Independent Airways. The next winter he was flying

fish at 1 ½ cents a pound from Cold Lake to the nearest railroad at Bonnyville. After changes in both his company and his aircraft, McConachie sold his Yukon Southern Air Transport to Canadian Pacific Railways and Canadian Pacific Airlines was formed on May 16, 1942. Five years later, Grant McConachie, at age 37, became president of this airline, the second largest in the country (behind Canada's first trans-continental air service, Trans-Canada Air Lines, which began in 1937). His knowledge and experience of northern flying, along with his courage and determination to fly new horizons, enabled CP Air to pioneer the Polar Route in February, 1958, flying from Vancouver, Calgary, and Edmonton over the Arctic Circle direct to Amsterdam.

Before his death in June, 1965, McConachie's vision of the future included supersonic aircraft. He said "I don't expect to see the hypersonic model off the drawing board before 1980 or 1985, but when it comes, we'll be right there to buy it".

[1936] **Unlike most merchants,** the Army and Navy store accepted the new Social Credit scrip certificates.

When the Social Credit government came into power in August, 1935, the province was bankrupt. Banks refused to honour civil servants' pay cheques in September, 1935, and roads throughout the province were quagmires in wet

weather. In order to pay the builders of the much-needed roads, and to get around the laws saying only the federal government could print money, Premier Aberhart passed the Prosperity Certificates Act in 1936 and issued about $200,000 worth of scrip in 25-cent, $1 and $5 denominations. The Prosperity Certificates were redeemable in two years provided that there were attached to the back 104 stamps each representing one percent of the denomination of the certificate. If a person held onto a $1 scrip certificate, each week he had to buy and paste onto the back of it a one-cent stamp. So the game people played was either not to accept the certificates or to get rid of them as fast as possible.

Most merchants and bankers maintained that there was only one currency in Canada, the notes issued by the Bank of Canada containing the picture of the King. Finally, the Supreme Court of Canada decided Alberta had no business creating what amounted to its own currency. So after two years, the scheme was dropped, although the Act remained in the Alberta statutes until November, 1977.

[1936] **Although the buildings of Edmonton** changed very little during the two decades following World War I, clothing fashions did change, as Moses Pollack's store at 10324 82 Avenue shows.

Prices during the Depression years were nothing like those of the inflationary 1970s. In 1936, men could buy ready-made pure wool suits at the Bond Clothes Shop for $15.75, while La Fleche Brothers Ltd. were selling custom tailored suits for as low as $27.50. Woodward's sold men's boots for $8.95 a pair and Oxfords for 50¢ less. The Army and Navy department store advertised men's all-leather work boots and Oxfords on sale for $1.00 a pair while they offered two-pant suits for $7.00 and all-wool tweed topcoats for $10.00.

Ladies could buy the latest in tweed suits from Thompson and Dynes Ltd. at regular prices ranging from $25-$35, or at the sale price of $18.88. The same store offered imported tweed suits, that many ladies could not afford at the regular prices from $29.75 to $49.75, at a sale price of $24.88. At the Hudson's Bay Company store, ladies were buying three-piece wool knitted suits for $7.95, imported sweaters for $1.95 and nightgowns for 89¢. Eaton's sold lace trimmed rayon slips for 60¢, summer cotton dresses for $.98, silk stockings at 59¢ a pair and goatskin gloves for $1.59. For the ladies who found these prices too dear, the Army and Navy offered silk dresses at $1.00 each and tweed spring coats at $3.00

Food prices were even better. Prime sirloin beef cost 13¢ a pound, while roast veal sold at 7¢. Butter was 24¢ a pound, sugar 7 lb. for 40¢, flour $2.55 for 98 pounds, coffee 29¢ a pound and tea a mere 42¢ a pound.

[May 13, 1937] **Local farmers had long since** junked their buggies, buckboards and democrats in favour of the plush and prestigious Fords and Chevrolets, but when the Depression left them without money for gasoline, they simply brought the horses back from the pasture and

created the "Bennett Buggies", named after the then Prime Minister of Canada. Times were tough. The consumer index dropped 22 percent from 1929 to 1933, farmers' wheat prices dropped 40 percent, while other prices doubled. In 1927, Alberta farmers had received 98 cents a bushel for wheat, but in 1932 the price dropped to 38 cents (with half of this paying for storage, transportation and marketing costs). By 1939, wheat sold at 52 cents a bushel, but the total provincial farm value of wheat was only half of what it was in 1928.

[June, 1930] **On a lovely summer day** during the Depression, families gather to concern themselves with a leisurely game of draughts on the grounds of Riverside Park, on the south bank of the river opposite the power plant. The park started with 27 acres in 1910 and over the years improved and expanded to include an area of about 75 acres, extending from near the High Level Bridge down-river to Scona Road. The park was renamed Queen Elizabeth Park on June 2, 1939, to commemorate the royal visit of the King and Queen.

[1931] **Whereas their parents had romped** in a dammed up hollow in Mill Creek in pre-war days, these children of the thirties enjoyed the comforts of a concrete pool in Riverside Park, thanks to a scheme known as The Rocky Rapids Development.

In 1915, an enterprising group of individuals formed the Edmonton Power Company with the idea of building a 108-foot-high hydroelectric dam at Rocky Rapids, a turbulent portion of the North Saskatchewan River about 70 miles upstream, near Drayton Valley. Their plan was to sell the electricity to the City of Edmonton, but since the City already had its own coal-burning power plant, opposition was so intense that the new company put up a $50,000 guarantee. After the plebiscite on November 22, 1915, the citizens approved the agreement to buy the proposed hydroelectric power. Subsequently the Edmonton Power Co. was unsuccessful in raising the $5.5 million capital required to build its dam and the company was dissolved, leaving the City of Edmonton with the $50,000 guarantee. With this money, the City built its first three swimming pools, in Riverside park, Borden Park, and the West End at 119 Street and 103 Avenue.

[April, 1936] **The decade of the 1930s** saw the continued worldwide success of the Commercial Grads. This photo of the Grads in action against their sister farm team, the Gradettes, shows two of the reasons for their phenomenal success – their disciplined teamwork and the short passing game. Dr. Naismith described the Grads' style of play: "As for the Grads, one notices most their general teamwork. There is no disposition to 'star' any one player, the whole team playing with a precision of movement, and general understanding of their plays which is beautiful to watch. Their ability to get into position, and to make accurate and rapid passes to each other under the most trying conditions is little short of uncanny."

Percy Page's coaching made the Grads the great team they were. He was a perfectionist, who in turn expected perfection from his girls. Explaining his reason for success, he said: "I first insist on teamwork, next comes shooting accuracy. My logic is that success may be achieved by continuous, hard practice of the fundamentals of basketball. We engage in 65 practice drills per year, many of which are against our Boy Grad Club. We strive for perfection of elemental plays, and in so doing, the tempo of our play is speeded up tremendously. We practiced 90 minutes twice a week. The last 30 minutes of each practice was devoted to perfecting our shooting. We

[June 6, 1940] **The last game the Grads played** – and won – was on June 5, 1940, before a capacity home crowd of 6,200. All the former Grads but three were in attendance. The following day the team celebrated their Silver Anniversary and announced that they were disbanding and withdrawing from active competition. Poor attendance at home games, the outbreak of World War II which placed restrictions on travel for non-essential reasons, the Air Force take-over of the Edmonton Arena (where the Grads played their games), and the successful entry of Mr. Page into provincial politics all combined to "defeat" one of the most outstanding teams in the history of sport.

In their 25 years of Canadian, Olympic and international competition, the Grads won 96.2 per cent of the 522 games they played, losing only 20. From 1915 to 1922, they played 147 consecutive games without a loss, and after losing one game they won 78 more before thier next loss in 1930. They won the provincial title 23 times out of 24, played in eleven western Canada playoffs and won them all, entered 13 Canadian finals and won them

played percentage basketball; whenever we got an opening we took a shot." On the occasion of their 21st anniversary, Dr. Naismith wrote: "My admiration and respect go to you also because you have remained unspoiled by your success, and

all, played 27 games on three European tours without a loss, won 7 of 9 official games played against men's teams, and monopolized the Underwood Trophy by winning 112 of 118 games played against the best amateur American teams. While the team was compiling some of the greatest records in sports history, it was given permanent possession of the provincial, Canadian, Underwood international, French and world championship trophies. In 1938, Noel

have retained the womanly graces notwithstanding your participation in a strenuous game. You are not only an inspiration to basketball players throughout the world, but a model for all girls' teams...."

MacDonald Robertson, team captain during the 1930s, was voted Canada's top woman athlete; in 1971 she was admitted to Canada's Sports Hall of Fame. In 1950, the team was selected in a press poll as Canada's best basketball team of the half-century. On April 18, 1973, two months after the death of Mr. Page, the Grads were admitted to Edmonton's Sports Hall of Fame and a year later they were admitted to the Alberta Sports Hall of Fame.

[June, 1940] **A modest 2,040-seat grandstand,** complete with open-air press box on top and dressing rooms underneath, marked the beginning of Clarke Stadium.

Prior to World War I, a more substantial fence surrounded the area, which then housed the old federal penitentiary established on that site in 1906. In 1930, the penitentiary walls and buildings were torn down and 25 of the 95 acres of the penn site were transferred to the city for an athletic field.

Eight years later, this stadium was erected from old bridge timbers at a cost of $55,500, with light standards containing eighty 1,500-watt fixtures, making it the "finest lighted field in western Canada". For the official opening on August 27, 1938, the I.O.D.E. ladies sold, at 15¢ a copy, the first sports program ever published for an Edmonton sports event. At that first game, a sell-out crowd saw the Eskimo football team lose to the Calgary Broncs 35-1. The local team ended the season without a single win and subsequently disbanded for the duration of the Second World War.

With the resurgence of the modern day Eskimos in 1949, Clarke Stadium underwent several expansions, particularly in 1954 when the original west stands were demolished to make way for a new 16,000-seat concrete structure facing the 4,000-seat east stands erected in 1949. With the opening of the 42,000-seat Commonwealth Stadium to the north in 1978, Clarke Stadium became a facility for amateur sport. On August 23, 1978, 25,000 fans saw the Eskimos play their last game at Clarke Stadium, beating the Winnipeg Blue Bombers 14-8.

[July 16, 1935] **Dressed to head the revival** of the Exhibition parade (the first since 1927) is Mayor Joe Clarke, known as "Fighting Joe" because of his years of campaigning for civic office. This champion of the underdog and promoter of a wide-open, free-wheeling type of city, the "Stormy Petrel" of Edmonton politics, served five years as mayor and eight years as alderman.

During his school years in Ontario, athletic Joe played lacrosse and rugby and while attending law school in Toronto, starred for the varsity football team. Upon graduation, he came to Regina to join the N.W.M.P. in 1892. At a track meet for the Mounties that year, he won all nine events and covered a distance of 47 feet 11 inches in the hop, step and jump.

Six years later, he left the police force and joined the thousands of goldseekers bound for the Yukon in 1897. There he was admitted to the bar and assisted in drafting laws and regulations for that part of the wild west.

In 1908, he settled in Edmonton to practice law. He first served as alderman in 1912 and as mayor in 1919 and 1920 (elections were held annually then). He was elected mayor again from 1935 to 1937. Always a promoter of local athletes and sports, Edmonton's first stadium was named after him because he had engineered the deal with his friend Prime Minister W. L. Mackenzie King to have the old federal penitentiary site transferred to the city for an athletic field on a 99-year lease for one dollar – a very neat bit of political maneuvering.

[May 12, 1937] **Streetcar No. 1 received special** treatment as Edmonton celebrated the coronation of His Majesty King George VI. This was the third time a streetcar was decorated with bunting and lights, the two previous occasions being the amalgamation of Edmonton and Strathcona in 1912 and Canada's 60th birthday in 1927.

On the hot May coronation day, 30,000 loyal subjects declared their allegiance to the King in the largest mass gathering ever held at the Exhibition Grounds. The patriotic program was preceded by a great parade down Jasper Avenue to the Legislative Grounds for the 21-gun Royal Salute. That evening the streetcar was gaily illuminated and the skies over the airport were filled with spectacular displays of fireworks.

[June 2, 1939] **As 68,000 Albertans waved** and cheered the first visit of a reigning monarch to Canada, a motorcade escorted King George VI and Queen Elizabeth down Portage Avenue, which that day was renamed Kingsway. Two miles of grandstands filled with loyal subjects not only impressed Their Majesties but also hid from their view the absence of buildings along this unique street.

The streetcar tracks, from the time of their installation in 1912 to their removal forty years later, never carried a streetcar. During that time, Portage Avenue served visiting aviators, the King and Queen and local citizens, who needed a quiet street on which to practice the new skill of driving an automobile.

[May 31, 1939] **Beside the Royal George Hotel,** the old Woodward's department store stands proudly fitted with flags and bunting, ready to celebrate the royal visit. While Sam Cherniak sells popcorn to passersby on the 102 Avenue corner, the new Eaton's department store is in the midst of construction on the other side of 101 Street (lower left corner).

The building shown here includes the original Woodward's store, which opened on this site on October 15, 1926, and the three additional bays built onto the north, nearest the Royal George Hotel, in 1929 and 1932. By September, 1940, fourth and fifth storeys were added as well. In June, 1974, the building was demolished to be replaced by the new Edmonton Centre complex.

[March, 1938] **At the southwest corner** of 101 Street and Jasper Avenue, the old Windsor Hotel has become the Selkirk Hotel, with the very popular Johnson's Cafe conveniently located at the centre of the business district. The hotel suffered severe fire damage on December 18, 1962, and was subsequently demolished in September, 1963, along with its two neighbouring buildings, to allow the construction of the Royal Bank Building.

At the right stands the sidewalk clock of Irving Kline, Alberta's first credit jeweller. This clock, which Kline bought in 1927 for $4,000, moved along Jasper Avenue with the business several times. Whereas Kline's previous stores were eventually demolished, this historic piece of street furniture kept moving and changing with the times and remained for over 50 years as a familiar fixture on Jasper Avenue.

[c1938] **The Canadian Bank of Commerce Building,** on the left, with its elaborate Neo-Renaissance cornice, and the old Empire Block, on the right, flank 101 Street north of Jasper Avenue.

Beside the street car are a Chevrolet (foreground) and a Ford with a Terraplane following. Parked along the curb behind the Ford truck is a Buick.

[July 2, 1947] **After ten years,** in the Tegler Building, the T. Eaton Co. erected a streamlined two-storey department store in 1939 on the northwest corner of the same intersection. The store featured almost an eighth of a mile of ground-floor show windows protected by a wide, stainless-steel canopy. Inside the building, customers could make use of the two widest unsupported steel stairways in Canada, in addition to the 4-foot-wide escalator, the widest available at that time. Ten years later, a third storey was added. With its curved corners, travertine and limestone cladding and custom nickel-plated doors, the Eaton's store was one of the best examples of streamlined Modern architecture on the Canadian prairies.

[May 10, 1945] **The new T. Eaton department store** reflected the cool, streamlined approach of the new International Style of architecture that was gradually reaching to the farthest corners of the western world. The terrazzo floors, plaster columns, and flush-recessed lighting system accompanied well-lit glass and plastic laminate display counters. The block-style lettering complemented the new clean, utilitarian effect.

[December, 1939] **In September, 1939,** Edmonton began its first use of trolley buses, like this one ignoring the streetcar tracks on Jasper Avenue east of 100 Street. The only horses found in town now pulled the milk wagons (right). Directly behind the bus are, from right to left, the Sandison Block of 1904 with its decorative arches and pediment, the Blowey Henry furniture store of 1908, and the adjacent Northern Building. Standing out above the buildings are huge signs advertising the two largest meat packing establishments in the city.

[1940s] **An ever more familiar** sound and sight to Edmontonians during the war years was the drone and shimmer of new types of airplanes making low flights over the city to the municipal airport. Here a DC-4 flies over the Macdonald Hotel and the central business district along Jasper Avenue west of 100 Street.

[c.autumn, 1942] **A Boeing 247 (left)** and a Lockheed Hudson (right) park on the runway behind the new Administration Building at Blatchford Field. This terminal, built in 1942, served international flights until 1959 when the new International Airport west of Leduc opened. After that time this building continued to handle passengers on western Canadian flights while the control tower monitored the traffic of local commercial and private aircraft. On November 24, 1975, a new terminal building, capable of handling a million passengers per year, was officially opened to provide more spacious and up-to-date facilities for local air traffic.

[c 1941] **Pyramidal tents dominated** the space between new hangars erected by the Department of National Defence after Blatchford Field was transferred to Dominion jurisdiciton during the war. The airport became the busiest on the continent and was especially strategic in United States plans for defending Alaska against the Japanese. This new significance led to the lengthening of old runways and the construction of new ones.

[June 19, 1942] **Following the Japanese** attack on Dutch Harbour in the Aleutian Islands on June 3, 1942, the United States immediately sent through the Edmonton airport 30 U.S.A.F. DC-3's. These were soon followed by hundreds more. In one day in June, 1942, five hundred planes were ferried through Blatchford. Later came hundreds of Lend-Lease planes to Russia, uncluding some 1,500 P-39 Bell Airacobras. With planes arriving and leaving every minute or so, what is believed to be a North American record was established when 860 planes passed through the busy airport in one day.

To relieve the pressure on Blatchford Field, the American armed forces opened the Namao air base ten miles north of Edmonton in September, 1944. Taking in 2,560 acres, with runways 7,000 feet long, the Namao field became the largest airport on the continent.

[February, 1943] **While the men fought** the war overseas, women filled the overhauls in the hangars at home. Crippled planes from the Battle of Britain were shipped to the new aircraft-repair branch of the Edmonton airport.

[April, 1943] **Here at the Air Observers' School,** Link Trainers are used for basic ground training. Women shared duties with men at the A.O.S., operated by Canadian Pacific Airlines during the war. C.P.A. called upon Wop May to round up a group of experienced pilots to staff the new school for the hundreds of young men who had volunteered to join the Royal Canadian Air Force. The R.C.A.F. used the Exhibition Grounds as a Manning Depot and also used the university residences to house air force personnel.

[November, 1942] **While planes were flying** off to Alaska daily, convoys of trucks and military vehicles were rushing up the new Alaska Highway. Edmonton was the supply base for the construction of the Alaska Highway, which was the largest single project since the building of the Panama Canal. Following the Japanese attack on Pearl Harbour on December 7, 1941, the 1523-mile road north from Dawson Creek was built through some of the world's roughest country in nine months at a cost of $139,000,000. Then goods and machinery passed through Edmonton daily by truck, track and air transport. During the war years, more freight passed through the local airport than through any other air terminal in North America.

[April, 1943] **Even the navy was active** in this prairie city during the war. These naval recruits paraded down Jasper Avenue past Mike's News Agency at the northwest corner of 100A Street. They belonged to a local group formed in 1923 as a naval half-company. A week after Canada entered the Second World War in 1939, the reserve unit became a basic training ground for thousands of naval recruits. Their training quarters were set up in the old Hudson's Bay Company horse barns in Rossdale at 102 Street and 97 Avenue. (When the H.B.C. was converting its horse-drawn delivery vans to mechanized units, the old barns became available to the navy.)

This unit adopted the name "HMCS Nonsuch" after the small 50-ton ketch that brought such a valuable load of furs from the Hudson's Bay area that it convinced King Charles II to grant a charter in 1670 for the Hudson's Bay Co. to trade into the Canadian Northwest. After the war, the unit returned to peace-time reserve status and in 1960 lived up to its name by winning the national competition trophy for being the best naval division in Canada.

[August 10, 1945] **The interior of Mike's News** had space to accommodate browsers and buyers regardless of the weather outside. On the right, newspapers and old magazine favourites, such as the *Saturday Evening Post, Life, Cosmopolitan, Redbook,* and *Reader's Digest* await a steady clientele. On the left, counters and shelves are stocked with candy and tobacco products. At the rear is the door leading to the Post Office and local ticket-selling outlet and, just to the left, cubby-holes are filled with the latest foreign newspapers. Modern fluorescent fixtures, which came into Edmonton during the war years, cause the old pressed metal ceiling to add a glistening touch to the popular shop, which closed in 1980 to make way for the huge Scotia Place complex.

[January, 1944] **Temporary lights were strung** down the centre of Convocation Hall to enable University of Alberta engineering students to work at improving their drafting skills.

The wartime demand for people trained in engineering, science, medicine and dentistry resulted in an increased enrolment in these courses at the university. In the fall session of 1944, there were 650 students in the Faculty of Applied Science and 367 in the Science program. The faculties of Medicine and Dentistry adopted accelerated courses to meet the heavy demand for graduates. During the war, both classroom and residence accommodation were filled to overflowing.

[October, 1941] **This experiment in radio frequency** induction is ready for students in electrical engineering in the Radio Technology Laboratory at the University of Alberta. This lab was situated in the upper floor of the campus power plant, located just behind the Arts Building. During the winter, the room was so cold that the students had to work wearing their mitts and parkas. Occasionally, in very cold weather, the innovative students would go downstairs, where the power generating equipment was housed, and make connection to allow large resistive load boxes to act as electric radiant heaters for the cold lab upstairs.

In 1978, the 69-year-old Power Plant was renovated to become the Graduate Students' social centre, including their restaurant, bar and games facilities.

[March, 1940] **Young scholars enjoy the latest** in techniques and the newest in teachers in this class at the Normal School (now Corbett Hall). The Alberta Normal School was organized in August, 1927, and formally opened its new building, south of the U. of A. hospital, in January, 1930. In 1944, the Normal Schools were closed and all future teachers took their training at the university.

[November 4, 1942] **Fire-fighters work frantically** to save the old Empire Block at 101 Street and Jasper Avenue from fire, while signs on the neighboring Banque Canadienne Nationale advertises Victory Bonds to help save the world from totalitarianism. The spectacular fire caused a half-million-dollars damage, but the four-storey brick structure was repaired, renovated and reopened three months later. The grand old building, which stood on the corner since 1905, survived fire and changing times until January, 1962, when it was demolished to make way for the new 11-storey Empire Building which now occupies that corner.

[November, 1942] **Two weeks later,** military personnel and civilians alike survey the problem on Jasper Avenue just east of Mike's News Agency. On Sunday, November 15, 1942, a record-breaking 19 ½ inches of heavy snow fell, causing drifts waist-deep in the city and as high as 15 feet in the surrounding countryside. While some adventurous folk used skis and snowshoes to negotiate around the drifts and stranded vehicles, more serious-minded businessmen questioned why the city had absolutely no snow-removal equipment. Fortunately, the American Air Force and Alaska Highway crews were in the city and after a day or two, their scrapers, trucks and loaders were able to get traffic rolling again. The city fathers vowed they would never be caught without snow-removal equipment again.

[June, 1943] **A Ford, Pontiac, Dodge,** and Chevrolet (left to right) line the curb beside the new King Edward Hotel on 101 Street.

When the city straightened out the intersection in the late 1930s so that 102 Avenue would be in alignment on each side of 101 Street, the King Edward was left with an additional 50 feet on which it built its third one-storey wing (at the right) in 1940. In 1951, the old pre-World-War-I facades were covered with this modern Art Deco styled facing. The King Edward's service to the city ended on April 23, 1978, when an extensive fire, which killed two persons, forced its closure and subsequent demolition the following year.

In 1981, construction began on a 36-storey office tower on this once-popular corner of 101 Street and 102 Avenue.

[March 29, 1940] **All is quiet in the** King Edward Hotel beer parlour as the wicker chairs await their afternoon and evening clientele.

After seven years of prohibition, liquor was voted back in 1923. Hard liquor could be bought from government operated vendors and beer could be obtained by the glass only in hotel "Beer Parlours". Men and women had to drink their beer in separate rooms, however, until the law was changed following a provincial plebiscite in October, 1957. Shortly after mixed drinking became legal, the visual and social amenities within beer parlours and liquor lounges improved and some of the better hotels obtained licences to serve alcoholic beverages with meals.

[Spring, 1943] **The staff of the Rialto Theatre** at 10134 101 Street proudly have their picture taken under the bright lights of the large marquee.

The building itself has a long and varied career going all the way back to its construction in 1910 at a cost of $30,000. Originally called the Bijou, it first opened its doors to the movie-going public on November 1, 1910. In 1914, a Calgary-based corporation took over the operation with a policy of a mixed program of motion picture and vaudeville. A temporary closure occurred in 1916, but after the war years the theatre re-opened in 1919 and was known for a time as Allen's 101 Street Theatre. The next year it operated for a short time as the Family Theatre before new owners in 1920 renamed the house the Rialto Theatre. On July 8, 1929, the theatre re-opened after extensive renovations. To keep up with the changing equipment and demands of the times, another $60,000 worth of renovations were carried out in August, 1938. This gave the old movie house a modernistic, streamlined appearance both inside and out.

[July 3, 1943] **Wartime theatre crowds consisted** mainly of women and children who contributed to the economy of the time by bringing salvage fat for soap production. During the period of scarcity and rationing that ran concurrent with the war years, Albertans even complied with the government's advice to return used toothpaste tubes so the lead could be recycled. Comedies like "Happy Go Lucky" helped brighten the day.

[August, 1943] **While the women were saving** the bacon and the fat during the war years, the men found enough gas to tear around the racetrack to the delight of the hot summer crowds at the Exhibition Grounds. These classy chassis are stock Model T Fords dressed up for speedy action at the track.

184

[April, 1944] **On a lovely spring day,**
the view north from the Macdonald Hotel
shows, counter-clockwise from the bottom
right, the Imperial Bank, the clock tower
of the Post Office, the Court House, the
McLeod Building, Woodward's store, the
Tegler Building, the C.P.R. Building on
Jasper Avenue next to the Gariepy Block
at the corner of 100 Street. At the bottom
left corner is the Dominion Bank Building.

[May 12, 1944] **No peonies and petunias here** at the U.S. Army Camp at 127 Street and 114 Avenue. A snowstorm on May 9, 1944, dumped 4.2 inches of the heavy white stuff in 13 hours over the city that was readying itself for another good ol' summertime of ice cream and lemonade. This snowfall was the heaviest May snowfall since 1930, but it was not the all-time record for Edmonton. The greatest May 24-hour snowfall was on May 2, 1920, when 7.5. inches of snow fell on the city!

[August 14, 1945] **Parade crowds jam 101 Street** in celebration of V-J Day, which ended World War II. Following the huge parade came street dancing in several designated areas. The market square filled with old time dances, while 100A Street north of Jasper Avenue was filled with younger and livelier dances. At the corner of 100A Street and 101 Avenue, the Edmonton Regiment Band held a singalong, as the jubilant celebrants whooped and hollered and sang "Roll Out the Barrel", "Waltzing Matilda", "The Old Grey Mare", "Over There" and other popular songs that filled the radio waves during the war days. The liquor store at 10160 103 Street had a queue two blocks long. Many believe this was the city's greatest celebration ever, even exceeding the May 8, 1945, V-E Day festivities.

[October 4, 1945] **With the Immigration Hall** of 1907 and Alberta Grain Co. elevators of 1905 rising in the background, the C.N. station platform fills with happy people as relatives come to welcome home from the war the Edmonton contingent of the Royal Canadian Engineers. Two days later, the Loyal Edmonton Regiment returned and was greeted with civic welcoming ceremonies. The war was over! Many veterans returned to the university residences, this time as students. Others walked the streets looking for employment in a world that was rapidly changing toward a new era of automation and recreation.

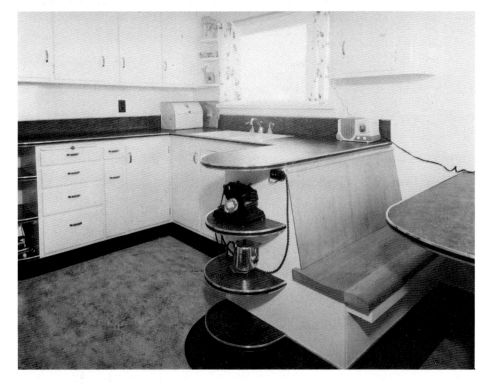

[October, 1946] **With the average annual income** in Alberta at $666, postwar houses for most families had to be compact and frugal. The abundance of stucco and absence of sheltering overhangs contributed little to the amenities of the new residential streets. Only time and the growth of new landscape materials would soften the visual effect for the generation born on the threshold of an era of relative peace and optimism. Baby bonuses and other welfare measures brought in by the federal government in 1945 helped carry the ambitions of returned soldiers to build a better Edmonton than the one that had remained essentially the same since the boom days before the First World War.

[October, 1946] **Interiors were likewise sparse** and sober, although the plush uphostery, imitation fireplace and streamlined radio cabinet mellowed the otherwise austere environment. Wool area carpets likewise added a softer touch to the oak floors.

[October, 1946] **Studebaker cars set** the streamlining pace in 1946 and soon buildings, interiors and appliances followed. Dream homes began to be serviced by shiny electrical toasters, coffee pots, radios as well as large vacuum cleaners, washers and dryers. To match, kitchen counters were lined with polished chrome or aluminum trim. The new efficient, streamlined look became the fad, replacing the tedious, cluttered heritage of the Victorian age.

9 Oil Capital (1947 – 1957)

The treasures that were lying under the farm lands surrounding Edmonton were finally discovered in February, 1947, when the Leduc oilfield started producing. Within a decade, the sleepy city based on an agricultural economy awakened to become a bustling industrial centre. During that time, Canada became one of the world's most sought-after areas for investment. Russia's acquisition of the atomic bomb in 1949, and later the Korean War from 1950 to 1953 created a need in the western world, and especially in the United States, for increasing military preparedness. The United States needed iron, uranium, aluminum and petroleum. The discovery of oil in central Alberta was a boon to both Canada and her southern neighbour, but especially to Alberta and Edmonton.

In the decade following the Leduc discovery, the number of Alberta's producing oil wells increased from 418 to 7,390, with three-quarters of these in the farming region surrounding Edmonton. During that period, the petroleum industry pumped $2.5 billion into the Alberta economy. More billions of dollars of largely U.S. investments set up petroleum-related industries and manufacturing plants, most of these on the eastern edge of Edmonton. In the Clover Bar area, some $400 million was spent on constructing new manufacturing plants. Within a few years, pipelines were delivering oil to the west coast and the Great Lakes. All of these investments created jobs and opportunities, and thousands of Canadians, Americans and European immigrants poured into Edmonton. The city's population doubled in these ten years to 226,000 in 1956, while in that same period the average annual income increased from $666 to $1,539. By 1956, Edmonton was the sixth largest city in Canada and shared with Calgary the distinction of being the fastest growing metropolitan area in the country.

In this booming period of growth and urbanization, many changes occurred in the life style of Edmontonians, and indeed of all Canadians. Following a decade and a half of depression and war austerity measures, people now had money in their pockets and were anxious to buy and improve their standard of living. Modern technology and mass marketing brought in the consumer revolution, and the *gadget* revolution. Large suburban homes, enormous chrome-trimmed cars, slick service stations, automatic washers and dryers, portable radios, hi-fidelity recordings, aerosol spray cans and nylon clothing soon became commonplace. This period saw the arrival of the shopping centre, drive-in movies, laundromats and the new stone and glass skyscrapers of Edmonton, including the Macdonald Hotel addition, the Milner Building, the Financial Building and a new City Hall.

The innovation which changed the lives of everyone most was television, which came to Edmonton in 1954. It added to the already strong Americanizing influence everywhere. TV not only gave a broader understanding of the world, but also helped teenagers relate to the new heroes, like Paul Anka and Elvis Presley, to rock 'n' roll, and made the older generation more aware of culture, the fine arts and professional sports, which were all revived following the war years.

In this period when almost everyone wanted fun and freedom, moral and social values changed. Bikinis became common, segregated beer parlours were supplemented at the decade's end by mixed cocktail lounges, censorship loosened, respect for authority waned in this permissive, affluent, consumer-oriented age. Many of the old traditional values went out of existence, as did the Edmonton *Bulletin,* the streetcars and the E. Y. & P. railway tracks.

The dynamic decade ended with the opening of a new City Hall and the Northern Alberta Jubilee Auditorium. But high overhead, Edmontonians watched a new portentous light. In 1957 Russia launched the world's first space satellite, Sputnik I. For the first time western technological superiority was challenged. It was a time for everyone to get serious, forget the fads, and live with the awesome possibility of sudden attack, even extermination.

[July, 1950] **On February 13, 1947,** a new era began for Alberta and Edmonton. On that cold winter day, Leduc Oil Well No. 1 blew in 20 miles south of Edmonton. It was the beginning of thousands of producing oil wells surrounding the Edmonton region. Alberta and the oil companies had hit the jackpot.

Edmonton became the centre of the oil refining industries and the source of pipelines that sent oil to Ontario, Vancouver and Los Angeles. By August, 1948, the Imperial Oil Company began operating the first part of its new refinery. Also the British American Oil Co. refinery was completed in Clover Bar in 1951. Later that year, the McColl Frontenac Company was in operation just across the highway. Within three years of the Leduc discovery, Edmonton became a major refining centre.

[March 31, 1948] **Melting snows signal** the arrival of spring and the prospects of another sunny Alberta summer, but woe to the motorist who has to navigate the mud holes, ruts and water puddles found along most of the residential streets of the post-war period. By the end of the war, only 70 miles of the city's 400 miles of streets were paved. Only 59 miles of sidewalk were of concrete, compared to 228 miles of wooden walks. Of the 28,000 homes in the city, 11,000 had been built before 1920. The city was in need of a stimulus to prosperity.

[October 18, 1948] **Few buildings stand out** in the sprawling city which saw little new construction since the boom years just prior to World War I. That real estate boom had set out numerous satellite subdivisions in all directions around the turn-of-the-century city, but the sudden end to growth left a 1910-1912 appearance that remained for four decades. This left a city that could accommodate about 300,000 people, but counted only 113,116 in 1946.

In 1947, Edmonton imported from England Noel Dant, its first town planner. Following his new concepts, several old, unbuilt subdivisions and many new ones were redesigned and built on the basis of curves, crescents, cul-de-sacs and service roads, in marked contrast to the existing rectangular grid pattern of city blocks. Another new idea he inserted into the street patterns was the traffic circle, which brought with it more problems than solutions to the rapidly increasing volume of vehicles in the streets of the reawakened boom town.

In 1949, the Low Level Bridge was twinned immediately north of its original span of 1900. This was just an indication that soon a new cityscape would arise on each side of the previously tranquil river valley.

[October 27, 1951] **While Lieutenant-Governor J.J. Bowlen** stands bareheaded at the left and distinguished guests look on, Premier Ernest Manning reads a greeting to the royal visitors, Princess Elizabeth and Prince Philip, the Duke of Edinburgh. This was their first visit to Edmonton and the first visit by British royalty since the visit of the King and Queen in 1939.

[1954] **In this view north along 101 Street,** the downtown area spreads to the east. The large central park is the future site of the new City Hall proposed to replace the old Civic Block, standing to the east of the city market square, filled with cars. Along the river bank, from left to right, are the Journal Building, McDougall church, Alberta College, Memorial Hall at the north end of the bowling greens, Public Library, Edmonton Club, 100 Street leading down into McDougall Hill and the Macdonald Hotel complete with the new addition. In the distance, two grandstands flank the Clarke Stadium playing field.

[July 25, 1953] **To meet the pressing need, caused by the oil boom,** for more hotels, tourist and convention facilities in the city, the C.N.R. hotel officials built this 16-storey, 300-bedroom addition to the old Macdonald Hotel. In order to provide accommodation as fast as possible, the hotel management opened the top three floors on January 12, 1953, and as each successive floor was completed, at the rate of about one floor per week, the remaining 13 floors were opened to the public. The ground and mezzanine floors of the $5 million addition contained a cafeteria, banqueting and convention facilities. The very marked change in style from the original chateau-type hotel of 1915 caused startled Edmontonians to refer to the enlarged hotel as "the Mac and the box it came in"!

Adjacent to the east of the hotel, Canada's first underground public parking garage was opened on February 12, 1955.

[April 11, 1954] **As this view of the new** lobby shows, the interiors of the addition were as much in contrast to those of the original building as were the exterior expressions. Gone were the coffered ceilings, wood panelling and graceful intricate detailing. Streamlined flat planes provided the new "functional" look.

[December 24, 1952] **The new bedrooms featured** the last word in hotel accommodation. Every room had a bedside radio and a built-in unit which combined the dressing table, writing desk, bureau and luggage rack. Instead of the old brass bedsteads, many of the bedrooms contained the latest vogue in other cities in eastern Canada and the United States, the fold-away chesterfield bed.

[January 11, 1953] **Cars of the early fifties** accompany the Macdonald Hotel addition as newcomers to the old Jasper Avenue scene west of 100 Street. Two new items of street furniture also appear. In 1948, the city introduced 800 parking meters along downtown curbs. These were increased to 2,000 by 1954, and thereafter, as city traffic increased, these pesky "hitching posts" seemed to emerge as fast as mushrooms along all the city's business streets. Furthermore, in 1947, Edmonton became the first city in Canada to replace the old incandescent street lights with mercury vapor fixtures. The first to receive the change were the lights along Jasper Avenue, three blocks east of 100 Street. In 1956, the city decided to install these fixtures in all new sub-divisions, and that year they established another record by being the first city in the world to order a large quantity of an even better mercury vapor luminaire. In a few years, Edmonton became one of the best lit cities in the world.

Most Edmontonians, however, were too busy becoming "modern" to realize that in another decade the old Edwardian and Victorian faces would be gone forever. The Dominion Bank erected in 1910, along with the Shasta Cafe and Yale Hotel of 1902 vintage, was razed in June, 1967. The Royal Bank of Canada, with its imposing Corinthian columns and pseudo-cornice, was demolished in October, 1967.

[February, 1944] **The lofty banking chamber** of the Royal Bank still retained the original 30-year-old incandescent fixtures that were described as an excellent system of lighting when the building opened on April 21, 1913. Likewise, the marble-faced counters, bronze tellers' cages, terrazzo floor and coffered ceiling preserved the original feeling of economic confidence and security that filled the air during the 1912 land boom.

[1957] **The conical tower-roof** of the Alberta Hotel forms a sharp contrast with the new Macdonald Hotel addition in this view of Jasper Avenue, looking west from approximately 96 Street. The Hub Hotel identifies the location of the original Jasper House hotel.

[July 10, 1948] **Prominent in this photo** of Jasper Avenue, looking east from 106 Street, is the Seven Seas Restaurant. When it opened in July, 1948, it was the only licensed restaurant in the city. With seating for 650 people and a staff of 100, it was one of the largest restaurants in western Canada. Soon it came to have one of the best reputations in western Canada, also. In 1952, expansion doubled the floor area and a $50,000 renovation in 1967 provided two additional lounges and banquet rooms. A constant feature from the time of its opening until its closing in December, 1977, was the large color-photo mural of Hawaii's famed Diamond Head located on the rear wall of the main dining room. Long before jet travel made possible the popular Hawaiian winter vacations enjoyed by many Edmontonians, this beautiful photo-mural brought a bit of sunny Hawaii to this northern city of short summers and long cold winters.

[October 2, 1947] **The new Hudson's Bay Company** store dominates this view of Jasper Avenue looking east past the intersection at 103 Street.

On November 14, 1939, 20,000 people attended the official opening of the new $1,000,000 Hudson's Bay Company store. Since the new store occupied the entire length of the block, it could be built in three stages so that a gradual shift of facilities from the old to the new could take place without losing a single day's business.

In order to make way for the new building, Poole Construction Co. had to remove 1,715 tons of 30-year-old concrete from the walls and foundations of the previous buildings occupying the site. Under the old 6-storey annex alone there were fifteen concrete footings weighing 22 tons each. Some of Edmonton's early buildings were certainly built to last a long time, but even sturdy construction was no guarantee of extended longevity.

Faced with light Manitoba Tyndal stone, jet black Swedish granite, satin-finish stainless-steel trim and glass-block windows, the new store expressed the very latest in modern merchandising appearance.

In 1948, a third storey was added to the H.B.C. store at a cost of $500,000. Six years later, a $3,250,000 extension to the north side doubled the floor area of the store. To make way for this, the popular "Barn" was demolished.

The Barn was an annex to the old store that originally housed the smelly raw-fur department, and later served as a barn. In 1940 it was transformed to become the most popular dance hall and rendezvous location during the remainder of the war years.

To further accommodate their customers, the Bay built a 600-car Parkade between 103 and 104 Streets south of Jasper Avenue.

[1953] **The Journal Building** and McDougall United Church stand prominently at the top of Bellamy Hill at 101 Street.

This church, the third one erected on this site, is named after Rev. George McDougall who built the first log church here in 1873. In 1910, this $90,000 brick church was built to replace the white frame church of 1892. Inside, the 1,200-seat auditorium contains a very fine English organ.

The Edmonton *Journal* moved its newspaper business to this location when its four-storey building was completed in 1921. Edmonton's second major newspaper began with 1,000 copies of a 4-page edition on November 11, 1903. In two years, it moved from its original location in an old fruit store at 101 Street north of Jasper Avenue to a nearby location just south of the Tegler Building. From 1906 to 1911, the *Journal* published both morning and evening editions. Circulation increased from 4,300 in 1910 and 95,881 in 1956 to 126,830 in 1963. (For some issues in 1980, up to 230,000 copies were printed). To keep pace with this growth, the original building on Macdonald Drive was doubled by an addition to the north in 1952 and within three years of that, a press building was added to the west. In 1938, the Edmonton *Journal* became the first newspaper outside the U.S. to win the prestigious Pulitzer Prize.

With the termination of the Edmonton *Bulletin* on January 20, 1951, the *Journal* remained as the city's only daily newspaper until the emergence of the morning tabloid, the Edmonton *Sun,* on April 2, 1978.

[October 18, 1948] **On looking west over** the University of Alberta, just prior to the period of post-war expansion, we have a last glimpse of the old pre-World-War-I campus. In thirty years, almost nothing had changed.

At the bottom left, we see the old Strathcona Hospital and the Col. Mewburn Veterans' Hospital nearby. Just to the north is 87 Avenue with the Varsity Rink and the old Drill Hall flanking the avenue one block to the west. Further north lie the three original residences. Surrounding the steel framing of the new Rutherford Library to the south are St. Stephen's College to the south, the Medical Building to the west, and the Arts Building to the north. Across 88 Avenue, south of the Medical Building, is St. Joseph's College.

At the extreme left of the photo, Corbett Hall, the old Normal School, indicates the southern edge of the campus.

In the foreground, the community of Garneau presses against the campus east boundary, 112 Street, while the space from the western edge of the campus to the river lies largely undeveloped. In 1948, when the university had 4,605 full-time students and 223 faculty, no one realized that in thirty years the enrolment would increase to 18,764, the faculty to 1,300 and the institution could well use that bushland to the west.

[c1951] **In front of the semi-circular** driveway sits the original Strathcona Hospital which opened in February, 1914. The southern half (left of the entrance canopy) was completed in October, 1930. South of the original five-storey Strathcona Hospital, a six-storey Polio Wing, with curved corners, was opened in 1950. The H-shaped building to the right is the 250-bed Colonel Mewburn Pavilion of 1945, named in memory of the university's first professor of surgery, Dr. F. H. Mewburn. The two-storey brick building to the left, between the small, hip-roofed Red Cross Wing of 1934 and the Varsity Rink (top), is the Alberta Public Health Institute.

Just south of the Varsity Rink is the tiny observatory of the university. This 12 ½-inch telescope, a gift from Mr. Wates, was a popular instrument on the campus after its opening in May, 1943, During the final stages of construction of the Jubilee Auditorium parking lot (1957-58), the telescope was moved south of the city beyond the interference of the multitude of city lights.

[September 9, 1948] **Continuing the streamlined style** set by the Studebaker car and the local T. Eaton's department store, Waterloo Motors erected this classy show room and garage at 107 Street and Jasper Avenue in 1946. In 1956, the company sold 2,600 cars to lead all dealers in North America. In June, 1975, the firm moved to its new location at 114 Street and 107 Avenue. This Jasper Avenue landmark was demolished in December, 1977.

[December 18, 1949] **The Edmonton Mercury Hockey Club,** sponsored by Waterloo Motors, gather around their coach, Jimmy Graham, in the centre.

In 1950, they represented Canada in the world title tournament at London, England. Competing against teams from the United States, Britain, Switzerland, Sweden and Norway, the Edmonton team scored 42 goals against 3 and came back with the 1950 world title. Two years later at Oslo, Norway, they captured the 1952 Olympic title, the last Canadian team to win the gold medal in Olympic hockey competition.

[March 14, 1950] **The Edmonton Flyers await** the start of another game before a capacity crowd at the Edmonton Gardens.

Under the successful coaching of Frank Currie and alert goaltending of Al Rollins, the team won the national Allan Cup in 1948. In 1955, the Flyers won the Western Canada Hockey League title under coach Bud Poile with such all-star personnel as 50-goal scorer Bronco Horvath, Vic Stasiuk, and Johnny Bucyk, who were later dubbed the "Uke Line" with the Boston Bruins. In goal was Glenn Hall, who later entered the National Hockey League Hall of Fame. In 1962, the team again won the W.C.H.L. title, but after a dismal season the following year, the Detroit Red Wings of the N.H.L. withdrew their sponsorship and pro hockey in Edmonton ended for several years.

[November 14, 1949] **The old Edmonton Exhibition Arena** in 1949 sported a new addition and a new name, the Edmonton Gardens. The four-storey addition to the western end of the old stock pavilion, costing a third of a million dollars, increased the seating capacity to over 7,700, thereby preparing the building for numerous other exciting sporting events in the years of the city's modern-day expansion during the 1950s and 1960s. Another million dollars worth of renovations in 1967, which reduced the seating to 5,200, prevented any closure and removal of this popular "sports palace".

Edmonton Gardens' visitors during those years included world champion figure skaters Sonja Henie, Karen Magnussen, Trixie Schuba, Janet Lynn, Barbara Wagner and Bob Paul, Otto and Marie Jelinek, world boxing champion Muhammad Ali and the legendary basketball team, the Harlem Globetrotters. In addition to sports events, other activities such as rodeos, circuses, concerts by bands, orchestras and singing stars and political rallies made the Gardens a popular social centre in the community.

[March 5, 1948] **Speedskater Pat Gunn** wins the Alberta senior women's title on the artificial ice of the Edmonton Gardens. That same day, Doreen McLeod won the intermediate ladies' championship.

Pat began her speedskating career in 1935, competing in local community league races. In 1956, she held the senior ladies' outdoor Alberta and Canadian titles and went on to win the North American indoor senior women's title by winning all four races. Before retiring in 1961, Mrs. Pat (Gunn) Underhill was three times Canadian senior women's speedskating champion. In 1971, she was inducted into Edmonton's Sports Hall of Fame.

Doreen McLeod started her speedskating career at the age of six and in 1947 won her first Canadian title in the junior girls' mass start class. That year also, the Canadian Track and Field Championships were held in Edmonton and Doreen, competing as a junior, scored the highest number of points in the meet. Concentrating primarily on speedskating after that, she later represented Canada in the Olympic Games of 1960 and 1964, and at some point in her career, Doreen held each of the Canadian women's speedskating records. In 1960, Mrs. Doreen (McLeod) Ryan was named Edmonton's Female Athlete-of-the-Year. Two years later, she was named Alberta's Woman Athlete-of-the-Year. She retired from competition in January, 1965.

[March 6, 1954] **On the ice of the Gardens**, hometown hero Matt Baldwin raises his broom in triumph as his team wins the 1954 national Macdonald Brier Curling Championship. With the Gardens filled to the rafters and 3,000 enthusiastic fans yelling "We want a slide!", the 27-year-old champion obliged by demonstrating his characteristic slide down the ice to deliver his last shot precisely on the button. The personable champion went on to win the national crown again in 1957 and for a third time in 1958. The "roaring game" had come a long way in Edmonton since the early days when local Scotsmen swept weighted kettles over the frozen surface of the North Saskatchewan River.

[August 15, 1950] **After a vigorous field workout,** the newly reorganized Edmonton Eskimo football team crowd together in their tiny dressing room under the Clarke Stadium stands to absorb the chalkboard tactics of coach and place-kicker, Annis Stukas.

Following two unsuccessful attempts to win the Grey Cup in 1921 and 1922, the Eskimo football team dropped out of senior ball in 1924. The team was revived in 1928 for four years and again in 1936, only to be disbanded at the outbreak of World War II. After Calgary's Grey Cup win in 1948, the Edmonton Eskimo team was reorganized for the 1949 season with Tiger Goldstick as trainer. In 1952, they made their first appearance in modern times in the Grey Cup final, losing to Toronto. In their next opportunity in 1954, they were successful.

[November 28, 1954] **The Eskimos won their first** Grey Cup in 1954 by defeating the heavily favoured Montreal Alouettes. To do it required the most famous play in Grey Cup history. With less than 3 minutes to play and losing 25-20, the Eskimos were on the defensive near their own goal line. Suddenly Montreal fumbled and Jackie Parker picked up the loose ball and ran 85 yards for the touchdown that tied the game. Tackle Bob Dean kicked the convert and the Eskimos won 26-25. To prove they were one of the greatest teams in Edmonton Eskimo history, they won the Grey Cup the next year and again in 1956, beating the same Alouettes 34-19 and 50-27. During those great years of the mid-fifties, Normie Kwong was selected as Canada's outstanding male athlete for 1955, Johnny Bright won the Schenley Award as the nation's most outstanding football player, and Parker won the Schenley Award three times.

[November 26, 1955] **Before the largest crowd** to see a football game in Canada up to that time (39,417), the Edmonton Eskimos challenge the powerful Montreal Alouettes in the Grey Cup final. Here the fleet-footed halfback Rollie Miles (98) receives a pass from quarterback Jackie Parker as Montreal defenders give chase. Like 1921 Eskimo captain Jimmy Enright, the multi-talented Miles was discovered while playing baseball on the northern prairies. He became the first black football player in Edmonton and went on to star on many outstanding Eskimo teams. Along with teammates Johnny Bright, Normie Kwong and Jackie Parker, he was inducted into Canada's Football Hall of Fame.

[October 2, 1947] **Outside the Capitol Pipe Shop** at 10063 Jasper Avenue, people tune their ears to the radio broadcast of the World Series. Although these annual autumn finals were played thousands of miles away, avid Edmonton baseball fans eagerly awaited the broadcasts, which began when CJCA celebrated its 10th anniversary in 1932 with a re-broadcast of the 1931 series. Before radio, baseball enthusiasts used to stand in front of the Empress Theatre where the progress of the World Series was posted on the huge bulletin board as results came in over the telegraph.

[July, 1949] **Breath-taking new rides** and provocative displays by worldfamous actress and dancer Gypsy Rose Lee help raise the temperatures of both the young boys and the old boys as crowds enjoy the warm summer evenings at the annual week-long Exhibition midway.

[June, 1943] **Young girls hang on firmly** as they enjoy the thrill of their first ferris-wheel ride at the midway. Every summer the Royal American Shows brought the world's largest midway through the prairies, bringing a once-a-year opportunity for daring adventure and sensational amusements.

[May 27, 1947] **Here on Jasper Avenue,** east from 97 Street, cars jostle with trolley buses and streetcars.

Streetcars rattled along Edmonton streets from November, 1908, until the city had completed the conversion to the quieter trolley buses on September 1, 1951. During this time, Edmonton had the distinction of having North America's most northerly electric streetcar system. By 1919, all of the original two-man (operator and conductor) cars were converted to one-man operation.

The first motor buses were put into service in 1932 on 102 Avenue between 124 and 142 Streets, to replace the single-track shuttle streetcar service. In September, 1939, Edmonton became the third city in Canada, following Montreal and Winnipeg, to institute trolley bus transportation. In 1964, Edmonton became the first city in Canada to purchase Japanese-built buses.

On October 10, 1941, the Edmonton Radial Railway and the Public Library introduced the world's first streetcar library. When streetcars ended their runs in 1951, this library service continued with two "Book-mobile" buses.

After the war, in 1946, the name of the system was changed from the Edmonton Radial Railway to the Edmonton Transportation System, and the following year another change gave it its present name, the Edmonton Transit System.

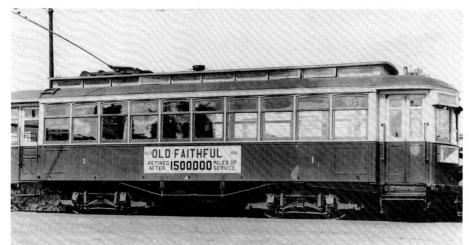

[September 1, 1951] **Streetcar No. 1 retires,** after 43 years of continuous service since November 9, 1908. Thirty years later, this car was again put into service for visitors at Fort Edmonton Park.

[1954] **Edmontonians' last look** at horses working regularly in the city streets was of the faithful plodders that pulled the early-morning milk delivery wagons. The last horse-drawn milk wagon made its final run on May 11, 1961.

[1953] **This Greyhound Bus Depot** at the northwest corner of 102 Street and 102 Avenue opened in June, 1949. The half-million-dollar terminal building of Indiana limestone continued to serve all four western Canadian bus lines until the new bus terminal was opened one block north in March, 1981.

The steady improvement of Alberta highways resulted in the emergence of buses as the chief means of inter-urban transportation, besides the private passenger car. The oldest of the motor coach companies is Greyhound Lines, which was formed with horse-drawn vehicles in 1914. The name Greyhound, which well described their sleek and trim grey buses, was established in 1922 by the Safety Motor Coach Lines, who made the first inter-city bus. The Greyhound company set up its prairie operation in May, 1929, when it inaugurated two daily runs between Calgary and Edmonton.

[August 10, 1956] **This sleek, efficient Railiner** at the old C.N.R. station at 100 Street and 104 Avenue was one of several of these units put into operation by the C.N.R. to compete with buses, private automobiles and airplanes. After about a quarter of a century, the competition proved too much and in April and May, 1977, these modern passenger "trains" made their last runs on the various rail lines which radiated from Edmonton.

To fill the need for better Edmonton to Calgary passenger transportation, Canada's third largest airline, Pacific Western Airlines, on May 22, 1963, inaugurated airbus service between the two Alberta cities, the first of its kind in Canada. In 1963, the service provided three daily flights for a fare of $11 one way. By 1981, service had increased to 19 flights a day at $50.95 one way.

[August 20, 1957] **Edmonton City Hall,** built at a cost of $3.5 million, was among the first of a wave of modern buildings to be erected after the war.

In 1913, the city administration, sitting in the "temporary" quarters of their newly completed Civic Block, had intentions of planning and building a proud civic centre and a new city hall worthy of their great city. Shortly thereafter, the boom ended, followed by the Depression and the austerity of two world wars, and the civic centre plans were continually postponed. Finally, on October 8, 1954, the city highlighted its golden anniversary celebrations with a site dedication and tree-planting ceremony for a new city hall at 100 Street and 103 Avenue. The following September, Mayor William Hawrelak unveiled the cornerstone as a highlight of the provincial jubilee celebrations, and on May 31, 1957, he formally opened the new city hall.

The nine-storey building features, on the outside, polished red Swedish granite and ivory-toned Italian travertine. Projecting on columns at the entrance is the 2,400-square-foot Council Chamber. On the inside, more travertine and green marble from Italy and slate flagstone from the central United States is featured. Inside the rotunda is a 4-by-14-foot cast aluminum mural designed by local artist Henry G. Glyde which depicts the builders of the Edmonton community from the days of the fort to the modern industrial age. The windows of the ninth-floor cafeteria afford a fine view of the downtown area.

[September 1, 1955] **The period which saw** the development of Edmonton into a progressive modern city coincided with the time William Hawrelak spent in public office as the mayor of the city he loved. After graduating from Victoria High School and then caring for the family farm for a few years, he returned to Edmonton in 1945 and became a successful businessman, a multi-millionaire and an energetic community worker.

When in 1951 he was first elected as mayor with a margin of victory considered the largest in Canada at that time, he brought to that office the youthfulness, vitality, ambition and administrative ability that the city required as it entered a decade of unprecedented growth. He won the next two elections by acclamation, setting a record that few, if any, other Canadian metropolitan mayors have matched. In 1959 and again in 1964, after his re-election in 1963, Mayor Hawreluk left his office after alleged involvements in land transactions. Although he twice lost his job as mayor, he never lost the popularity and support of many of the city's citizens. In 1974, he was again re-elected, for the fifth time, by the greatest mandate given a mayor of Edmonton up to that time.

In 1972, he was declared an honorary citizen of the province of Saskatchewan in

For the pool in front of the granite-faced Council Chamber, Lionel J. Thomas of Vancouver designed his $16,900 bronze fountain on the theme of the Canada goose, as a symbol of flight appropriate to Edmonton's position in the northern airlanes of the world. Edmontonians, not yet accustomed to abstract modern art, nicknamed the tubular sculpture "The

Spaghetti Tree" and composed a popular song about the work of art they couldn't understand.

In 1980, City Council held an architectural competition, won by ex-alderman Gene Dub, for a design to demolish this 25-year-old building in order to erect a much larger city hall at the same location.

recognition of his endeavors in promoting the Yellowhead Highway. He declined an offer from Prime Minister Louis St. Laurent for a cabinet post and when Prime Minister John Diefenbaker offered the opportunity to become the Canadian ambassador in Moscow, his answer was "No, my place is in Edmonton. . . . This is my city – this is where I want to serve."

After serving as mayor for over ten years, Mr. Hawrelak died while in office on November 7, 1975. Citizens showed their recognition and respect for this popular mayor at his funeral (which was attended by the entire provincial government) to the extent that the funeral cortege included more than 800 cars.

[c1957] **The Northern Alberta Jubilee** Auditorium, at 114 Street and 87 Avenue, was built to commemorate the fiftieth anniversary of the province of Alberta. The provincial government erected identical auditoriums in Edmonton and Calgary. These 2,695-seat concert halls, each costing $4 ½ million, were formally opened on April 28, 1957. Designed to provide a facility that could accommodate the widest possible range of presentations, including drama, vocal and instrumental performances and a host of other community assembly functions, the auditoriums featured one of the largest stages on the continent. The 120-foot-wide by 48-foot-deep stages could be increased to 65 feet in depth by covering the orchestra pit, which itself accommodated 75 musicians. Vermont and Italian marble and American black walnut decorate the lobbies, while the 50-foot-high, fan-shaped auditorium, which contains two balconies, is sheathed in French walnut.

The first public concert on April 29, 1957, opened with Beethoven's *Consecration of the House* overture and featured Edmonton-born concert violinist Betty Jean Hagen who played Brahms' Violin Concerto with the Edmonton Symphony Orchestra under local conductor Lee Hepner. Included in the opening week of entertainment was the Edmonton Civic Opera Society's presentation of Bizet's *Carmen*, under the direction and baton of Mrs. J.B. Carmichael.

[April, 1957] **The main lobby** of the Edmonton Jubilee Auditorium.

[1957] **The main auditorium** of the Edmonton Jubilee Auditorium.

[September 23, 1954] **The first open-air drive-in** movie theatre in Edmonton was the Starlight Drive-in at 156 Street and 87 Avenue, which could accommodate 1,000 cars and opened on June 6, 1949 with the film "Perils of Pauline". The Belmont Drive-in, shown here, located on the north bank of the river past the east end of the Fort Trail, opened on September 29, 1954, with what was believed to be the first curved screen in Alberta. That same year, the Twin Drive-in Theatre in Namao opened with one of the first screens constructed in Canada to accommodate wide screen pictures. Their screen measured 40 feet high by 100 wide, compared to the earlier Starlight screen of 45 by 57 feet, which was claimed to be the largest and highest in North America when it opened. With the wide panorama screens, piped-in car speakers, privacy for your own car party, and convenient snack-bar and restroom facilities, all for the price of a dollar a car, the drive-in theatres soon became a multi-million-dollar enterprise that easily outdrew live theatres and concert-hall production. By 1977, the city had ten of these open-air theatres, more than any other Canadian city. (Toronto had 6, Winnipeg 5, Saskatoon 4.) Edmonton had become the drive-in capital of Canada.

[December 7, 1954] **In this view looking northeast** over the Westmount shopping centre, the Bel-Air Apartments lie east of Groat Road and north of 114 Avenue. The $8 million Bel-Air Apartments, consisting of 25 apartment blocks in a landscaped setting, opened in 1954 and were among the first of many new multiple-dwelling buildings erected after the war to fill the growing need for residential facilities.

The open space in the background is the municipally owned Blatchford Field, called the Industrial Airport after 1957.

[August 20, 1957] **With traffic and parking** problems becoming more acute in the downtown area, merchants began to establish shopping centres in the suburbs, where more land was available for automobile-oriented consumers. The city's first shopping centre opened on August 18, 1955. Westmount Shoppers' Park, at 111 Avenue and Groat Road, was built at a cost of approximately five million dollars and provided parking for 3,000 cars. Forty one-storey stores and shops were assembled along its long, outdoor, uncovered sidewalk. At the north end, Woodward's Stores Ltd. occupied the only two-storey portion of the complex. In 1966, the centre was expanded and the entire sidewalk area was enclosed to provide an air-conditioned covered mall for the comfort and convenience of customers and merchants alike.

[February, 1956] **The cash registers jingle** and the check-out counters of Woodward's Westmount Food Floor bustle with activity as northwest residents adapt to the new style shopping carts. Before these four-wheeled grocery carts were adopted, shoppers had to use small wire arm baskets, and often a housewife with a large order would fill over two dozen of these small baskets. There weren't any cash registers either. The checkout girl used adding machines and gave the customer the paper tape on which was printed each price and the total. In the days before plastic credit cards, payment was made by cheque or usually by cash.

Another change, which occurred in the 1950s, was self-serve meats, which were pre-cut, pre-wrapped in cellophane and pre-priced. These various innovations in food marketing speeded up the shopping routine and provided more convenience for the all-important buyer.

10 Growing Up (1958 - 1970)

While the children of the post-World-War-II baby boom were growing up during the 1960s, the city of Edmonton was growing up with them. The city nearly doubled in area from 44 square miles in 1956 to over 85 square miles by 1967, while the population likewise nearly doubled from 226,000 in 1956 to over 436,000 in 1971, when the population of the metrpolitan area of Edmonton and its satellite communities combined was just under a half million.

A more visible sign of the city's rapid growth and expansion was seen in the dozens of new office buildings and hotels of concrete, steel, aluminum and glass, many of them skyscrapers that replaced the small old brick buildings of pre-World-War-I vintage. In the suburbs, more shopping centres, hotels, motels and trailer parks sprang up. And along the north bank of the river west of the Legislative Building, dozens of new high-rise apartments emerged, along with several more on the south river bank east of 109 Street. Building permit values increased from $72.5 million in 1958 to $136.7 million in 1970. By 1971 the city was attracting one new manufacturing plant every five and a half days.

This rapid growth both horizontally and vertically, as well as in numbers, was due partly to the increased national immigration, which peaked in 1957, and partly to the shift of many people from rural areas to the city. But it was mainly the continued development and export of the natural resources of Alberta and the North that created the affluence characteristic of the period. Following a decade of oil discoveries around Edmonton came continued discoveries in northern Alberta. By 1970, the number of oil wells in Alberta had doubled the 1957 total, and a similar increase occurred in the number of natural gas wells. By 1971, the huge Alberta Gas Trunk Line was ready to deliver natural gas to eastern and western Canadian markets and into California. Adding to this flurry of acitivity around Edmonton was the construction of the world's first commercial oil sands plant near Fort McMurray by Great Canadian Oil Sands Ltd. In 1967, production started in this new plant and began piping synthetic crude oil to the expanding Edmonton refineries. The development of the Pine Point lead and zinc mines led to an expansion of the Northern Alberta Railways in 1964 and resulted in more business for Edmontonians. Although rising inflation reduced the purchasing value of the dollar by one third, the per capita income doubled during the decade.

As the pace of the technological revolution quickened, and as the post-war babies grew up, educational facilities grew in importance and in size. The number of school children doubled in the decade and portable classrooms appeared beside most of the older schools. A similar doubling of the university population resulted in extensive expansion of facilities at the University of Alberta. During the sixties, several high-rise buildings gave a vertical accent to the old low-slung campus. The Northern Alberta Institute of Technology opened just east of the Industrial Airport and became in size, if not in the number of students, the largest polytechnical institute in Canada.

The continued expansion of Canada's northern frontier, and the increasing importance of Edmonton as the gateway to the north on the new international polar air route between Europe and North America resulted in the opening of the new International Airport near Leduc, and the return of Blatchford Field to national and private flights under the new name of the Industrial Airport. Modern bush pilot Max Ward, in 1961, acquired an international charter license and began flying Canadians around the world. To accommodate the increased traffic of over 150,000 cars and trucks, Edmonton, with Canada's highest vehicle-to-population ratio, had to construct more bridges over the river that divided the expanding city.

Similarly, in the 1960s the arts in Edmonton were beginning to flourish, expand and reach professional calibre. For years the Women's Musical Club's Celebrity Concerts had been bringing the world's best musical talent to the city and now other groups were joining in this endeavor. The Edmonton Professional Opera Association, formed in 1963, brought to local audiences some of the world's top performers. The Edmonton Symphony Orchestra, revived in 1952, was becoming fully professional and gaining increasing recognition across the country. In 1962, the Alberta Ballet Company was formed and in 1969 the new Edmonton Art Gallery opened and private galleries were beginning to spring up. Amateur theatre groups were thriving too, including the Walterdale Playhouse, the Yardbird Suite, Studio Theatre and the summer Torches Theatre. Edmonton's first professional theatre, the Citadel, opened in 1965, and was soon acclaimed one of the finest theatres in Canada. Culturally, economically and physically Edmonton was growing up during the sixties to become a cosmopolitan metropolis.

[June 14, 1960] **In June, 1960,** Jasper
Avenue east of 101 Street still had not
changed very much from the pre-war
years. A couple of small curtain-wall
buildings and the modern cinema marquee
are the only significant changes – except
for the cars, of course! The prosperous
fifties produced luxurious vehicles that
were longer, lower, faster and adorned
with fins and chrome. Since Edmonton
had one of the highest ratios of cars per
capita on the continent, traffic safety
needed promotion and to help achieve
this, a corps of traffic police on
motorcycles patrolled the streets.

[1962] **Television first came into** the lives of Edmontonians on Sunday, October 17, 1954, when Dick Rice's Sunwapta Broadcasting Company began broadcasting live on CFRN-TV, Channel 3. In hundreds of homes eager viewers turned on their brand new sets to see for the first time, in living black and white, some of their favorite entertainers: Burns & Allen, Amos 'n' Andy, Syd Caesar, Ed Sullivan, Lucille Ball, Roy Rogers, Jackie Gleason, "Our Miss Brooks", "The Plouffe Family", and "Disneyland".

In those early days of telecasting, there was no microwave link to bring network programs to our screens within a matter of seconds. Instead, programs were "kinescoped" by the CBC in Toronto and sent by air express to CFRN, then a CBC affiliate, for broadcasting at a later date. In the beginning, the station scheduled only forty hours of programs a week, signing on at 6:00 each weekday evening and at 3:30 on Sunday afternoons.

By 1957, the network's microwave link was ready and on October 5th local baseball fans were able to watch the World Series live for the first time. When Edmonton's second television channel, CBXT, came on the air as the new CBC

affiliate in 1961, CFRN gave up its CBC programming and joined the private CTV network. It was not until October 1, 1966, that network programs began to be telecast in color and it was 1970 before CFRN was able to produce its own programs and commercials in color. Cablevision arrived in 1971 and expanded the range of programs available until by 1976 all twelve channels were in use. Alberta's first independent station, CITV, began broadcasting in September, 1974.

[1962] **The studios of Alberta's first** television station, CFRN, are located on Edmonton's western outskirts in this building combining modern design with rustic adornments to reflect the Sunwapta Broadcasting Company's Stony Indian name meaning "rippling or radiating waves". This Indian theme was also incorporated in the Indian-head test pattern adopted by the station.

[March 10, 1970] **Mezzo soprano Huguette Tourangeau,** accompanied by the Edmonton Symphony Orchestra, was one of several French-Canadian stars who entertained at the official opening of CBXFT, Channel 11, Edmonton's new CBC French-language station which first went on the air on March 1st, 1970.

Channel 11, Edmonton's third TV channel, was unique in Canadian television history. The French network shared the channel with English-language educational programming provided by the Metropolitan Edmonton Educational Television Association (MEETA), making Channel 11 the first bilingual channel in Canada and MEETA the first non-commercial educational station in Canada to broadcast on a regular VHF channel. In 1973, however, MEETA became part of the Alberta Educational Communications Corporation (ACCESS) and Channel 11 became a full-time French-language station.

[August 17, 1964] **On August 17, 1964,** this mini-park at 100 Street and Jasper Avenue in front of the Macdonald Hotel was dedicated as a memorial to the Hon. Frank Oliver, who had once published Alberta's first newspaper, the *Bulletin,* in his little log printshop not far from this site. In appreciation of his relentless efforts to help Edmonton survive and thrive and in recognition of his significant contributions to the development and settlement of the Canadian West as federal Minister of the Interior, the Government of Canada and the City of Edmonton erected commemorative plaques to honor him as a person of national historic importance.

[August, 1966] **With peanuts roasted** in the shell and bags of popcorn neatly packaged, Austrian-born Sam Cherniak's pushcart is ready for the day's customers. This amiable entrepreneur started selling popcorn in 1938 and for well over a quarter century he and his cart were a popular and reliable feature along the sidewalks of 101 Street and 102 Avenue. The thousands of passersby appreciated his friendly smile as well as the flavour and fragrance of his tasty treats.

[November 27, 1952] **North America's only** self-appointed, unofficial town crier was Edmonton's own Pete Jamieson, a Scotsman who came to Alberta in 1913 at the age of five. His sidewalk advertising career began in 1935, when the desperate manager of the Dreamland Theatre, wanting to attract more customers, sent talkative Pete down the street with a placard. His booming voice and flair for the dramatic proved so successful that soon other businessmen were hiring "Sandwich-Board Pete" too. He continued his career as early morning sidewalk sweeper and town crier, always including the weather forecast and local news events in his barrage of information. He wore a different hat for every occasion and made his beat Jasper Avenue between the Alberta Hotel and the Cecil Hotel, where he could occasionally lubricate his vocal cords with a cool beer. With head held high behind an old Edmonton Eskimos megaphone, ramrod straight, shoulders back, chest out, Pete strutted the streets with a brisk marching stride that for nearly half a century was a tradition unique to Edmonton.

[1965] **In 1965, with the post-war** baby boom generation reaching university age, the University of Alberta was beginning a new growth spurt. The huge Math-Physics complex, the Cameron Library and a new Engineering wing (right to left), filled in much of the open space between the old Arts Building, in the foreground, and the original three student residences. Across 87 Avenue from the Jubilee Auditorium, a new Physical Education Building and arena replaced the old Varsity Rink and Drill Hall. Beside the Jubilee Auditorium, two (soon to be three) 11-storey student residences were built flanking the new

cafeteria in Lister Hall to accommodate the influx of students. The 10-storey Education Building on 87 Avenue began a new trend as high-rise buildings became the only solution to the space squeeze faced by the rapidly growing university. West of the campus (centre right), the Windsor Park subdivision is now well developed, while the Garneau district east of the campus is beginning to suffer the first encroachments of an expanding campus where the enrolment had lept from 3,565 full-time students and 228 faculty members in 1950 to 11,515 students and 850 faculty members in 1966.

[July, 1964] **In response to a pressing** need for qualified technicians and skilled tradesmen, the federal and provincial governments cooperated to finance construction of the Northern Alberta Institute of Technology on a 26-acre site next to the municipally owned Industrial Airport.

NAIT opened its doors to students in October, 1962, with 67 students in only one program, telecommunications. By the fall of 1963, when the institute first became fully operational, 300 qualified potential students had to be turned away because of a shortage of openings and

already expansion had to be considered. NAIT's success and popularity continued to far surpass expectations and by 1970 enrolment had reached the level originally estimated for 1980. Facilities were taxed to the limit and further expansion was planned. By 1980 NAIT had become one of the largest polytechnical institutes in Canada, with a 45-acre main campus, four satellite campuses and a staff of 1030 serving over 4,700 full-time students and an additional 32,000 part-time students and apprentices.

[January 14, 1970] **School designs and classrooms** were changing too. Round schools, windowless schools, portable classrooms and "open classrooms" had replaced the more traditional styles of bygone days. Tubular-steel desks have eased out the wooden desks of the forties and ink wells have long since disappeared. Amid this modern school in a modern suburb of a burgeoning modern city, these children of Athlone Elementary School enjoy the visit of an old-timer, Alberta's Lieutenant-Governor Grant MacEwan, to tell them about life in "the olden days".

[c1964] **The terminal building** of the Edmonton International Airport opened in February, 1964, and handled an average of 55 scheduled flights daily.

In front of the central tower, at the far left of the photo, a 60-foot stainless-steel revolving beacon, with sixteen spiral arms lit by natural gas flames, stands almost atop the Leduc oilfield that ushered in Alberta's age of prosperity. The beacon, designed by Montreal sculptor Norman Slater, was one of four works of art commissioned to decorate the new airport terminal.

In 1957, the federal Department of Transport began construction of a new Edmonton International Airport near Nisku, about 15 miles south of the city, clear of the air routes of the municipal and Namao airports and well away from the high-rise office towers that would soon begin to sprout in the downtown area. With jet aircraft going into service in 1958 and the shorter polar route now providing Edmontonians with direct flights to Europe, this new, larger facility was needed and in November, 1960, the majority of regularly scheduled flights switched from the municipal to the International airport, where a hangar acted as a temporary passenger terminal until February, 1964, when the glistening new glass and steel terminal was ready for use.

Designed by local architects Rensaa & Minsos, the terminal building consists of a three-storey passenger terminal and an eight-storey office tower housing a weather office, telecommunications centre and air traffic control centre--a far cry from the primitive landing fields that greeted the pioneering bush pilots forty years earlier.

Trans-Canada Air Lines (now Air Canada) started regular service to and from Edmonton in 1939 using Lockheed 14H2's that carried only fourteen passengers, but by 1964 they had graduated to 130-passenger DC-8's. Canadian Pacific Airlines was created in Edmonton in 1942 with the amalgamation of several small independent airlines established by various early bush pilots. In 1964, CPA still offered daily flights to Fort Smith, but since 1958 polar flights to Amsterdam were also featured several times a week. Wardair, another airline that began in Edmonton, was the largest charter carrier using the new airport, with flights into the Mackenzie River area as well as to Britain and western Europe.

[c1964] **Inside the ultra-modern** terminal building, in the main waiting area, is Vancouver artist Jack Shadbolt's controversial mural commemorating the daring bush pilots who pioneered navigation in the North and helped secure Edmonton's role as Gateway to the North.

[August, 1973] **This unusual view of** Coronation Park, at the intersection of 111 Avenue and 142 Street, shows the layout of footpaths emanating concentrically from the Queen Elizabeth Planetarium in the foreground. To the left are the Coronation Park sports facilities, including an arena, tennis courts, and the award-winning swimming pool.

The Queen Elizabeth Planetarium was named to commemorate the 1959 visit of Her Majesty Queen Elizabeth and HRH Prince Philip, when the Queen officially opened the park and planted a tree at the Planetarium site. When the Planetarium opened its doors in September, 1960, it became the first civic planetarium in Canada, but now its 24-foot dome and seating capacity of only 75 make it one of the smallest and a new Space Sciences Centre is being planned. Meanwhile, inside the domed Star Theatre, daily multimedia star shows take school children and astronomy buffs on fascinating trips to distant galaxies and mind-stretching journeys through time past and future.

[October 5, 1964] **With the opening of** Storyland Valley Zoo in 1959, Edmonton's youngsters eagerly crossed the drawbridge over the moat and passed through the castle gateway into a fairytale land where some of their favourite nursery rhyme characters and animal friends were waiting to amuse them. Some of their parents no doubt remembered happy childhood visits to the Borden Park zoo, a major local attraction after its opening in 1928, with a $200 grant from the city.

[n.d.] **Inside the palisade,** a miniature train takes its passengers on a quarter-mile tour of storyland where they may recognize Old MacDonald's Farm, the Indian village, the Bremen Town Musicians, Peter Pumpkineater, the old woman who lived in a shoe, and the Crooked House before entering the tunnel under Goat Mountain. Twangy melodies from the only authentic street organ in North America, a Centennial gift from Edmonton's Dutch community, add to the festive mood.

[July, 1963] **The fun of make-believe** extends to the adult population as well during the last two weeks of each July when Edmonton revives the excitement of the Klondike Gold Rush, which in 1898 jolted the town out of an economic slump and launched it firmly on the way to a prosperous and promising future.

The Klondike theme was first introduced for the 1962 Edmonton Exhibition in an effort to infuse the annual summer fair with new vitality and to encourage greater community participation. With considerable support from the business community, the idea caught on, and Klondike Days became an annual frolic rated among the ten best festivals in North America.

Townsfolk and shopkeepers dress in the finery of saloon gamblers and dance hall queens, businesses put on false storefronts to recapture the look of boom town '98, honky-tonk pianos and barbershop quartets serenade shoppers, a stagecoach escorted by a posse of trigger-happy out-riders brings the winner of the Bonanza gate prize to the bank to deposit his bundle of silver dollars, a flotilla of fanciful rafts (reminiscent of the inventive craft of the original Klondikers) race down the river, and beard-growing contests, beer-tray races, and melodramas add to the fun.

The Exhibition Grounds offer an additional 90-acre feast for funseekers: Raffles offer the chance to strike it rich by winning a car, a holiday, a dream home, or a gold brick. The Chilkoot Mine offers the would-be prospector the chance to try his hand at gold panning and he can have his take appraised by government assayers. Then he may gamble his poke away at the Golden Garter Casino, bet it on the horses at the Northlands race track, or simply, choose to tour the exhibits and watch the free entertainment at the Coliseum until the nightly fireworks signal the close of another Klondike day.

[July 20, 1967] **A very special Klondike Mike** joined in the fun in 1967. Prime Minister Lester Pearson and his wife Maryon were in town to officially open the festival in Canada's Centennial year and to ride at the head of the parade in a vintage Rolls Royce.

[July 20, 1967] **Thousands of people packed** the sidewalks and perched on the rooftops along Jasper Avenue to view the annual parade of floats, marching bands and majorettes that marked the beginning of Klondike Days in 1967 and also paid tribute to Canada's 100th birthday.

[July 31, 1971] **For many years** the Royal American Shows' mile-long midway attracted thrillseekers to the Exhibition Grounds to sample the spine-chilling rides and exotic sideshows and to meander amid the smell of cotton candy, popcorn and hot dogs, the shouting of carnival barkers, and the visual cacophony of bright colours and flashing lights.

[July 1, 1967] **For Edmonton's salute** to Canada's 100th birthday on July 1st, 1967, about 5,000 celebrators thronged into Sir Winston Churchill Square to enjoy the entertainment and a piece of the city's 1,600-pound Centennial birthday cake, baked by the apprentice bakers at NAIT.

Fireworks, balloons, community "coming-out parties", carillon music, military bands, ethnic costumes and dances, parades, speeches, choral singing, an RCAF fly-past and a 101-gun salute were all part of the fun of Edmonton's Centennial festivities, but there were more lasting contributions as well. The provincial government began work on the Provincial Museum and Archives, the City opened the new Centennial Library, the Kinsmen Club commenced its fieldhouse, and the Rotary Club helped initiate the reconstruction of Fort Edmonton, to name but a few of the many significant projects undertaken to celebrate Canada's 100-year history.

[September 29, 1965] **Edmonton's skyline was indeed** growing up by 1965 and the Macdonald Hotel no longer stands out as the lone sentinel on the river bank as the replica sternwheeler *Little Klondike Queen* takes its cargo of tourists on a nostalgic tour along the old fur-trade highway.

[June 9, 1966] **In this aerial view** looking north from the 105 Street traffic circle in June, 1966, the city's earliest high-rise towers add a bold new relief to the texture of the city while at the left the Legislative Building and the new Terrace Building, curving along the brow of the hill above River Valley Road, remain unchanged. Improved roadways in the flats help traffic avoid downtown congestion.

[June 20, 1967] **In 1962, Mayor Elmer Roper** and City Council approved plans for a refurbished civic centre to revitalize a decaying city core and by Canada's Centennial year progress was well underway. Behind City Hall the new CN Tower rises 27 storeys above 100 Street and dominates the skyline. To its right is the new post office, and to its left are the 24-storey Avord Arms apartment building and the 19-storey Centennial Building which tower over the Land Titles Building and the old Court House. In front of City Hall is the new Sir Winston Churchill Square. On its southern edge, a spacious new public library, built on the site of the old farmers' market, is the City's tribute to Canada's Centennial. Just south of the library, the proud tower of the old post office enjoys its last days of glory. Facing Churchill Square on the east, Chancery Hall provides a new backdrop for the renovated facade of the police station which disguises the original 1913 Civic Block. In the foreground, just east of the Macdonald Hotel, Thornton Court balances on the cliff edge and towers over a tiny street on its west side once reported by Ripley's *Believe It or Not* to be the shortest street in the world.

216

[October 18, 1968] **In the Council Chamber** of City Hall, the newly elected aldermen of the 1968-71 Council concentrate on the increasingly more difficult business of administrating one of the continent's most rapidly growing cities.

[July 28, 1973] **The CN Tower replaced** the former C.N.R. station in 1966 and in turn replaced the "grand hall" concept of earlier railway stations with the streamlined efficiency and glossy plastic functionalism of the second half of the twentieth century.

[1965] **On the evening of November 10,** 1965, Edmonton's first resident professional theatre opened with a production of Edward Albee's *Who's Afraid of Virginia Woolf?* in the remodelled Salvation Army Citadel on 102 Street south of Jasper Avenue. The impetus for bringing professional theatre to Edmonton came from The Citadel's founder and first president and executive producer, Joe Shoctor, a local lawyer with an unquenchable love for the theatre, experience in producing plays on Broadway, and unshakable faith in the ability of Edmontonians to finance and support a professional theatre. Edmonton audiences were quick to justify his faith and to welcome this major achievement in the city's artistic life.

The Citadel soon established a reputation as one of Canada's major theatres and expanded steadily, adding drama workshops, a touring company (The Citadel-on-Wheels), lunch-time specials, and a second stage (Citadel Too) for more innovative productions. Performances were practically sold out with season's tickets alone and the intimate 275-seat theatre could not accommodate the demand for seats. So Joe Shoctor and his backers launched another campaign to plan and finance a new home for The Citadel.

[March, 1970] **With the help of scholarships** from the local musical societies and service clubs, the very gifted Edmontonian, Marek Jablonski, became a world-acclaimed concert pianist.

Born in Poland in 1939, he began picking out tunes on the piano by ear at the age of four and at age six began his formal training at the Krakow Conservatory. During the War, his family lost their possessions and when they moved to Edmonton in 1949, he had to practice on a neighbor's piano. His exceptional talent was soon recognized,

though. In 1951, he received the first scholarship offered by the Women's Musical Club and in 1952 the Active Club presented him with a piano. He continued to win top marks in music festivals and

won scholarships to spend his summers studying at the Banff School of Fine Arts. In 1955, he auditioned for Arthur Rubinstein and in 1957 he won a scholarship to the summer school at Aspen, Colorado, where he met Mme Rosina Lhevinne who invited him to become her pupil at the Juilliard School of Music in New York. Just to be on the safe side, though, he also studied toward a degree in Science!

In 1961, at age 21, he won the $1000 Lhevinne Award at Juilliard and the Jeunesses Musicales of Canada Grand Prize, which included radio and TV performances and concert tours of Canada and Europe as well a debuts in New York and Paris. During these tours he received international acclaim and his career as a concert pianist was firmly established. Concert tours of Canada, the United States, the Soviet Union and South America are now a way of life for him and for the Edmonton girl he married. When he returns to Edmonton periodically to give a recital or as guest soloist with the Symphony, his masterful performances are warmly received by proud Edmontonians who witnessed the early triumphs in his brilliant career.

[September 28, 1968] **Spread out over 300 acres** west of 127 Street and 137 Avenue is Edmonton International Speedway, one of the most complete motorcar racing tracks in Canada. The facility, which opened in May, 1967, featured a two-mile sports car circuit and a quarter-mile banked oval. In its heyday, the complex housed almost every major stock car race in addition to drag racing and the racing of Formula A and Group 7 cars. Despite the postponement of many races due to fickle summer rainstorms, auto-racing rapidly grew to be the second-largest spectator sport in the city, second only to football.

Automobile racing was often seen at the Exhibition Ground race track in the 1920s, when Alex Sloan used to tour the west on half-mile dirt tracks. After about a twenty-year absence, during the Depression and the War, auto racing was revived at the Exhibition track in 1949.

Soon after, in 1951, stock car racing got its start in Edmonton when Gavin Breckenridge and Oscar Green built Breckenridge Speedway. A few years later, the four Booth brothers started the original Speedway Park with a quarter-mile dirt oval. The success and popularity of auto racing rapidly increased and about ten years later they built the new, enlarged version of Speedway Park so that international races could be held in Edmonton. The new facility held several seasons of races in the Can-Am series for Group 7 cars and also held races in the world championship drag racing series. The last major auto race was held in 1973. Eight years later, wealthy city sportsman Peter Pocklington revived the Can-Am race here in 1981.

[June 20, 1970] **This is the view** from the Sky Paddock of the Northlands lounge atop the renovated Exhibition grandstand. In 1963, the Edmonton Exhibition Association enclosed this upper part of the race track grandstand so well-heeled patrons could watch their favourites in all kinds of weather within the comfort of this spacious lounge. That year, too, the grandstand was renamed Northlands, and in 1967 the association began to call its entire operation Edmonton Northlands.

The association could well afford the new look. For years Edmonton horse-racing enthusiasts had filled the Exhibition coffers well. In recent years local bettors wagered, on the average, over $100 per person per day at the race track. In 1978, they wagered $73 million, producing a $330,000 profit for Northlands and $730,000 in provincial taxes. During the 168 days of thoroughbred and harness racing, local bettors wagered over $102.7 million.

Surprisingly, one of the few enterprises keeping ahead of inflation is gambling on the horses at Northlands. In 1980, the per person amount spent at the mutuals averaged over $137, and during the 24-day spring harness meet of 1981 the average increased to $147, rated by some observers as the highest on the continent. Because of these high per capita betting statistics, Edmonton lays claim to the title of the gambling centre of North America.

[July, 1970] **The remarkable Swimming Smiths** are the children of U. of A. physical education professor Dr. Donald Smith and his wife Gwen, who is also a University of Toronto graduate in physical education. Their eight phenomenal swimmers are, from the top, George, Susan, Sandra, Graham, Lewis, Alison, Becky and Scott. All eight children reached at least the nationl level in competitive swimming, and five competed internationally, taking part in three different Olympics. (It would have been four if Canada had participated in the Moscow Olympics in 1980).

The family's incredible climb to Olympian heights began modestly in 1960 when eldest son George, at age 10, became the first Albertan ever to break a national age-class record. He continued to earn recognition and in 1967 competed, along with his sister Sandra, in the Pan-American Games in Winnipeg. The next year, Don was along as team manager when George placed a highly respectable fifth in the 200-metre individual medley at the Olympics in Mexico City. It was

Susan's year for glory in 1969 when she became the first of the Smiths to be named Edmonton's Athlete of the Year. In 1970 the family was off to the Commonwealth Games in Edinburgh where Don coached the Canadian swim team, including George, Susan, and Sandra, and savoured his son's triumphs as George won two gold and two silver medals. The following June, however, a near-fatal motorcycle crash ended George's competitive swimming career and left sisters Susan and Sandra to compete in the Pan-Am Games in Cali, Colombia.

Then it was Susan's turn for the Olympics in Munich in 1972, before little Becky, despite an allergy to chlorine, burst onto the international scene in 1973 at age 14 after winning five golds and a silver at the Canadian Summer Games and a gold and two silvers in her first major international competition at the Commonwealth Games in Christchurch, New Zealand, in January, 1974. These victories led her to become the second Smith to be named Edmonton's Athlete of the Year. In addition, both Don and Becky were inducted into Alberta's amateur Sports Hall of Fame, where they were joined in 1975 by George.

The Montreal Olympics were a time of triumph and tragedy for the family as Graham and Becky succeeded in winning the family's first Olympic medals as a last tribute to their father who was dying of cancer. Graham won a silver as part of the relay team, while Becky won two bronze medals (with Edmonton's Cheryl Gibson beating her for the silver in the 400-metre individual medley).

The next year, Graham set a world record in the 200-metre individual medley at the national championships before going on to win two golds and one silver at the World Student Games in Sofia, Bulgaria. But Graham's best year was 1978. At the Commonwealth Games in Edmonton, swimming in the pool dedicated to their father, Becky chalked up another silver medal and Graham became the first athlete in the 48-year history of the Games to win six gold medals. From this triumph, he went on to even greater victories at the World Aquatic Championships in West Berlin, where he set a new world record and became the first Canadian swimmer ever to win both a gold and silver in the world championships. As a result of these feats, he was voted Canadian male athlete of the year and co-winner (with Calgary skier Ken Read) of the Lou Marsh Award as outstanding athlete of the year and he was named to the Order of Canada.

What a remarkable record of achievement by a truly remarkable family!

[July 9, 1970] **Sizzling summer temperatures** combined with disagreeably high humidity are sometimes the ingredients for spectacular thunder and lightning displays and torrential rains that can douse the city with as much as two inches of rain in a couple of hours, swamping the sewers and converting streets into Venetian canals. That's what happened to 118 Avenue on July 9, 1970, when over one and a half inches of rain drenched the city in less than an hour leaving up to three feet of water on parts of the avenue. Basements flooded, transformers blew throwing large areas of the city into darkness and putting traffic lights out of operation, underpasses filled with up to eight feet of water, some streets caved in, trolley wires broke, cars stalled, and wet brakes and poor visibility led to accidents.

A similar storm on July 16, 1949, claimed two lives when a taxi plunged into four feet of water covering a country road just south of the city. On that occasion, over a half-inch of rain fell in ten minutes at the peak of the two-hour storm. The rainiest day in Edmonton's recorded history occurred on July 31, 1953, when 4 ½ inches fell on the city in a 24-hour period.

[August 12, 1970] **When the Southgate Shopping Centre** opened on this date at 111 Street and 51 Avenue, it was the largest shopping centre west of Toronto and marked the first time in Canada that two of the nation's largest merchandising companies, Woodward's and the Hudson's Bay Company, combined to produce a shopping complex. At Southgate, the Bay made history on the 300th anniversary of its company, by opening its first suburban store, whereas for Woodward's and Johnstone Walker's, it was their fourth local outlet.

The $25 million complex was designed by a consortium of some of Edmonton's finest contemporary architects, Don Bittorf, Peter Hemingway, Don Pinckston and James Wensley. The central feature of the 600-foot-long mall is this pool with fountains programmed to leap to a height of 25 feet accompanied by a sequence of coloured lighting effects. Outside, the 40-acre site offered parking for 3,500 cars, until the complex was enlarged in 1981.

11 Metropolis (1971-1981)

The 1970s saw Edmonton begin to emerge as a major world energy centre. Soon after Peter Lougheed formed Alberta's first Conservative government in 1971, he instituted large increases in oil royalties, so that in two years the provincial net oil and gas revenues doubled to over $500 million per year. Then the OPEC countries substantially increased world oil prices, and suddenly Alberta's petroleum reserves increased dramatically in value. During the decade, synthetic crude oil began to be extracted from vast Athabasca Tar Sands, and Edmonton refineries again had to expand. The spiralling demands for energy and the realization that the world's petroleum reserves would rapidly diminish caused Alberta's vast coal reserves to take on increased importance. With Alberta possessing over 85 percent of Canada's sources of fossil energy, Edmonton was now not only the oil capital of Canada, but also the centre of Canada's entire energy empire.

Concurrently, Alberta's largest electric power station, located 25 miles west of Edmonton, and Edmonton Power's new 800-megawatt Genesee power plant (scheduled to open in 1987) were increasing the demands for the world's second largest coal reserves in the foothills of western Alberta. With all these developments of Alberta's energy resources occurring, in addition to the expansion of the forestry industry caused by the spiralling demands for paper, it was not surprising that Edmonton, located at the centre of all this activity, would experience significant growth and change.

During the decade, Edmonton's metropolitan population increased from 496,000 in 1971 to 665,000 by 1980, and was expected to double by the year 2000. In 1981, Edmonton, with a city area of over 120 square miles, annexed another 134 square miles, making Edmonton larger in area than any other major city in Canada.

The seventies were a period of extensive construction activity in Edmonton. Between 1971 and 1979, twenty-six new office buildings were added to the downtown area. Earlier in the decade, the AGT Tower, the Imperial Oil Building, Edmonton House, the twin towers of Petroleum Plaza and the four towers of Edmonton Centre emerged, and later, in 1979, high rise office towers sprang up like mushrooms in the downtown area. In 1978, the value of building permits in the metropolitan region surpassed the one billion dollar mark. During the decade, the high-rise apartment building boom continued, with several designed for senior citizens. Several large shopping centres opened, with two more, including Canada's largest, scheduled for opening in 1981. At Canada's third largest university, where enrolment peaked at over 20,000 full-time students in 1976, many new buildings appeared, including the block-long HUB mall, and construction began on an over $200 million ultra-modern health sciences centre. The opening of the Northlands Coliseum, Muttart Conservatory and Citadel Theatre added excellent new public facilities. East of the Macdonald Hotel, more of the city's early buildings were removed to allow the construction of the controversial convention centre, which will house Canada's Aviation Hall of Fame.

The rapid and extensive redevelopment of the older regions of the city led to the realization that, as block after block of the old city was being demolished, Edmonton was quickly losing its architectural heritage. Fortunately, a few of the city's old buildings were preserved, including several commercial and residential structures in old Strathcona, Rutherford House, St. Stephen's College and the old student residences at the university, and the Le Marchand Mansion and McLean Block north of the river. The revival of interest in Edmonton's past also resulted in the construction of Fort Edmonton Park.

Continuing to expand its important role as a transportation centre, Edmonton opened a new terminal building at the Industrial Airport, and the three-fold increase in the number of passengers using the new International Airport south of the city resulted in extensive expansion plans for that facility. Within the city, more freeways were constructed and in 1978 the Light Rail Transit line opened.

Leading other Canadian cities, Edmonton became the first to put into operation a commercial fibre optics telephone system, and the only city in North America to develop its own resource development research park facilities. In addition, North America's largest central park opened in 1978 along the river banks. And to show the world that Edmonton was of world-class stature, in 1978 the city staged the very successful Commonwealth Games, attended by Queen Elizabeth II.

With a large affluent population and excellent mass entertainment facilities, Edmonton became one of the continent's major stopping points for popular and rock music performers, such as ABBA and Rod Stewart, who each started their North American tour here. The large Northlands Coliseum enabled Edmonton to set North American attendance records for professional hockey, to win a North American indoor professional soccer championship and to stage indoor track meets that produced several Canadian and world records. In several other sports, Edmontonians achieved standards of international excellence.

Playing its role as the gateway to the north, the crossroads of the world, the oil capital of Canada, and the centre of Canada's energy empire, Edmonton expects to experience many more years of growth. But Edmontonians must beware of over-confidence. Their past history shows that future events on the local and world scene can dramatically change a boom into a bust. But while the good times last, this expanding metropolis on the banks of the North Saskatchewan River is sure to increase in world prominence.

[June, 1971] **At the left,** the cylindrical towers of the 45-storey Edmonton House, the city's tallest building, and of the Chateau Lacombe Hotel add distinctive landmarks to the river bank. The Chateau's revolving restaurant on the 24th floor offers a spectacular view of the river valley and of the city spreading out for miles around its base. In the centre, the prominent, white AGT Tower, which opened in 1971, rises 33 storeys to a record height of 441 feet. It towers over the new Edmonton Club, on the site that once held Matt McCauley's livery stable, and dwarfs the Macdonald Hotel that for so long dominated the skyline. Above the Macdonald, just behind Chancery Hall, the unique shape of the new Law Courts Building adds variety to the civic centre. Thornton Court stands on the high bank just to the right of the Macdonald Hotel. In the right foreground, the James Macdonald bridge is under construction and a network of freeways crisscross one another at the approach to the Low Level Bridge.

[September, 1971] **In this view of the downtown** skyline seen from the east, a few impressive high-rise office towers and several apartment buildings dominate the city-scape. Immediately behind the old chateau landmark looms the Alberta Government Telephones Building and the adjacent 24-storey Imperial Oil Building. To their left is the cylindrical tower of the C.P.R. hotel, the Chateau Lacombe, and the slightly higher apartment and office building called Edmonton House. The two prominent buildings on the skyline at the right are the A.G.T. Toll building and, at the extreme right, the Centennial Building.

[September 16, 1974] **In just a few years,** the skyline filled with many high-rise office towers and apartment buildings. The tall buildings which appear from right to left are: the CN Tower, the Law Courts Building, Centennial Building, Century Place under construction with the first Edmonton Centre Tower behind, the A.G.T. Toll Building, Plaza Hotel (renamed the Westin Hotel in 1981), Cambridge Building, Macdonald Place office and apartment complex blocking the view of the Imperial Oil Building, the A.G.T. Tower, the Chateau Lacombe, Edmonton House and several apartment buildings striving to catch a view of the impressive river valley parkland.

[June 3, 1971] **In this view looking southwest** over Rossdale, the James Macdonald Bridge and its sprawling roadways dwarf the nearby Low Level Bridge.

To help solve the steadily increasing traffic problems in the river valley, in 1970-71 the city constructed the James Macdonald Bridge just south of Edmonton's first bridge, the Low Level. This new 1,180-foot-long, six-lane bridge, which opened on October 4, 1971, is named after University of Alberta civil engineering graduate, James Macdonald, who was appointed city engineer in 1949 and died in 1966. When he began working for the city in 1923, there were only four bridges across the North Saskatchewan River at Edmonton, three of which are seen in this photo. They were the Low Level, completed in 1900 and twinned in 1949, the Dawson, built in 1912, the 105 Street and the High Level, both completed in 1913. Engineer James Macdonald had a hand in the next five which opened: the Clover Bar Bridge in 1952, Groat in 1955, Quesnell in 1968, Capilano in 1969, and the James Macdonald in 1971. In 1972, the local engineering firm T. Lamb, McManus and Associates, Ltd., received the Award of Merit from the Association of Consulting Engineers in Canada for the design of this $9,355,000 James Macdonald Bridge.

[August 4, 1973] **On the northeast corner** of 101 Street and Jasper Avenue stands the new Empire Building and to its right is the 18-storey Cambridge Building.

In January, 1962, McDougall & Secord's original four-storey Empire Block, which stood on this corner since 1905, was demolished to make way for this $2.5 million, 11-storey office building. The building is faced with 8-by-12-foot slabs of grey Minnesota granite that project no more than one and one-half inches. This minimal projection was requested by the owners, McDougall & Secord Ltd., who wanted to eliminate their previous problems with pigeons roosting and "decorating" the facade. When the building opened on June 12, 1963, the office spaces rented at a rate of $5.35 per square foot, including maintenance and janitorial services. Although the owners desired a tall building that would be fairly imposing, city and Department of Transport regulations at that time would not permit anything higher than this 11-storey tower.

The remaining buildings in this downtown block were demolished late in 1980 to allow the construction of the huge Scotia Place complex.

[August 12, 1973] **The new City Market,** located at 97 Street and 102 Avenue, now carries on all its business indoors.

In the spring of 1965, the $293,000 market opened and allowed for the clearing of Sir Winston Churchill Park and the construction of the new public library. When the new market opened, farmers' produce sold at the following prices: small bunches of beets and carrots at 10¢ each, two large bunches of onions for 25¢, vegetable marrow and zucchini squash at 15¢ a pound, 2 pounds of pickling cucumbers for 25¢, beans and peas at 20 and 25¢ per pound respectively, 4 pounds of potatoes for 25¢ or 100-pound sacks of potatoes for $4, and large cobs of corn at 5¢ each. The busiest day is Saturday and the hustle of activity begins very early in the morning.

[August 16, 1972] **When it opened on August 16,** 1972, the $22 million Londonderry Mall shopping centre at 66 Street and 137 Avenue was again the largest west of Toronto. The complex accommodated three major department stores, a food store, two movie theatres and about 80 shops and boutiques. The 500-foot-long mall was the first two-level mall built in Western Canada. The 52-acre site was arranged to accommodate 3,500 cars. In 1980, new owners announced a proposed $15 million expansion to the Londonderry Mall.

The original owners, Western Realty Projects Ltd., had previously constructed western Canada's first covered regional shopping centre, the $4 million Meadowlark Park Shopping Centre, which opened on September 26, 1963.

In August, 1980, construction began on what is believed to be Canada's largest shopping centre, the West Edmonton Mall at 87 Avenue west of 170 Street, constructed at a projected cost of over $200 million. When phase two is completed, the complex will contain over 2 million square feet of retail services, including four major department stores, six movie theatres, and over 440 shops and boutiques, plus a medical centre and year-round recreational centre. With more than 100 clothing stores, the new mall will contain the largest collection of high-fashion stores in North America under one roof.

[August 10, 1972] **Old-timers watch** the demolition of the old Court House and ponder the metamorphosis of the downtown area, as towering skyscrapers replace the grand, but diminutive, landmarks of the pre-World-War-I boom period. Here the old buildings give way to the Edmonton Centre development. This was the first of several projects constructed in the 1970s, which saw entire city blocks demolished to make way for the rapid expansion of the metropolis.

[April 26, 1974] **This is downtown Edmonton** looking northwest toward the new Edmonton Centre complex located on the west side of Sir Winston Churchill Square.

The first phase of the Edmonton Centre complex, shown here, opened on May 1, 1974. This phase, costing $40 million, included the 20-storey Royal Trust Tower,

the new 5-storey Woodward's store, and a 900-car parking garage to the north. This was the first major downtown retail development in Edmonton since the completion of the T. Eaton's department store in 1939.

On October 28, 1975, the second phase opened and featured the spacious 65-foot-high indoor "Garden Court" surrounded by three floors of shopping mall containing 100 boutiques. also included in phase two, but opened in August, 1976, was the 30-storey Toronto Dominion Tower, located just northeast of the 20-storey Royal Trust Tower. When the first and second phases were completed at a cost of $65 million, it was estimated that Edmontonians would spend up to $75 million annually at Edmonton Centre.

Phase three concluded with the opening of the 320-room, 27-storey Four Seasons Hotel on May 31, 1978, and the adjacent 25-storey Oxford Tower later that year. In 1979 plans were announced for three more towers to be located in the block just west of the Four Seasons Hotel on 101 Street.

[May 2, 1975] **After four years of construction,** costing nearly $65 million, the northeast portion of the Light Rail Transit opened. "Light" refers to the reduced capacity, speed and weight of cars in comparison with the "heavy" systems used in Toronto and Montreal. When the first stage officially opened on April 22, 1978, the system became the first LRT system in North America and only the third rapid transit system in Canada. Edmonton also had the distinction of being one of the few cities of the world, if not the only one, with a population of a half million to have a rapid transit system.

The construction attracted engineers from many parts of the world to observe the methods used to build the mile-long, 45-foot-deep underground portion with a minimum of traffic interruption on Jasper Avenue. First a series of concrete piles were poured along each side of the street. Then huge horizontal beams were built on the piles and precast concrete bridge

girders were set in place across the street to form the roof. Then the 45-foot excavation proceeded without interrupting the normal street traffic along Jasper Avenue. In addition, twin 700-foot-long tunnels were hollowed out between the Central and Churchill Stations.

During its first year of operation, the LRT gave over six million rides. The highest single-day passenger load was on

August 8, 1978, when over 69,000 persons rode the trains to Commonwealth Games events.

In October, 1980, the next one-mile, three-station extention west to the Legislative Buildings began. This $100 million addition was scheduled for opening in 1984. Meanwhile, in April, 1981, the $6 million northeast extension to Clareview opened.

[October 1, 1977] **This new LRT train** stands in Central Station ready for its test run on the new line. It took the two-car electrically powered trains only twelve minutes to make the 4-1/2-mile trip from the Jasper Avenue and 101 Street station to the original northeast terminus at 129 Avenue and Fort Road, pausing only about 40 seconds at each of the three intermediate stops (Churchill Square, Commonwealth Stadium and Northlands Coliseum).

[August 3, 1978] **Over 42,000 spectators** and television viewers around the world watched the opening of the Commonwealth Games on August 3, 1978. The staging of "the Friendly Games" was one of the outstanding success stories in the history of Edmonton. The official song of the games, composed by Edmonton's Tommy Banks, was appropriately titled "We're Gonna Show the World". The determination and hard work of a few enterprising Edmonton boosters who initiated the idea was soon well supported by the community. As a result of good organization, cooperation, and energetic help from over 10,000 volunteers, Edmonton enjoyed one of the most successful and exciting events ever held in the city.

With the federal and provincial governments each matching the city's $12 million contribution, the city's populace gained many fine facilities, including the stadium, velodrome, aquatic centre, lawn bowls and shooting range. Another facility that was rushed to completion before the games was the LRT line.

Several of Edmonton's world-class athletes achieved personal success in the games. Graham Smith and Cheryl Gibson in swimming and Diane Jones-Konihowski in track and field set Commonwealth Games records in winning their events, while John Primrose took the gold medal in trapshooting.

Beautiful weather, a visit from the Queen and Prince Philip and their sons for the opening days, the entertaining and colourful opening and closing ceremonies, and the warm friendship from people from around the world all made this ten-day event a happy and memorable one for Edmonton's half-million residents.

[September 10, 1978] **In order to host** the Commonwealth Games, the city had to construct the LRT line and several new sports facilities, the largest of which was this stadium. Just beyond Commonwealth Stadium, in this view looking northwest, is the LRT station. Further back in the distance is Northlands track and fair grounds, with the verdant Borden Park to the south. At the bottom right corner lies Clarke Stadium, while at the opposite corner along the LRT line is the cylindrical Northlands Coliseum.

The stadium was completed in October, 1977, within the $21 million budget. The official opening of the 42,500-seat stadium took place on July 15, 1978. The field, of natural turf, lies 35 feet below street level. Suspended 100 feet above the field is the seven-ton speaker cylinder, which gives living-room sound to all parts of the stadium.

This photograph was taken during the first Sunday afternoon football game played in the stadium after the Commonwealth Games. While the Eskimos played the Calgary Stampeders, the very limited parking facilities were filled with buses which, in addition to the LRT, provided transportation for the over 42,000 fans attending the game.

[c1978] **North of the Edmonton Gardens** and the broad pedestrian overpass across 118 Avenue is the Northlands Coliseum at 73 Street. The building in the left foreground is the Sales Pavilion; the Sportex Building can be seen on the extreme right.

With the Commonwealth Games and the World Hockey Association (WHA) coming to Edmonton in the 1970s, it became clear to the Edmonton Exhibition Association that they would have to build a large new sports complex to replace the 60-year-old Gardens. On November 10, 1974, after just 20 months of construction, the new $15 million Edmonton Coliseum (now Northlands Coliseum) was ready for its first hockey game between the Edmonton Oilers and the Cleveland Crusaders of the WHA. This spacious building, with a height of 80 feet from ice surface to the domed roof, could seat 15,326 spectators for professional hockey and 17,326 for stage performances during which 1,600 ice level seats could be added.

In March, 1975, a Canadian indoor rodeo attendance record was set when over 73,000 people came to see the world's champion cowboys in "Superrodeo '75". This made Edmonton the third largest rodeo city in the world. After eight months of use and the completion of construction, the Coliseum was officially opened with a day-long series of entertainment on July 1, 1975. After the merger of the WHA with the National Hockey League in 1979, constant sell-out crowds for hockey necessitated the installation of additional seats in the highest levels of the five-tier building.

[1971] **When the Detroit Red Wings** organization withdrew its sponsorship of the Edmonton Flyers hockey team in 1963, professional hockey in Edmonton came to a temporary end. In its place, the junior team, the Edmonton Oil Kings (shown here in the Edmonton Gardens) began a dynasty that saw them win seven Western Canada titles and two Memorial Cups, representative of the national championship title. The May, 1963, Memorial Cup victory against the Niagara Falls Flyers, Edmonton's first Canadian junior hockey championship, took place in the Gardens. In 1966, the Oil Kings became the first western team in 18 years to win the Memorial Cup on eastern ice. Perhaps the finest series ever played in the Gardens occurred in 1967, when the Oil Kings won the Western Canada Junior Hockey League semi-final against the Moose Jaw Canucks in nine games after four ties. The revival of professional hockey with the Oilers of the World Hockey Association in 1972 brought a sharp decrease in attendance for junior hockey games, and in 1976, the Oil Kings Tier One junior hockey team was sold to Portland, Oregon. Many Oil Kings graduates became prominent stars in the National Hockey League.

[October 14, 1973] **Gordie Howe (over the puck)** and the Houston Aeros play the Edmonton Oilers in a World Hockey Association game at the Edmonton Gardens.

After a decade-long absence, professional hockey returned to Edmonton in 1972 when the Edmonton-based Alberta Oilers were one of the original teams in the newly formed World Hockey Association. In the first regular season game of the WHA, the Alberta Oilers defeated the Ottawa Nationals 7-4 in Ottawa. Home games were played in the Edmonton Gardens until November, 1974, when the new Coliseum was ready for its first hockey game. In the summer of 1979, the WHA terminated its operations and the Edmonton Oilers (renamed in 1976) became one of the new additions to the expanded National Hockey League.

Shortly after the move of the Oilers to the Coliseum came the end of one of the most illustrious hockey careers of all time, that of the all-time scoring champion Gordie Howe. About a year before Howe retired, the Edmonton Oilers signed, to a 20-year contract, his likely successor, eighteen-year-old scoring wizard, Wayne "The Great" Gretzky.

[May 30, 1971] **During World War II,** the Edmonton Federation of Community Leagues inaugurated the Soap Box Derby, a race using gravity-powered homemade vehicles, for boys 11 to 15 years of age. In the early years, the annual event was run down McDougall Hill, but after Victoria Park Road (shown here) was paved, it provided a more convenient site because of the minimal interruption of normal city traffic. In later years, the sponsorship was taken over by the Active 20-30 Club, which raises funds for the Winnifred Stewart School for Retarded Children, Block Parents, and victims of cystic fibrosis.

When the derby began, the restriction on the homemade carts was a maximum cost of $10, but even do-it-yourself hobby sports like this one felt the effects of inflation. In 1978, when the 30th annual Soap Box Derby was held, the shiny four-wheeled carts were not allowed to exceed a value of $75. The winnings likewise increased over the years. In 1945, the winner received a bicycle and trophy; in 1978 first prize included $250, a large trophy, and the right to compete, with all expenses paid, in the Western Canadian Championships. Not bad rewards for rolling an eighth of a mile down Victoria Park Road in 47 seconds.

[May 24, 1971] **With the power wheels** burning rubber and the light front wheels keeping the car straight, another drag racer at Edmonton International Speedway attempts to roar down the ¼-mile of pavement in less than six seconds. In 1974, Edmontonian Gary Beck, at competitions in the United States, won the National Hot Rod Association world championship. That year he also received two "driver of the year" awards for his accomplishments in drag racing. By 1981, Gary had won his ninth (American) National Hot Rod Association title.

[February 7, 1974] **More than sixty years** after Reginal Hunt was making experiments in flying on the hillside south of the Legislative Building in 1909, another group of flying enthusiasts began to enjoy the new sport of hang gliding. A favourite location for this sport is the hill south of the Provincial Museum. Here we see ski flyer Terry Jones gliding over the trees near the slopes of Whitemud Creek.

[1972] **Dave Cutler kicks another** field goal for the Edmonton Eskimos, while quarterback Tom Wilkinson places the ball after the snap from centre Bob Howes. On August 26, 1980, Cutler kicked a 48-yard field goal to surpass George Blanda of the (American) National Football League as the most prolific field goal kicker in professional football. That evening in Commonwealth Stadium, Cutler, in his 12th season as a professional, kicked the 336th of this career.

[November, 1973] **The Edmonton Eskimos win** the western Canadian final and head for another Grey Cup game.

During the 1950s, the Eskimo football team was never out of the Western Conference playoffs, appearing in five national finals and winning the Grey Cup in three successive years, 1954-56. The next football dynasty to emerge with Eskimo teams began in 1973. Since then, the team finished first in western Canada in seven of the eight subsequent years, played in the national championships every year except one and won the Grey Cup in three successive years, 1978-80. The success of the community-owned team is attributed to excellent organization, good coaching, good players and good fans, who fill the stadium to capacity for every home game.

[July 23, 1973] **The young lads are just** as intent on the game as the professionals, as this photo of a playoff game in the City Senior Little League shows. Often the difference between winning is a matter of inches, or the decision of the umpire!

[October 19, 1971] **Susan Nattrass,** **following** in the footsteps of her father Floyd Nattrass, who represented Canada in trapshooting at the 1964 Olympic Games, began shooting four-inch-diameter clay pigeon targets with a twelve-gauge shotgun at the age of 13. Within two years, under the tutorship of her parents, she won her first trophy. In 1976, she became the first woman to ever compete in an Olympic trapshooting event. Susan broke the world record, when she won her first gold medal in 1974 and at the world championships in 1978, she set a new women's international record by hitting 195 of 200 targets. In 1979, she became the first woman ever to win the Canadian over-all title. By 1980, she had won the world women's title five consecutive times, a feat no trapshooter, either male or female, had ever accomplished in the history of the sport. For this achievement, she was honoured with the prestigious Order of Canada award in 1981. Fellow Edmontonian John Primrose won the world men's trapshooting championship in 1975.

233

[*March 3, 1972*] **The Ukrainian Shumka Dancers** troupe was founded in 1959 under the direction of Chester Kuc, who resigned in 1969 to organize the local Ukrainian Cheremosh Dance Ensemble. In 1967, he also organized the Ukrainian National Federation School of Dancing, the largest Ukrainian folk-dancing school in western Canada.

The Shumka Dancers began with 16 dancers and grew in numbers and renown until by 1981 the troupe consisted of 60 dancers and a 24-piece orchestra under the direction of conductor-arranger Gene Zwozdesky. The group performed at Expo '67 at Montreal, represented Canada in the Bi-Annual Folk Festival in Tunisia and gave yearly performances in Japan from 1974 to 1977. In 1978, they were the only Canadian ethno-cultural dance troup that performed on Parliament Hill, Ottawa, during the Canada Day festivities. In August, 1978, the Shumka Dancers highlighted the opening ceremonies of the Commonwealth Games, held in Commonwealth Stadium before a capacity audience of 42,500. A few days later, they were invited to dance a Command Performance for Her Majesty Queen Elizabeth. Later that year, at the 1978 Alberta Achievement Awards ceremony, this world-class dance group was presented with the Award of Excellence by the Government of the Province of Alberta.

[*July 1, 1972*] **Here, the Edmonton All-Girl** Drum and Bugle Band struts in formation during Canada Day celebrations at the Legislative Grounds.

In September, 1966, under the direction of conductor Bob Nagel and the sponsorship of Safeway Stores and the Edmonton Civic Centennial Committee, the Edmonton All-Girl Drum and Bugle Band was formed. The 100-girl band was the largest of its type in Canada when it began and by 1970, when they represented Edmonton in the Toronto Grey Cup parade, the 230-member organization was divided into senior (age 14-19) and junior (age 12-14) corps. In July, 1974, this accomplished group won the gold medal in the top division of the World Music Festival held in the Netherlands. A few years after they were organized, the bugles were phased out in favour of trumpets and other brass instruments, and in 1975 the band assumed its new name, the Edmonton All-Girl Ambassador Marching Band.

[March 24, 1972] **Conductor Tommy Banks** and the Edmonton Symphony Orchestra provide a musical interlude for a standing-room-only crowd at McCauley Plaza Shopping Centre.

For over a quarter century, Tommy Banks has successfully brought good music to the ears, hearts and minds of Edmontonians. Whether as a guest conductor of the Edmonton Symphony or as leader and pianist in his own band, Mr. Banks has, through the medium of the concert hall, popular on-site locations, radio, television, sound tapes and stereo disc recordings, maintained a high standard of musical achievement in the classical, popular and jazz idioms. In addition to his local popularity, Mr. Banks has received international plaudits which rank him as one of the fine musicians of our time. In July, 1978, the Tommy Banks Orchestra was the first western Canadian group to represent Canada at the prestigious Montreux (Switzerland) Jazz Festival. The double album made at that festival of the 16-piece Tommy Banks Orchestra along with vocalist Big Miller later won the Juno award given by the Canadian Academy of Recording Arts and Sciences for the best Canadian jazz recording of 1978. The same record album won the Grand Prix du Disque – Canada by the Canada Music Council, as the best jazz recording in Canada in 1978.

[n.d.] **The Citadel's impressive new** theatre complex, situated just east of the Centennial Library, won the Stelco Design Award for outstanding steel buildings. It welcomed its first audiences in the fall of 1976 and once again Edmontonians enthusiastically endorsed the new theatre and kept filling the house so that plays had to be held over.

With the farthest seat only 70 feet from the stage in the 675-seat main theatre, named for the Citadel's founder and executive producer, Joe Shoctor, the intimacy and immediacy that endeared audiences to the old Citadel Theatre is maintained. Furthermore, a 250-seat second theatre, named in honour of benefactor Dick Rice, continues to feature the type of innovative productions begun by Citadel Too, and a 230-seat cinema and lecture hall, named for benefactor W.R. Zeidler, expands the Citadel's range even further. In addition, the complex provides space for rehearsals, workshops, classrooms, wardrobe and design studios, a theatre library, a restaurant, and a large, inviting glass-enclosed lobby.

235

[c1978] **Hawrelak Park spreads out** between the Groat Road and the river, south of the Groat Bridge and the Mayfair Golf and County Club.

At a cost of one million dollars, the city transformed an old 140-acre gravel pit into Edmonton's first year-round park. This recreational area features a shallow 14-acre lake, used for boating and fishing in summer and skating in winter, together with picnic and playground facilities for thousands of year-round visitors. After about six years of construction, the park opened in 1967 and in 1971 it received the prestigious Vincent Massey Award for excellence in Canadian urban park design.

Originally called Mayfair Park, the spacious recreational facility was renamed in October, 1976, as a tribute to former mayor, William Hawrelak, who began the fund raising for this park and who previously had contributed many efforts toward the establishment of several other city parks, including the new Borden Park, Coronation Park, Queen Elizabeth Park, the Storyland Valley Zoo and Fort Edmonton Park.

[May 17, 1974] **Almost sixty years after** the demolition of the old fort below the Legislative Building, City Council finally (in September, 1968) approved in principle the long-range plan for Fort Edmonton Park. This 152-acre park, located on the south bank of the river just west of the Quesnell Bridge, began as a project of the local Rotary Club. Later the Fort Edmonton Historical Foundation was created to supervise the park, which is operated by the Edmonton Parks and Recreation Department. On October 13, 1970, the first formal opening of the fort palisades occurred. By May 17, 1974, the total reconstruction of the old fort was completed and the park was officially opened to the public at a modest admission charge of one dollar for adults and fifty cents for children.

By the end of 1976, almost $3.5 million was spent on carrying out the long-range plans of recreating street scenes representing the various eras of Edmonton's past: 1845 (the fort), 1885 (the town), 1905 (the new city), 1920 (the early years), 1947 to the present (present and future eras). In 1978, the park opened a 2 ½-mile railway, complete with vintage cars pulled by a reconditioned 1919 steam locomotive. This feature helps transport visitors back in space and time so they can begin their tour of the historical park at the gates of the old fort.

[September 28, 1972] **A hundred years after** prospectors first searched for gold along these banks of the North Saskatchewan, a few optimists, like Joe Biollo here, still sift through the gravel hunting for those elusive, but now far more valuable, grains of gold. Over the century, the price of gold, the motorized pump, and the city skyline have changed the scene considerably, but the goldseekers' goal remains the same.

[July 8, 1978] **Premier Peter Lougheed** leads a group of fellow Albertans for a leisurely stroll through the newly opened Capital City Recreation Park.

Along with deer, muskrat, rabbits, and 123 species of birds, Edmonton citizens and visitors can enjoy family recreation, exercise and the exhilaration of a nature walk through Capital City Recreation Park, North America's largest central park.

In 1907, Montreal landscape architect Frederick G. Todd recommended to Edmonton City Council a plan to set aside the city's river valley and ravines for parks. Although Council finally adopted the idea in 1915, it was not until 1974 that the city and provincial governments announced plans to make $34 million available to construct ten miles of recreational parks along each side of the river valley from the Legislative Grounds to the eastern edge of the city.

When it opened on July 8, 1978, the 3,000-acre park provided Edmontonians with 18 miles of paved bicycle trails and 16 miles of gravelled hiking trails. The four graceful pedestrian bridges that cross the river allow hikers, joggers, cyclists, snowshoeists and cross-country skiers to make round trips of varying lengths through the scenic nature trails of the park. Numerous shelters, benches, fountains, picnic tables, bicycle racks, educational signs, and other facilities make time spent in the vast park enjoyable, comfortable and unforgettable. One of Edmonton's greatest natural assets is now accessible to everyone.

Aberhart, William, 107, 164, 170
Agency Building, 106
Alaska Highway, 164, 179
Alberta: choice of capital, 18, 70, 75; Golden Jubilee, 64, 203, inauguration, 64, 65, 72-74; Legislature, 17, 75, 90, 116
Alberta Ballet Co., 206
Alberta College, 15, 74, 82, 124, 191
Alberta Gas Trunk Line Building, 105
Alberta Government Telephones, Toll Building, 224; Tower, 167, 223, 224
Aldridge, F.G., 157
Allan Cup, 196
Allen, John, 68
Allen, Max, 157
Ambulance service, 145
American Dairy Lunch, 106
Anderson, Tom, 26
Archibald, Arthur, 92
Armistice, 143
Armoury Restaurant, 40
Armstrong Block, 110
Armstrong, George, 148
Armstrong, Robert, 105
Army & Navy store, 170
Arts, the, 64, 80, 153-157, 203, 206, 211, 218, 235
Athabasca (Landing) Trail, 12, 14, 52
Baldwin, Matt, 197
Banks: Banque Canadienne Nationale, 182; of British North America, 106; Canadian Bank of Commerce, 165, 175; Dominion, 85, 86, 185, 193; Imperial Bank of Canada, 85, 86, 164, 185; of Montreal, 106; Royal, 83, 175, 193; Union, 106
Banks, Tommy, 229, 235
Barford, Vernon, 64, 153, 155, 156
Barn, the, 194
Barrooms, 20, 21, 31, 65, 84, 183
Battleford, 29
Beck, Gary, 231
Bel-Air Apartments, 204
Bell, Alexander Graham, 18
Bellamy Hill, 195
"Bennett Buggy", 170
Bennett, R.B., 164
Bennett, Thomas, 34
Berg, Gilbert, 47
Betting, 24, 67, 68, 219
Big 4 Transfer and Storage Co., 146
Big House: Hardisty's, 8, 10, 58, 68, 76, 116; Rowand's, 7, 8, 10
Big Island, 118
Biollo, Joe, 237
Bittorf, Don, 221
Blacksmiths, 22, 31, 34, 93
Blatchford Field, 138, 149, 150, 164, 168, 169, 177, 178, 204, 206, 222
Blatchford, Kenneth A., 149
Bleeker, Henry Y., 115
Blowey Henry furniture store, 85, 118, 132, 140, 177
Borden, Sir Robert, 71
Bow, Dr. M.R., 150
Bowen, J.C.F., 21, 117, 149
Bowen, J.J., 191
Boyle, J.R., 69
Breckenridge, Gavin, 219
Bridges, 26, 206, 225; Capilano, 225; Clover Bar, 225; Dawson, 225; Groat, 225; High Level, 28, 70, 87, 102, 122, 166, 225; James Macdonald, 223, 225; Low Level, 28, 38, 44, 54, 60, 77, 80, 111, 140, 190, 223, 225; Quesnell, 225; Walterdale (105 Street), 6, 28, 225
Bright, Johnny, 198
Brown Block, 106
Brown, George, 107
Brown, Harry P., 153
Brown, John, 16
Brown, Roy, 138
Buchanan, Rev. T.C., 74
Bucyk, Johnny, 196
Bulletin, 12, 14, 16, 18, 50, 55, 132, 142, 188, 195, 209
Bulletin Building, 16, 49
Bullock, R.A., 157
Bulyea, G.H.V., 72, 74, 75, 77, 81, 90, 107
Burbank, Luther, 19
Burns, Patrick, 26, 85, 93
Bury, A.U.C., 150
Bush pilots, 138, 148-150, 164, 169, 206, 211
Byng, Lord, 158
Byrnes, Patrick, 16
Cablevision, 208
Cahoun, Jack, 88
Cairn's brewery, 54
Calder, 77, 125
Calgary, 12, 21, 23, 24, 25, 26, 30, 31, 45, 68, 70, 75, 100, 132, 138, 148, 151, 159, 164, 188, 198, 203
Calgary-Edmonton stagecoach. See Edmonton-Calgary stagecoach
Calgary Trail, 11, 12, 25
Cambridge Building, 224, 225
Canada: Centennial, 167, 212-216; Diamond Jubilee, 151, 157, 174; purchase of Rupert's Land, 6, 12
Canada Permanent Building, 86, 106
Canadian Broadcasting Corporation, 164, 208
Canadian National Railway: CN Tower, 162, 216, 217, 224; station, 162, 186, 201, 217. See also

Railways: Canadian National
Canadian Pacific Airlines, 169, 179, 211
Canadian Pacific Railway Building, 70, 105, 152, 185
Capitol Pipe Shop, 199
Capitol Square, 157
Carlton Trail, 11, 45
Carmack, George, 44
Carmichael, Mrs. J.B., 153, 156, 203
Carnegie, Andrew, 40
Carrigan, Dan, 158
Carson, W.H., 17
Caverhill, E., 50
Centennial Building, 216, 224
Century Place, 224
Chancery Hall, 216, 223,
Cherniak, Sam, 175, 209
Christie, William J., 14
Churches: All Saints, 8, 14, 64, 82; Baptist, 33, 42, First Presbyterian, 62, 82, 83, 86, 116, 156; Holy Trinity, 42; Knox Presbyterian, 40; McDougall's Wesleyan Methodist, (log) 8, 12, 15, 17, 19, 42, 195; (frame) 15, 51, 59, 82, 195; McDougall United (brick) 15, 156, 191, 195; St. Anthony's, 43; St. Joachim's, 58, 59
Citadel Theatre, 206, 218, 235. See also Theatres, live: Citadel
City Hall, 188, 191, 202, 216, 217
Civic Block, 113, 114, 149, 166, 167, 191, 202, 216
Civic centre, 216, 223
Claim jumpers, 17
Clarke, Joe, 158, 173
Clarke Stadium, 13, 173, 191, 198, 229
Clarke, Walter, 71, 74-75
Clark, M.C., 33
Clover Bar, 23, 50, 51, 188, 189
Cloverdale, 28. See also Gallagher Flats.
Clover, Tom, 51
Coal, 18, 26, 27, 43, 50, 222
Coliseum, 222, 229, 230
Commercial Airways, 149
Commercial Grads. See Edmonton Grads
Commonwealth Games, 220, 222, 228, 229, 234
Commonwealth Stadium, 13, 173, 229, 232, 234
Connaught Armoury, 40
Connaught, Duke of, 36, 116
Convention Centre, 95, 222
Court House, 89, 185, 216, 227
Cristall, Abe, 85, 109
Cunningham, Rev. C., 100
Currie, Frank, 196
Cutler, Dave, 232
Daly, Philip, 48
Dant, Noel, 190
Davies, Arthur, 43
Day, Billy, 99
Dean, Bob, 198
Depression: of 1873-96, 44, 70; of 1913, 102, 106, 163; of 1930s, 138, 154, 155, 157, 164, 166, 170, 188
Derbyshire, Pete, 148, 149
Diamond Park, 87, 132, 140, 159
Dickins, C.H. "Punch", 138, 150, 169
Dominion Cigar Store, 137
Dominion Dining Hall, 88
Dominion Land Office, 17, 26, 79
Dominion Lands Act, 12
Dominion Land Survey, 12
Dominion Telegraph, 12, 18. See also Telegraph
Dorman, "Curly", 159
Dowling's Mill, 54
Drugstores, 48, 92
Dub, Gene, 202
Duggan, D.M., 151
Duggan, J.J., 34, 37, 40
Dunham, Cliff, 158
Eaton's, 163, 175, 176, 227
Edmiston, Herbert, 23
Edmiston, William, 59
Edmonton: area, 206, 222; first aeroplane flight, 98; first airmail, 148; first bridge, 44; first brick building, 21; first cable ferry, 28; first car, 66, 69; first cinema, 95, 109; first coal miner, 50; first electric light company, 18; first hospital, 56; first hotel, 19; first lawyer, 115; first livery stable, 17; first mayor, 17; first opera, 64; first school, 12, 17; first school board, 14, 17; first settlers, 12, 13-19 (See also Settlers); first streetcar, 38; first taxi, 145; first telephone system, 18; first traffic light, 165; first train, 60; gateway to north, 12, 44, 77, 164, 206, 211, 222; golden anniversary, 202; incorporation as city, 71, 80; incorporation as town, 17, 44; population, 6, 23, 62, 70, 78, 102, 103, 164, 188, 206, 222
Edmonton aeroplane, 148, 149
Edmonton Agricultural Society, 12. See also Edmonton Exhibition
Edmonton Airline Company, 149
Edmonton All-Girl Drum and Bugle Band, 234
Edmonton Art Gallery, 80, 206
Edmonton Brass Band, 46, 67
Edmonton Brewing and Malting Co., 34, 132
Edmonton-Calgary stagecoach, 12, 21, 25, 45. See also Transportation: stagecoach
Edmonton Centre, 89, 109, 175, 224, 227
Edmonton City Dairy, 125
Edmonton Civic Opera Society, 156, 203
Edmonton Club, 73, 94, 132, 140, 191, 223
Edmonton Coal Co., 50

Edmonton Drug Co., 85
Edmonton Eskimos: baseball team, 159; football team, 138, 153, 159, 173, 198, 232; hockey team, 138, 160; name, 132; rugby football team, 132
Edmonton Exhibition, 19, 67, 98, 99, 126, 128-131, 148, 158, 184, 199, 213-214; Arena, 126, 160, 161, 172, 197; Grounds, 23, 24, 67, 72, 73, 99, 174, 179, 213-214, 219, 229; Stock Pavilion, 71, 106, 126, 160
Edmonton Flyers, 196, 230
Edmonton Flying Club, 149, 168
Edmonton Gardens, 71, 106, 126, 160, 196, 197, 230
Edmonton Golf and Country Club, 68
Edmonton Grads, 138, 161, 172
Edmonton House (apartment building), 223, 224
Edmonton House (fort). See Fort Edmonton
Edmonton International Speedway, 219, 231
Edmonton Journal, 66, 109, 149, 151, 152, 157, 158, 195
Edmonton Journal Newsboys' Band. See Edmonton Newsboys' Band
Edmonton Mendelssohn Choir, 156
Edmonton Mercury Hockey Club, 196
Edmonton Newsboys' Band, 143, 157
Edmonton Oilers, 230
Edmonton Oil Kings, 230
Edmonton Opera House, 154
Edmonton Professional Opera Association, 206
Edmonton Protestant School District No. 7, 17. See also Schools
Edmonton Radial Railway, 38, 98, 125, 145
Edmonton Schoolboys' Band, 157
Edmonton Sun, 195
Edmonton Symphony Orchestra, 64, 155, 156, 203, 206, 208, 235
Edmonton Technical School, 124
Edmonton Telephones, 18, 96
Edmonton Transit System, 145, 200
Electrification, 12, 18, 52, 82, 222
Elevators, grain, 37, 186
Ellwood, J., 95
Empire Block, 82, 83, 86, 108, 175, 182, 225
Empire Building, 182, 225
Enright, Jimmy, 159, 198
Entwistle, Alex, 95, 107
Entwistle, Arnold, 95
Entwistle, Clarence, 95
Exhibition. See Edmonton Agricultural Society; Edmonton Exhibition
"Famous Five", 138, 142
Farming, 12, 14, 19, 70
Ferguson, R.B., 88
Ferries. See Transportation: ferries
Ferris, Dr. W.D., 39
Finch, H.A., 22
Fire Brigade Band, 46, 67
Fire Halls: No. 1, 45, 46, 88; No. 6, 40; No. 7, 115
Fires, 43, 62, 71, 83, 97, 126, 175, 182, 183
Fleming, Sandford, 12
Floods, 6, 7, 27, 54, 138, 140-141, 221
Fort Augustus, 6, 10
Fort Edmonton, 6-11, 12, 14, 15, 18, 27, 28, 45, 58, 67, 116; demolition, 139, 236
Fort Edmonton Park, 13, 15, 35, 54, 107, 155, 200, 215, 222, 236
Fort Garry, 11, 14. See also Winnipeg
Fort Saskatchewan, 6, 17, 23, 24, 26, 46, 47, 69, 111, 132
Frank Oliver Memorial Park, 209
Fraser, Jack, 159
Fratkin, Abe, 155
Fur trade, 6-11, 16, 45, 61, 73
Gainer, John, 26
Galician hay market, 66
Gallagher & Hull, 26, 54
Gallagher Flats, 54. See also Cloverdale
Gariepy Block, 86, 96, 105, 115, 185
Gatty, Harold, 168
George, Rev. W.R., 43
George VI, Coronation, 174. See also Royal visits
Gibbons, Jim, 51
Gibson, Cheryl, 220, 229
Glenora Rink, 160
Glyde, Henry G., 202
Gold, 19, 44, 49, 51-52, 116, 164, 237. See also Klondike Gold Rush
Gold dredges, 27, 51
Gold miners, 19, 44, 51, 237
Goodridge, James, 21
Gorman, George, 148, 149
Government House, 80, 81, 117
Graham, Jimmy, 196
Grant, W.W., 153
Graydon, George, 48
Great West Saddlery, 110
Gretzky, Wayne, 230
Grey Cup, 138, 159, 198, 232
Grey, Earl, 71, 72, 73, 76
Greyhound Bus Depot, 201
Grey Nuns. See Sisters of Charity of Ville-Marie
Griesbach, Maj. A.H., 26
Groat, Malcolm, 12, 14, 63, 66
Groat Ravine, 111, 127
Gunn, Pat, 197
Gyro Club, 134
Hagen, Betty Jean, 203
Hagmann, John, 149
Hall, Frank, 50
Hall, Glenn, 196

Hallgrimson, O.J., 95
Hambly, Charles, 115
Hardisty Big House. *See* Big House: Hardisty's
Hardisty, Mrs. Richard, 15, 24
Hardisty, Richard, 12, 15
Harness-makers, 13, 22
Haugen, John, 135
Hawrelak, William, 202, 236
Hemingway, Peter, 221
Hepner, Lee, 155, 203
Hilton, Matthew J., 124
HMCS Nonsuch, 180
Holgate, Bidwell A., 163
Hooker, Clara, 168
Horner, Vic, 138, 150
Horvath, "Bronco", 196
Hospitals: Col. Mewburn, 195; General, 56-58; Glenrose, 56; Misericordia, 80, 91; Public, 56, 91; Royal Alexandra, 56, 91, 106; St. Albert Mission, 56; Strathcona Municipal, 91, 195; University, 195
Hotels, 37; Alberta, 16, 46, 47, 54, 65, 88, 118, 194, 209; Cecil, 110, 118, 209; Chateau Lacombe, 25, 223, 224; Columbia House, 16, 45; Commercial, 31; Dominion, 38; Edmonton (Don Ross), 8, 19-20, 50, 82, 87, 140; Edmonton (Strathcona), 26, 31, 38 (See also Hotels: Strathcona); Four Seasons, 227; Grandview, 59, 118, 132; Hotel du Canada, 16; Hub, 21, 194; Imperial, 88; Jasper House, 21, 22, 25, 46, 62, 63, 194; King Edward, 88, 118, 145, 183; Macdonald, 25, 59, 66, 70, 109, 116, 118-119, 140, 145, 146, 156, 159, 162, 166, 177, 185, 191, 192, 193, 194, 209, 215, 216, 223; Mammoth, 45; Ontario House, 33; Plaza, 224; Raymond, 31-32, 34; Royal, 32; Royal George, 70, 109, 118, 152, 175; Selkirk, 83, 118, 175; Strathcona, 26, 31, 32, 34, 38, 43, 144 (See also Hotels: Edmonton [Strathcona]); Transit, 111; Westin, 97, 224; Windsor (in Edmonton), 82-84, 175; (in Strathcona), 37; Yale, 76, 193
Housing, 70, 78-79, 102, 120-121, 164, 187
Howard, Mrs. Wesley, 141
Howe, Gordie, 230
Howes, Bob, 232
Hudson's Bay Company, 6-17, 27, 34, 45, 47, 50, 52, 54, 56, 61, 90, 180; land sale (1881), 61; land sale (1912), 102, 104; Reserve, 12, 14, 17, 23, 58, 67, 102, 104, 169; sale of Rupert's Land, 6, 12; stores, 16, 52, 82, 88, 106, 154, 194, 221
Huff, J.W., 55
Hulbert, Russell A., 34
Humberstone, William, 27, 28, 50, 54
Hunt, Reginald, 98, 231
Hutchings & Riley, 22
Ibbotson, Bill, 17
Ice harvesting, 55
Immigration, 70, 78, 102, 164, 188, 206
Immigration Hall, 78, 186
Immigration Office, 73
Imperial Oil Building, 224
Imperial Oil Company, 189
Incline Railway, 80, 87
Independent Airways, 169
Indians, 6-10, 12, 15, 16, 24, 54, 71, 77, 100, 111
Industrial Airport. *See* Blatchford Field
International Airport, 178, 206, 211, 222
Inter-Urban Railway, 102, 125
Jablonski, Marek, 218
Jackson Brothers (foundry), 26
Jackson Brothers (jewellers), 49, 105
Jamieson, Pete, 209
Jennings, Milton R., 149, 157
Johnson, Henry D., 80
Johnson's Cafe, 83, 175
Johnstone Walker's stores, 53, 74, 86, 221
Jones-Konihowski, Diane, 229
Jones, Terry, 231
Journal Building, 15, 151, 153, 191, 195
Jubilee Auditorium, 188, 195, 203, 210
Keats, Duke, 160
Kelly, Luke, 54
Kernohan, Mrs., 22
King, W.L. Mackenzie, 173
Kinsmen Fieldhouse, 215
Kirkpatrick, G.R.F., 60, 68, 158
Kline, Herman B., 105, 157
Kline, Irving, 175
Klondike Days, 213-214
Klondike Gold Rush, 27, 44, 52-54, 107, 173, 213
Kuc, Chester, 234
Kwong, Normie, 198
Lacombe, Father Albert, 54
Lake, Sir James Winter, 6
Lamb, George, 43
Land Office. *See* Dominion Land Office
LaRose's livery stable, 31
Lauder, Billy, 100
Lauder, Clara, 69
Lauderdale, 47
Lauder, James, 47
Lauder, Jennie, 69
Lauder's Bakery, 45, 47
Lauder, Tommy, 45, 47
Laurier, Sir Wilfrid, 18, 26, 44, 65, 70, 71, 72, 73, 76, 81, 88
Law Courts Building, 89, 223, 224
Lawrence, Albert R. "Pop", 95
Leary, John, 108
Legislative Building, 6, 36, 68, 70, 75-76, 102, 116, 139, 216
LeMarchand Mansion, 81, 222

LeMarchand, René, 81
Library, public, 167, 191, 200, 215, 216, 226
Light Rail Transit, 99, 222, 228, 229
Lines, Roland, 106, 126
Lingas, Harry, 106
Liquor laws, 21, 138, 141, 183
Livery stables, 17, 31, 223
Livingstone, Sam, 51
Locklear, Ormer, 148
Londonderry Mall, 226
Looby, Edward, 22
Lougheed, Peter, 222, 237
Loveseth, Enoch, 167
Loveseth, Loyd, 167
Loveseth Service Station, 167
Lumber industry, 26-28, 34, 50
Lynch, Charles, 95
MacAlpine, Col., 150
McCauley, Matt, 12, 17, 26, 44, 71, 132, 223
McCauley Plaza, 17, 235
McClung, Nellie, 141, 142
McConachie, Grant, 149, 169
McCurdy, James, 98
MacDonald, A., & Co., 16
Macdonald, D.W., 48
Macdonald, James (carpenter), 73
Macdonald, James (city engineer), 225
Macdonald, Sir John A., 44, 118
McDonald, Kenneth, 13, 63, 73
Macdonald Place, 224
McDonald, Robert, 100
McDougall & Secord, 61, 80, 82, 108, 165, 225
McDougall Hill, 20, 44, 50, 82, 191, 231
McDougall, John A., 16, 39, 52, 53, 60, 61, 63, 80, 81, 82, 163
McDougall, Rev. George, 8, 12, 15, 19, 59, 74, 167, 195
McDougall, Rev. John, 15
MacEwan, Grant, 210
McIntyre, Dr. Wilbert, 40
McIntyre, Malcolm, 34
McIntyre Memorial Fountain, 40
MacKay, Dr. William M., 90
Mackenzie and Mann, 44, 60
MacKenzie, Duncan S., 33
McKenzie, J.J., 34
Mackenzie, K.W., 72
Mackenzie, Sir William, 44, 60
McKernan, James, 29
McKernan Lake, 29, 136
McKernan Lake streetcar, 136
McKernan, Robert, 29, 38
McLaughlin Motors, 147
McLean Block, 222
McLeod Building, 46, 86, 109, 146, 166, 185
McLeod, Donald, 25, 45, 55
McLeod, Doreen, 197
McLeod, Kenneth, 46, 109
McLeod, Murdoch, 73
McNamara, William S., 59, 114
McNeill, Alex, 145
McNeill, John, 145, 149
Magrath, William J., 163
Mail service, 12, 17, 28, 138, 148, 168
Manchester House, 53, 74
Manning, Ernest, 191
Mann, Sir Donald, 44, 60
Market, 88, 112-113, 124, 146, 166, 186, 191, 216, 226
Masonic Hall, 16
Mathers, C.W., 16, 46, 62
May, Charles, 97
May, Court, 148, 149
Mayfair Golf and Country Club, 68, 236
Mayors (Edmonton): Blatchford, K.A., 149; Bury, A.U.C., 150; Clarke, Joe, 158, 173; Duggan, D.M., 151; Edmiston, William, 59; Hawrelak, William, 202, 236; McCauley, Matt, 17, 44, 71; McDougall, John A., 16, 60; Mackenzie, K.W., 72; McNamara, William S., 59, 114; Roper, Elmer, 216; Short, William, 71, 107
Mayors (Strathcona): Bennett, Thomas, 34; Davies, Arthur, 43; Duggan, J.J., 34, 37; McKenzie, J.J., 34; Sheppard, William H., 32, 34
May, W.R. "Wop", 122, 138, 148, 149, 150, 169, 179
Meadowlark Park Shopping Centre, 226
Meat packing, 14, 26, 111, 177
Memorial Hall, 143, 191
Metis, 12, 15, 54, 61
Mewburn, Dr. F.H., 195
Michaels, Audrey, 157
Michaels, John "Mike", 108, 157, 158, 168
Michaels, Ruth, 157
Michener, Edward, 116
Midway, 198, 199, 214
Mike's news stand, 108, 180
Miles, Rollie, 198
Mill Creek, 44, 111, 171
Miller, "Pop", 145
Mills, John I., 62
Mills, Marion, 155
Minto, Earl of, 90
Mitchell, David, 149
Moore, Ernest A., 156
Moose team, 99
Moosewa, D., 24, 68
Morris, Joseph H., 66

Morris, Mrs. Joseph H., 69
Morrow, T.B., 136
Moser-Ryder Block, 109
Municipal Airport. *See* Blatchford Field
Murphy, Emily, 138, 142
Nagel, Bob, 234
Naismith, Dr. James, 161, 172
Namao Air Base, 178
Nattrass, Floyd, 233
Nattrass, Susan, 233
Natural gas, 81, 206
Neilson, Hans, 152
Newspapers, 76, 83, 108. *See also* Bulletin; Edmonton *Journal;* Edmonton *Sun*
Newton, Rev. William, 8
Normal School, 181, 195
North Edmonton, 77, 102, 111, 115
Northern Alberta Institute of Technology, 206, 210, 215
Northern Alberta Railways Building, 105
Northern Building, 177
Northlands, 219, 229. *See also* Edmonton Exhibition
North Saskatchewan River, 6, 11, 12, 25, 26, 28, 30, 49-51, 54, 55, 69, 116, 140, 171, 197, 225, 237
North West Company, 6, 9, 10, 11
North West Mounted Police, 10, 12, 24, 26, 29, 44, 47, 63, 173
North-West Rebellion, 12, 23, 25, 26, 73
O'Brian, Maj-Gen. Geoffrey, 168
Ochsner, Robert, 26
Oil, 138, 164, 188, 189, 206, 211, 222
Old Strathcona Foundation, 31, 40
Old Timers' Ball, 63
Oliver, Frank, 12, 16, 17, 18, 26, 70, 71, 81, 82, 209
Omand's brewery, 54
Orange Hall (Strathcona), 40
Oregon, Treaty of, 6
Osler, Hammond & Nanton, 26
Pace, W.J., 60
Pacific Western Airlines, 201
Page, J. Percy, 161, 172
Pakan. *See* Victoria (Pakan)
Pankhurst, Emmeline, 142
Pantages, Alexander, 107
Parker, Jackie, 198
Parks: Borden, 67, 99, 127, 133, 171, 212, 229, 236; Capital City Recreation Park, 222, 237; Coronation, 212, 236; East End, 99, 127; Frank Oliver Memorial Park, 209; Hawrelak Park (Mayfair), 236; Queen Elizabeth, 40, 127, 171, 236; Riverside, 127, 136, 171; Tipton, 127; Victoria, 133; West End, 127
Parrish, Sam, 31, 34
Pearson, Lester B., 213
Pearson, Maryon, 213
Pemmican, 6, 10
Penitentiary, 17, 50, 146, 173
"Persons" case, 138, 142
Pinckston, Don, 221
Pocklington, Peter, 219
Poile, Bud, 196
Police, 115, 129. *See also* North West Mounted Police
Pollack, Moses, 170
Pollard Brothers' brickyard, 26
Poole Construction Co., 167, 194
Popcorn vendor, 108, 175, 209
Post office (Edmonton): brick, 86, 97, 146, 185, 216; at fort, 12; frame, 97, 109; Sir Alexander Mackenzie, 97, 216
Post office (Strathcona), 36
Post, Wiley, 168
Prevey, Warren W., 125
Prices: airbus, 201, apartments, 81; beef, 14; billiards, 20; bread, 47; car repairs, 147; cars, 147; clothing, 170; coal, 50; electricity, 82; groceries, 61, 112, 170, 226; hospital, 56; hotels, 20, 65; ice, 55; live theatre, 154; meals, 19, 88; movies, 95, 107; property, 102; stagecoach, 25; taxis, 145; vaudeville, 107
Primrose, John, 229, 233
Prohibition, 138, 141, 142, 144
Prosperity Certificates, 164, 170
Provincial Museum and Archives of Alberta, 215, 231
Purvis Block, 165
Queen Elizabeth Planetarium, 212
Race track. *See* Edmonton Exhibition: Grounds
Radio, 138, 151-153, 164, 199
Radio stations: CFCK, 151, 153; CFCN (Calgary), 153; CFRN, 152; CFTP, 152; CHCY, 151; CJCA, 150-153, 199; CKUA, 153, 156
Railways, 12, 30, 44, 45, 60, 70; Calgary & Edmonton, 12, 26, 30, 31, 44, 60, 148; Canadian National, 162; Canadian Northern, 44, 60, 70, 77, 99, 102, 106; Canadian Pacific, 12, 26, 30, 31, 34, 37, 44, 60, 70, 77, 122, 169; Edmonton Radial, 38, 98, 125, 145, 200; Edmonton, Yukon & Pacific, 44, 60, 77, 111, 116, 188; Grand Trunk Pacific, 50, 70, 77, 99, 118; Inter-Urban, 102, 125; Northern Alberta, 105, 206. *See also* Transportation: railways
Railway stations: Calgary & Edmonton, 20, 26, 31; Canadian National, 162, 186, 201, 217; Canadian Northern, 77; Canadian Pacific (Strathcona), 37, 143; Edmonton, Yukon & Pacific, 44; Union station, 77
Ramsay, James, 163
Rankin, Bill, 159

Raymer, Emanuel, 16, 21, 49, 100, 105
Raymond, Erskine N., 32
Real estate, 16, 31, 34, 45, 61, 85, 102-104, 109, 163, 190
Red River carts. See Transportation: Red River carts
Rice, G.R.A. "Dick", 152, 208, 235
Riel Rebellion. See North-West Rebellion
Robertson, Annie, 69
Robertson Hall, 16, 62-63, 64, 89, 95
Robertson, Noel MacDonald, 172
Robertson, W. Scott, 62, 89
Robinson, Hugh, 98
Rockwell, "Klondike Kate", 107
Rodeo, 230
Rollins, Al, 196
Roper, Elmer, 216
Ross Brothers' hardware (Edmonton), 16
Rossdale, 7, 10, 17, 19, 24, 27, 28, 54, 72, 99, 132, 140-141, 160, 180, 225
Ross, Donald, 19-20, 50, 54, 60, 63, 82, 87, 140
Ross Flats. See Rossdale
Ross Grade, 73, 87
Ross, William E., 31, 36
Rotary Club, 155, 215, 236
Rowand, John, 6-9
Rowland, William, 13
Royal Canadian Air Force, 179, 215
Royal Canadian Navy, 180
Royal visits: Duke of Connaught, 36; Edward VIII (as Prince of Wales), 144; King George VI and Queen Elizabeth, 171, 174, 175; Princess Elizabeth and Prince Philip, 191; Queen Elizabeth II and Prince Philip, 212, 229
Roy, Georges, 79
Rupert's Land, 6, 12
Rutherford, Cecil, 35
Rutherford, Hazel, 35
Rutherford, Hon. A.C., 34-35, 39, 75, 90, 123, 144
Rutherford House, 123, 222
Rutherford, Mattie, 35
Ryan, Doreen McLeod, 197
Sache, F.H., 50
St. Albert, 17, 18, 47, 52, 56, 102, 125
St. Joachim's Catholic Separate School District No. 7, 58
St. Joseph's College, 124, 195
St. Stephen's College, 124, 222
Sanderson and Looby, 22
Sanderson, C., 50
Sanderson, George, 22
Sandison Block, 89, 177
Saskatoon, 96
Schools, 76, 210; Athlone Elementary, 210; Brother Scollen's, 58; Catholic boys' school, 59; College Avenue, 15, 51, 59, 82, 140; Donald Ross, 90; Duggan Street, 41; first public, 12, 17, 59, 80, 89, 90, 141; Grandin Street, 33; King Edward (old), 33; McDougall Commercial High School, 161; McKay Avenue, 17, 75, 82, 90, 111; Niblock Street, 33, 41; Normal School, 181; Norwood, 98; Old Scona Academic High School, 33, 41; Queen Alexandra, 41; Queen's Avenue, 59, 97, 110, 146, 162; St. Joachim's, 58, 59; South Edmonton's first, 33, 34; Strathcona Collegiate Institute, 33, 41; Victoria High School, 90
Scotia Place, 180, 225
Scrip: Metis, 54, 61; Social Credit, 164, 170
Secord, Richard, 16, 61, 69, 71, 80, 163
Settlers, 6, 12, 13-19, 23, 37, 44, 61, 66, 70, 78-79. See also Edmonton: first settlers
Seven Seas Restaurant, 194
Shadbolt, Jack, 211
Shaganappi, 11
Sharples, W.J., 31
Shasta Grill, 106, 193
Shaw, Angus, 6
Sheppard, William H., 32, 34
Shoctor, Joe, 218, 235
Short, A.H., 33
Short William, 71, 107
Shumka Dancers, 234
Sidewalks, 16, 62, 190
Sieberling, Jerry, 159
Sifton, Clifford, 44, 70
Sifton, Premier A.L., 116
Simpson, Isaac, 39
Simpson, Sir George, 6, 9
Sir Winston Churchill Square, 215, 216, 226, 227
Sisters of Charity of Ville-Marie (Grey Nuns), 56
Sisters of Misericorde, 91
Sisters of the Faithful Companions of Jesus, 58
Slater, Norman, 211
Sloan, Alex, 219
Smallpox, 6, 15, 58
Smith, C.L., 52
Smith, Donald (Lord Strathcona), 34, 41, 72
Smith, Dr. Donald, 220
Smith, Graham, 220, 229
Smith, Max, 145
Smith, S.H., & Co., 50
Smiths, "Swimming", 220
Soap box derby, 231
South Edmonton, 23, 26-34, 42, 69. See also Strathcona
South Edmonton News, 26
South Edmonton School District No. 216, 33
Southgate Shopping Centre, 221

South Side Covered Rink, 69
Spanish 'flu, 138, 143
Speedway Park, 219, 231
Spillios, George, 106
Sports: automobile racing, 184, 219; baseball, 24, 67, 134, 159, 198, 199, 208, 233; basketball, 138, 161, 172; bicycle racing, 158; boxing, 100, 159; Commonwealth Games, 220, 222, 228, 229, 234; cricket, 23, 132; curling, 29, 71, 136, 197; drag racing, 219, 231; football, 138, 153, 159, 198, 219, 229, 232; footraces, 24, 67, 68, 129-130; golf, 68; hang gliding, 231; hockey, 71, 136; ladies, 42, 69, 160; men, 69, 101, 126, 138, 159, 160, 196, 222, 230; horse racing, 67, 99, 131, 219; lacrosse, 67, 100; lawn bowling, 163; rifle shooting, 24; rodeo, 230; rugby football, 23, 132, 159; show jumping, 131; skating, 29, 69, 136, 160; skiing, 101; ski jumping, 101, 135; snowshoeing, 101; soap box derby, 231; soccer, 222; speedskating, 197; stock car racing, 219; swimming, 171, 220, 229; tennis, 42; tobogganing, 136; track and field, 68, 173, 197, 222, 229; trapshooting, 24, 67, 229, 233; tug-of-war, 67, 128
Sports days, 67, 128, 133
Sproule, Walter, 148, 149
Stagecoaches. See Transportation: stagecoaches
Stanley Cup, 101, 138, 160
Stark, W.J., 148
Stasiuk, Vic, 196
Steamboats: City of Edmonton, 27, 118; Lily, 8; Little Klondike Queen, 215; Northcote, 25; Northwest, 54, 115. See also Transportation: steamboats
Stephenson, "English Charlie", 51
Stewart & Bannerman, 16
Stinson, Katherine, 138, 148
Stores, 16, 47, 61, 205; Army & Navy, 170; Blowey Henry furniture, 85, 118, 132, 140, 177; Brown, John, 16; Douglas Brothers, 36; Eaton's, 163, 175, 176; Hudson's Bay Co., 16, 52, 82, 88, 106, 154, 194; Hulbert, Russell A., 34; Johnstone Walker, W., 53, 74, 86, 221; MacDonald, A., & Co., 16; MacDonald, D.W., drugstore, 48; McDougall & Secord, 61, 82, 165; McDougall, John A., 16, 52; MacLaren's 31; Oliver, Frank, 16, 18; Parrish, Sam, 31; Pollack, Moses, 170; Raymer's jewellery, 16, 49, 105; Ross Brothers' hardware, 16; Ross, W.E., hardware, 31; Stewart & Bannerman, 16; Walter, John, 27; Woodward's 175, 205. See also Drugstores
Storyland Valley Zoo, 212, 236
Strange, Gen., 26
Strathcona, 26-43, 34, 50, 60, 69, 70, 77, 101, 132, 160, 222; amalgamation, 26, 34, 38, 43, 102, 103, 174; City Hall, 26, 40, 43; Fire Halls, 26, 40; first town council, 34; hospital, 26; incorporation (as city), 26, (as town), 26, 34, 38; land office steal, 17, 26; last council meeting, 43; population, 26, 36, 70, 103; post office, 36; public library, 26, 40, 167. See also South Edmonton
Strathcona Brewing & Malting Co., 26
Strathcona, Lord (Donald Smith). See Smith, Donald (Lord Strathcona)
Strathcona Plaindealer, 26
Street lights, 193
Streets, 190; Boyle Street (103A Avenue), 56, 134; College Avenue, 59; Fort Trail, 111; Jasper Avenue, 12, 16, 45, 61, 62, 73, 86, 103, 104, 105, 106, 141, 165, 182, 193, 194, 207, 214; McKay Avenue, 90; Main Street (east Jasper Avenue), 16, 23, 62, 67; Portage Avenue (Kingsway), 104, 149, 158, 168, 169, 174; Victoria Park Road, 231; Whyte Avenue, 26, 31, 36, 38; 101 Street, 108, 109; 110 Street, 58
Stukas, Annis, 198
Subdivisions: Garneau, 195, 210; Highlands, 102, 163; Inglewood, 102; Lauderdale, 47; McKernan, 29, 102; Norwood, 61; Windsor Park, 210
Sunwapta Broadcasting Co., 152, 208
Surveys, 12, 90
Sutherland, Cecil, 53
Swanson, S., 95
Tait, C.M., 75
T. Eaton Co. See Eaton's
Tate, Bill, 161
Taylor, Alex, 12, 18, 52, 68, 87, 96
Taylor, Charles, 87
Taylor, E., 158
Taylor, Gariepy and Boyle, 115
Tegler Building, 86, 109, 163, 166, 176, 185
Tegler, Robert, 109
Telegraph, 12, 18, 24, 29, 137, 199. See also Dominion Telegraph
Telephones, 12, 18, 70, 96, 222. See also Edmonton Telephones
Television, 152, 188, 208
Television stations, 208
Terrace Building (old), 75; (new) 216
Theatre, cinema: Allen, 106, 157; Bijou, 95, 97, 109, 154, 184; Capitol, 106, 155, 157; Dreamland, 95, 209; Empress, 95, 199; Family, 184; Garneau, 95; Monarch, 95, 107, 157; Princess, 95; Rialto, 184; Strand, 95, 107, 155
Theatre, live, 63; Citadel, 206, 218, 235; Empire, 154-155; Lyceum, 154; Metropolitan, 107; Pantages, 106-107, 153, 155; Walterdale Playhouse, 40, 206
Theatre, drive-in, 204

Thistle Rink, 64, 69, 71, 74, 75, 80, 82, 100, 126
Thomas, Lionel J., 202
Thornton Court, 216, 223
Todd, Frederick G., 237
Tomison, William, 6
Tory, Dr. Henry Marshall, 39, 41, 144
Tourangeau, Huguette, 208
Town crier, 209
Traffic lights, 165
Trans-Canada Air Lines, 169, 211
Trans-Canada Air Pageant, 168
Transportation: airplanes, 98, 138, 148-150, 164, 168-169, 177, 178, 206, 211; bicycles, 22, 158; buses, 201, 229; canoes, 11; cars, 66, 70, 85, 145, 146, 147, 175, 193, 200, 201, 206, 207; covered wagons, 29; ferries, 12, 27-28, 44, 54, 58; horse and wagon, 20, 30, 38, 44, 83, 85, 87, 125, 145, 146; hotel buses, 37; milk wagons, 165, 177, 200; pack horses, 14; railiner, 201; railways, 11, 12, 20, 23, 25, 45, 236. (See also Railways); Red River carts, 11, 14, 25, 29, 53, 73, 77, 80; sleighs, 27, 52, 53, 55, 83; stagecoaches, 12, 17, 21, 24, 25, 45, 63 (See also Edmonton-Calgary stagecoach); steamboats, 12, 25, 27, 54, 115, 118 (See also Steamboats); streetcars, 38, 70, 85, 86, 98, 102, 104, 122, 136, 163, 166, 174, 188, 200; taxis, 145; trolley buses, 177; trucks, 145, 146, 168, 200; York boats, 6, 11
Treaty No. 8, 54
Treaty of Oregon, 6
Trocadero Ballroom, 154
Truscott, Lyn, 100
Tryon, Robert M., 145
Turnbull, Jessie, 56
Tyrell, Joe, 160
Underhill, Pat Gunn, 197
United States Army Camp, 186
University of Alberta, 16, 26, 35, 39, 41, 70, 122-124, 144, 153, 156, 179, 181, 195, 206, 210, 222

Vancouver, 23
V-E Day, 186
Victoria Armories, 79
Victoria (Pakan), 15
V-J Day, 186
Vogel Meat & Packing Co., 26
Volunteer Fire Brigade, 46
Wages, 17, 19, 27, 33, 40, 46, 56, 70, 80, 96, 187, 188, 206
Wainwright, undertaker, 43
Walker, Maj. James, 54
Walker, W. Johnstone, 53. See also Johnstone Walker's stores; Stores, Johnstone Walker, W.
Walsh, W.L., 117
Walter, Annie, 28
Walterdale, 26-28, 54
Walterdale Playhouse, 40, 206
Walter, John, 8, 12, 18, 26, 27-28, 34, 143, 50, 54, 118, 140
Wardair, 211
Ward, Max, 206
Waterloo Motors, 196
Water man, 17, 55
Waterworks, 62
Weaver-Winston, Albert, 155
Welch, Paul, 147
Welling-Fisher, Charles, 116
Wensley, James, 221
West Edmonton Mall, 226
Western Canada Airways, 150
Western Canada Realty Co., 104
Westminster Ladies' College, 144
Westmount Shoppers' Park, 204-205
Wheat, 12, 70, 170
Whisky traders, 6, 12
White, Deacon, 159
Whoop-Up Trail, 11
Whyte Avenue. See Streets: Whyte Avenue
Whyte, Sir William, 26
Wild, Mr., 41
Wilkinson, Tom, 232
Williams, Edgar, 151, 153
Wilson, Dr. H.C., 23, 48
Winnipeg, 12, 16, 18, 29, 37, 45, 47, 55, 66, 71, 77, 142, 150, 168, 220. See also Fort Garry
Women, 138, 142, 179
Women's Musical Club, 64, 156, 206, 218
Wood, Dorothy, 158
Woodward, Charles, 109
Woodward's, 175, 185, 205, 221, 227
World War I, 102, 137, 138, 143, 150
World War II, 117, 150, 164, 172, 173, 178-180, 184, 186
Wright, Bob, 108
Wright, E.H. (residence), 120-121
Yellow Cabs, 145
York, Anna Ada (Mrs. Richard Secord), 80
York boats. See Transportation: York boats
Young, Campbell, 23
Young, Harrison S., 15, 16
Zeidler, W.R., 235
Zwozdesky, Gene, 234